DATE DUE

LOW-TECH ASSISTIVE DEVICES:

A HANDBOOK FOR THE SCHOOL SETTING

Lynn Ciampa Stoller,
M.S., OTR/L, BCP

Published
by
Therapro

LOW-TECH ASSISTIVE DEVICES:
A HANDBOOK FOR THE SCHOOL SETTING
Lynn Ciampa Stoller, M.S., OTR/L, BCP

Therapro, Inc.
225 Arlingto Street
Framingham, MA 01702
508 - 872 - 9494

Developmental Editor: Karen Conrad, Therapro, Inc.
Copy Editor: Mariam E. Grossman, Affinity Art
Illustration and Design: Marcella Gallardo, Affinity Art
Cover Design: Marcella Gallardo, Affinity Art

Dedication

**Special recognition and appreciation is expressed to
Cotting School in Lexington, Massachusetts.**

Cotting School is a nonprofit charitable corporation providing specialized services and education to students with special needs. Cotting School, which was founded in 1893, has been a pioneer in the development of methods and technologies to better serve individuals with disabilities. Without the commitment of Cotting School and its staff, this book would never have become a reality.

Acknowledgements

*The completion of this book would not be possible without the assistance
of the following individuals and facilities, to whom I am greatly indebted:*

Dr. Carl Mores, Executive Director and President of Cotting School,
for his professional advice and support, which helped to transform the idea for this project
into an actual book contract.

Karen Conrad, Sc.D., OTR/L,
for believing in this book enough to publish it, and for providing invaluable editorial assistance
from her unique position as both a highly respected occupational therapist and book publisher.

Meg Grossman, my editor,
for her terrific job transforming the written manuscript so it was more clear, concise,
and readable.

Marcella Gallardo, my illustrator,
for the excellent illustrations which brought the words to life.

The Contributors,
whose names are listed on the following page and throughout this book, for taking time out
from their busy schedules to share their successful assistive device solutions so others could
benefit from them. I greatly appreciate every piece of information I received that helped to
make this a better book.

**Paulette Binder, Virginia Birmingham, Molly Campbell, Suzi Collins, Jeanette Harney,
Amy Houghton, Lucy Kulis, Eileen Kiernan, Nancy McClintock, Kate Moore,
Noreen Murphy, Micki Rosenberg, Sue Shannon, Rosanne Trolan, Alex Truesdell,
Scott Whidden, Sheryl Zelten, and a** *special thank you* **to Val Greene**
for donating many additional hours to this project by sharing their expertise, reviewing
chapters, taking photographs, and/or identifying resources.

Kennedy Day School at Franciscan Children's Hospital, Brighton, Ma.
Perkins School for the Blind, Watertown, Ma.
The United Cerebral Palsy Association, Watertown, Ma.
for generously opening their doors to let me view some of their successful hand-made
or modified assistive devices. I hope we will continue to share information between schools
in the future.

Lela Llorens, Ph.D., OTR, FAOTA,
teacher and mentor, for her visionary insights into the purpose and nature of occupational
therapy which continue to strongly influence my professional practice to this day.

My husband Ken,
for providing a great deal of assistance on the homefront, without which this book
would have taken much, much longer to complete.

My children, Jason and Melissa,
for their great patience and for motivating me to finish this book so I could spend
more time with them.

Contributors

Rucker Ashmore
Subhashini Balagopal, M.Ed.
Dina Becze, SLP
Barbara Berberian, MA, OTR/L
Paulette E. Binder
Virginia Birmingham, P.T.
Sharon Bridson, COTA
Molly Campbell, M.S., OTR/L
Thomas E. Capps, Jr.
Martha Carr, P.T.
Suzi Collins, M.S., OTR/L
Karen Conrad, ScD, OTR/L
David Creesy, MBA
Helen Denham
Cynthia Furbish, PT
David Gilbert, COTA
Val Greene, B.S. Ed.
Deena Gulezian, M.S., CCC-SLP
Patricia Harlow, B.S. Ed.
Jeanette Harney, OTR/L, BCP
Kathleen D. Hickey, M.Ed.
Amy A. Houghton, OTR/L
Beth Jackson, M.S., OTR/L
Eileen Kiernan, M.Ed.
JoAnn Kluzik, M.S., PT., PCS
Lucy Kulis, M.S. Ed.

Robin Levy, OTR/L
Melissa Litton, OTR/L
Diane Long, M.S., OTR,
Kristine Lopes, COTA
Nancy F. McClintock, Ed. M.
Frances Maggiore, COTA/L
Cathy Mayo, M.Ed.
Elizabeth Miller, M.S., CCC-SLP
Amy B. Milne, B.S. Sp.Ed.
Kate Moore, M.S., CCC-SLP
Noreen Murphy, M.Ed.
Kristen Taylor Rooney, M.S.
Micki Rosenberg, M.Ed.
Bob Rudolph
Faith Saftler, P.T.
Sue Shannon, OTR/L
Marissa Shindell, M.Ed.
Staff and Therapists at the
    United Cerebral Palsy Association
Barbara Steva, OTR/L
Michael Talbot, Ed.D.
Marcie A. Theriault
Joseph E. Trickett
Rosanne Trolan, B.F.A.
Alex Truesdell, M.Ed.
Scott Whidden
Sheryl Zelten, OTR/L

Table of Contents

Introduction

Frequently, the only thing preventing a student from performing a desired or necessary activity is the lack of the right assistive device. Often the particular device that is needed is not commercially available; is available but needs to be modified; or is prohibitive in cost when a simpler and less expensive solution would do. As a result, professionals who work with special needs students spend a significant amount of their working time and energy trying to come up with just the right gadget, activity set-up, or modification that will enable their students to function as independently as possible.

Unfortunately, it is rare for teachers and other professionals to publish or otherwise advertise their successful solutions so others can benefit from them. As a result, professionals end up continuously "reinventing the wheel". This uses up excessive staff time as well as student treatment time which could be put to better use. A major purpose of this book is to inform people that in many cases, the wheel has already been built. Rather than invent it (once again) from scratch, why not take advantage of the knowledge that is already out there and help to evolve it to a higher state of art?

This book appears, at first glance, to epitomize a "cookbook approach" to treatment, since it includes very specific directions on how one might fabricate various devices. This is in fact not the case. Specific directions are provided simply to show one way that the device has been constructed, to assist in generating ideas. Specific information should be particularly helpful for those teachers and therapists who feel they lack sufficient knowledge or intuition regarding which materials and processes might be used to make particular devices. If, following an activity analysis, it appears that a certain device would provide a good starting point for solving a particular problem, it is hoped that the device will be modified as necessary in order to best meet the needs of the particular student and situation.

This book does not list every possible solution that exists, nor necessarily the best solutions presently available for the specific problems presented. However, since the solutions included in this book come from the clinical community, it does give the reader a taste of where the current state of the art is. Sharing these devices with others will help them evolve to new uses and better designs. Nevertheless, there will always be the need to design some devices from scratch, as many students have very unique needs.

By publishing a book of this nature, there is a risk that the devices that are included will be designed or used inappropriately for some students. This is more apt to occur when the device is made by someone who is not properly trained in how to assess the student's needs; who may not be aware of relevant precautions pertaining to a particular student's medical condition; or who are not aware of the physical effects that mechanical stressors can have on particular body parts. Care has been taken to address these issues in Part I: Design Philosophy.

The section on Design Philosophy also provides a theoretical understanding of how the appropriate use of low tech assistive devices may affect human occupation. The common goals of assistive devices directly emanate from the concepts presented in this theory. This unit also discusses activity analyses, constructional considerations, as well as specific materials, tools, and procedures used when making low tech assistive devices.

Part II: Devices Used Throughout the School Setting, describes hand made or modified assistive devices which may be used in a variety of settings throughout the school or assist with transitions from class to class. It includes chapters on Positioning, Mobility, Communication, Switches & Switch Mounts, Computers, Pointers & Mouthsticks, and Time Management & Organizational Aids. It is suggested that the reader review this section first before proceeding to the classroom subject of interest, as many of the solutions to student problems will be found here.

Part III: Devices Used in Specific Curriculum Subject Areas, describes hand made or modified assistive devices which have helped some students increase their level of performance in specific school subjects. It includes chapters on Reading, Writing, Math, Art & Craft Activities, Music, Home Economics, Industrial Arts, and The Lunch Room.

Each chapter in Part II and Part III follows a specific organizational format, in this sequential order:
1. Text of the Chapter
2. Quick Tips
3. Directions for Fabricating Selected Devices

The Quick Tips sections are written in a Problem/Possible Solution format. They include some problems encountered by students (which may or may not have been addressed in the general text) along with one or more solutions that have been successful for certain students. The modifications and aids discussed in the Quick Tips sections can be understood and implemented without illustrations and lengthy directions. Devices which do require detailed instructions and illustrations are found at the end of each chapter.

Included in parentheses after each Quick Tip solution is the name of the person who contributed the idea to the book. These contributors are not necessarily the designers of the devices or the first ones who thought of the particular solution. However, if the designer's name was known, it was listed as the contributor. In the last section of each chapter, the names of the designers, builders, and/or contributors are listed after each device. Great pains were taken to ensure that the design and credit information was as accurate as possible. All contributors and designers were given the opportunity to review the first draft of the write-ups to reduce the chances of error. However, with a project of this size there is bound to be errors despite all efforts taken to avoid them, and for these the author apologizes. Please use your own clinical judgment when fabricating any of the devices or modifications presented in this book.

Following Part 3 is the Resource Directory. All products mentioned in the book have the company's name provided directly after them. These companies are all listed with addresses and phone numbers in the Resource Directory.

The Additional Reading and Reference lists follow, and are organized by chapter.

This book is designed for people who are familiar with working with students who have physical, communication, or developmental challenges to learning. It is presumed that the reader possesses basic knowledge regarding common student diagnoses, treatment approaches, as well as the underlying theories that support use of these approaches. An effort has been made to define terms within the body of this book. However, a medical dictionary may also be useful for those who find some of the medical terms confusing.

The author welcomes your comments and experiences with this book. She can be contacted in care of Therapro, Inc. at 225 Arlington Street, Framingham, MA 01702.

Important Note for Chapter 1: Theory & Goals

Although many different school professionals use assistive devices to help students succeed in school, the ideas presented here will be most familiar and most applicable to occupational therapists. This is because many of the theoretical concepts discussed in this chapter are those that help to define the occupational therapy profession. These concepts are discussed in order to more fully articulate the relationship of assistive devices to human occupation.

In the context of the school setting, the terms "human occupation", "occupational behaviors", and "occupational performance" refer to those functional activities that a student needs to perform to be successful in his or her occupational role as student. (Most of the chapter titles of this book explain specifically what these are!) The term "remediate" means to develop missing component skills that are necessary for performing a functional activity. These component skills fall under five major categories: motor functioning, sensory-integrative functioning, cognitive functioning, psychological functioning, and social functioning [1]. The term "compensate" means to use adapted techniques and/or devices to enable an individual to perform a functional activity in spite of his or her deficits in underlying component skills. Other terms are defined in the course of the first chapter's text.

Readers who are not familiar with the theoretical concepts presented may find this chapter more difficult to read, but may gain a greater understanding of the occupational therapy profession and the therapeutic use of assistive devices by doing so.

Part I

DESIGN PHILOSOPHY

This section of the book provides a theoretical framework for understanding the relationship of low-tech assistive devices to human occupation.

Common goals of assistive devices are presented which directly emanate from this theory.

This section also discusses activity analyses, constructional considerations, as well as specific materials, tools, and procedures used when making low tech assistive devices.

Chapter 1
Theory & Goals

THEORY AND GOALS
UNDERLYING THE USE OF ASSISTIVE DEVICES

The purpose of this chapter is to provide the reader with a clear and useful framework from which to better understand the relationship of assistive devices to human occupation. This framework is based on an integration of premises put forth by Llorens in her conceptualization of developmental theory [2,3,4] and Kielhofner in his conceptualization of systems theory [5,6,7,8,9]. The synthesis of Llorens' and Kielhofner's theories was not only the topic of the author's dissertation for her Master's Degree many years ago, but is also the theoretical lens that guides her practice in the school setting. A portion of this synthesis is briefly summarized on the next page using a model depicting a developmental cycle of human occupation.

A DEVELOPMENTAL CYCLE OF HUMAN OCCUPATION

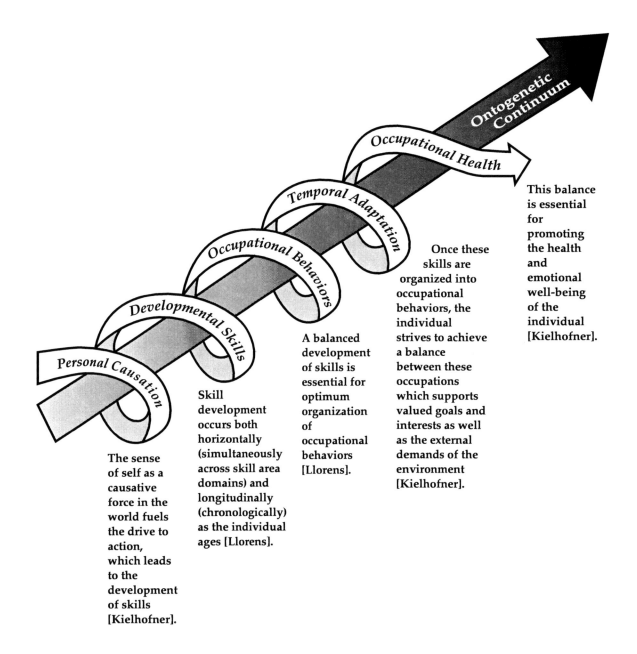

Ontogenetic Continuum

Occupational Health

Temporal Adaptation

Occupational Behaviors

Developmental Skills

Personal Causation

The sense of self as a causative force in the world fuels the drive to action, which leads to the development of skills [Kielhofner].

Skill development occurs both horizontally (simultaneously across skill area domains) and longitudinally (chronologically) as the individual ages [Llorens].

A balanced development of skills is essential for optimum organization of occupational behaviors [Llorens].

Once these skills are organized into occupational behaviors, the individual strives to achieve a balance between these occupations which supports valued goals and interests as well as the external demands of the environment [Kielhofner].

This balance is essential for promoting the health and emotional well-being of the individual [Kielhofner].

Children are born with an innate drive to move and explore their environment. Through these explorations, they discover cause and effect, and more importantly, that they themselves are a causative force in the world. This sense of "personal causation" further fuels the drive for action, which leads to the development of skills.

Skill development occurs simultaneously across skill area domains (i.e. sensory-integrative, motor, cognitive, psychological, and social) as well as chronologically as the individual ages. As these skills develop, they become organized into occupational behaviors- such as eating, dressing, playing, reading, writing, and so on.

2   Theory & Goals

A balanced development of skills is essential for optimum organization of occupational behaviors. For example, a child who has achieved a developmental level of 3 years in all skills areas will be able to organize these skills into occupational behaviors that are typical of the average 3 year old. In contrast, a child who has scattered developmental skills ranging from 1 year to 5 years will not find it as easy to organize these widely disparate skills into organizational behaviors.

Once developmental skills are organized into occupational behaviors, the individual strives to achieve a balance between occupations which supports valued goals and interests as well as the external demands of the environment. Kielhofner refers to this balance as temporal adaptation. This balance is essential for promoting the health and emotional well-being of the individual.

Each part of the above process is continuous throughout the lifespan. As new skills are acquired, they reorganize existing occupational behaviors, and a new balance is achieved between them. For example, a child who has cerebral palsy may learn new skills which help her to better feed herself. This in turn shortens the amount of time spent at the dinner table, thus allowing her more time to perform schoolwork or engage in a favorite leisure activity.

Please note that, although the cycle is depicted as a "one way street" in the model, in fact all levels influence each other. This influence may be positive or negative. For example, spending more time performing an occupational task such as gymnastics will undoubtedly lead to improved skills in this area, and when these skills emerge the gymnast will be able to reorganize all of his or her existing skills for improved performance on the various gymnastic equipment.

Similarly, disruption at any level of the cycle may result in disruption at all other levels. A lack of skills due to a disability may result in failure to meet personal goals (such as to walk, read, or write), despite hard effort, which can erode the sense of "personal causation" and subsequently self-esteem. Some start to believe their actions are futile, and so they lose all motivation for school-related tasks. As any teacher or therapist knows, it is extremely difficult to teach skills to students who lack motivation. And so the developmental cycle of human occupation becomes stalled.

The Relationship of Low-Tech Assistive Devices to the Development Cycle of Human Occupation

When the developmental cycle of human occupation has been disrupted, the skilled application of purposeful activities and personal relationships can promote or restore a healthy cycle [2,3]. Purposeful activities may (or may not) incorporate the use of assistive devices as tools to help meet this objective. On the following page is a model which describes how the use of assistive devices during purposeful activity, *when appropriate,* may affect the developmental cycle of human occupation.

THE INFLUENCE OF ASSISTIVE DEVICES
ON THE DEVELOPMENTAL CYCLE
OF HUMAN OCCUPATION

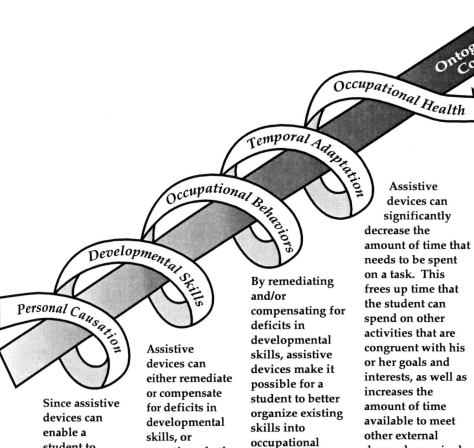

Personal Causation

Since assistive devices can enable a student to accomplish previously unattainable tasks, they can be powerful tools which help a child view him or herself as competent and able to master the world and meet its demands.

Developmental Skills

Assistive devices can either remediate or compensate for deficits in developmental skills, or sometimes both (e.g. a large magnetic checkerboard with adapted game pieces placed on an angled surface may help to remediate range of motion and grasp limitations while providing compensation for impaired release skills.)

Occupational Behaviors

By remediating and/or compensating for deficits in developmental skills, assistive devices make it possible for a student to better organize existing skills into occupational behaviors. This enables the student to better meet society's expectations for occupational performance.

Temporal Adaptation

Assistive devices can significantly decrease the amount of time that needs to be spent on a task. This frees up time that the student can spend on other activities that are congruent with his or her goals and interests, as well as increases the amount of time available to meet other external demands required by the occupational role of student.

Occupational Health

Ontogenetic Continuum

A healthy balance of occupational activities is essential in order to promote the health and well-being of the student, and will help the student gain optimal benefit from the educational experience.

Common Goals of Assistive Devices

Major goals of assistive devices in the school setting coincide with the concepts presented in the Development Cycle of Human Occupation, and are presented below along with case study examples:

GOAL #1. To help develop a student's view of him or herself as competent and able to master the world and meet its demands. (Personal Causation)

CASE STUDY #1: A 17 year old female student (with a history of organizational and motor planning difficulties) refused to try using a regular ruler or scissors. Her teacher requested the O.T. to address these skills. It was evident that she had the skills to use these tools (even considering her history), but the student viewed herself as being incapable of performing many motor tasks. She would often state, "I can't do it: it's part of my disability!" and would frequently break down in tears before even trying the task. She was given the magnetic notebook and ruler to reduce the task demands, and within two treatment sessions she progressed to using a regular ruler without adaptations. Scissor skills were also broken down into tiny steps which were mastered within a couple of sessions, with the help of loop scissors. By breaking these (and several other tasks) down into tiny steps and initially providing her with assistive devices, she learned to be independent (usually without devices) in several new skills.

GOAL #2: To remediate developmental skill deficits interfering with occupational performance by encouraging use of higher level skills in any of the component areas: sensory-integrative, motor, cognitive, psychological, or social. (Developmental Skills)

CASE STUDY #2: A student with neurological involvement was in need of motivating activities to facilitate shoulder flexion and elbow extension. His teacher constructed an Easel Switch (page 98) to use for playing fun computer games while simultaneously addressing this motor goal.

GOAL #3. To compensate for missing developmental skills to enable the student to better organize existing skills occupational behaviors. (Occupational Behaviors)

CASE STUDY #3: A student with impaired hand strength demonstrated very light, wavy lines when printing. His occupational therapist provided him with a weighted pencil (page 192) to compensate for his light pencil pressure, which significantly improved his quality of writing skills.

GOAL #4. To help increase a student's speed or efficiency in an occupational performance area thereby allowing for a better balance of time spent between the occupational roles in the student's life. (Temporal Adaptation)

CASE STUDY #4: A high school senior was routinely very late for O.T. following aerobics class because she was spending over 10 minutes in the locker room buttoning her shirt. She was subsequently trained in the use of a button hook to reduce the amount of time it took her to dress herself.

The following case example demonstrates the integration of remedial goals into a solution to enable a student to perform a functional, school-related activity. It tackles the student's cycle of human occupation on at least two levels, and for this it wins special brownie points:

CASE STUDY #5: A 7 year old student with a diagnosis of cerebral palsy with spastic quadriplegia was unable to hold a marker, paintbrush, or other drawing implement to participate in art class. Evaluation (which included the Erhardt Developmental Prehension Assessment[10]) revealed that she needed to work on developing a radial palmar grasp (page 128) to fill in some of the major gaps in her hand development. Therefore, she was provided with a marker/paintbrush holder that incorporated a horizontal, cylindrical handle to assist in developing this grasp.

Implications for Practice

The above case examples (as well as many others described later in this book) show that assistive devices are routinely used for purposes beyond simply helping a student to compensate for missing skills in order to be able to perform a given task. They are also often used to help develop these missing skills, as well as to reduce the time it takes to perform a task so the student can better balance the various occupational tasks in his or her life. On occasion, they are even used as "cycle starters" to help promote a sense of self-competence for those students who are sure they cannot perform a task and are unwilling to try. Just like the "magic slippers" used by the ballerina, the devices are often soon discarded when they have served this purpose. Therefore, the following is a proposed definition of assistive/adaptive equipment for use by the occupational therapy profession:

Assistive/Adaptive Equipment refers to the provision of special devices or structural changes that promote a sense of self competence, the further acquisition of developmental skills (or prevention of lost skills), improved ability to organize existing skills into occupational behaviors, and/or an improved balance of time spent between the occupational roles in an individual's life as determined by the individual's goals and interests and the external demands of the environment.

The adoption of such a definition would affect how assistive devices are used in occupational therapy practice by recognizing that the following common assumptions are *false:*

ASSUMPTION #1: Assistive devices should only be used as an absolute last resort in treatment, after remedial techniques have failed.

Although this statement is false, the intention behind this statement is valid, which is to ensure that assistive devices are not provided that would hinder the development of skills. An example would be to adapt a ruler so that it does not require stabilization by the non-dominant hand, when in fact the student has potential to develop this skill. This would constitute a misuse of assistive devices, which would result in a grave disservice to the student. However, if a ruler was adapted to provide just enough stabilization to ensure success as long as the student used the non-dominant hand to the best of his or her ability, now that's an ideal device! It would remediate this skill while enabling occupational performance. (See page 202, Quick Tip #9, for two ways to make this device.)

ASSUMPTION #2: Assistive devices are only provided when sensory-integrative, motor, and/or cognitive skills are insufficient for task performance.

On occasion, an assistive device may need to be provided initially for psychosocial reasons (e.g. lack of self-confidence, history of failure, anxiety), just to get the ball rolling (or cycle rolling), even though the student has the sensorimotor skills to perform the task without devices. When used for this purpose, the device is usually quickly out-grown (psychologically) and discarded. An example of this is Case Study #1.

ASSUMPTION #3: An assistive device should only be provided when the individual is unable to perform the particular activity without one.

It is important to recognize that time factors also play a role in determining whether or not an assistive device is needed. This helps to ensure that a balance of occupational roles is achieved which supports valued goals and interests in addition to the external demands of the environment. As shown in Case Study #4, the student was able to perform the skill (buttoning) without devices, but not within the time constraints necessary to meet her school schedule. Of course, if the individual has the potential to perform the task within an appropriate amount of time without devices, it should be set as a goal and addressed.

ASSUMPTION #4: Decisions regarding the use or design of assistive devices need only take account of the discrepancies between an individual's present level of skills and the skills demanded by the activity.

The definition above recognizes that the ultimate goal of intervention is a health-promoting balance between occupational activities that is congruent with the individual's valued goals and interests as well as the demands of society. This necessitates taking into account an individual's valued goals and interests when deciding whether and how to make an assistive device. For example, in some cultures, it is a valued norm for individuals with disabilities to be fed by family members. This may cause the individual and/or family members to resist the use of adaptive feeding equipment, even if this equipment would allow the individual to be independent in self-feeding. Many students also do not use their wheelchairs in the home setting, and some prefer to be pushed in their wheelchairs when venturing out in public, even though they are proficient in using a manual or power chair within the school setting. These differing attitudes regarding assistive devices need to be taken into account and respected when making equipment decisions. The design of a device (including the aesthetics) should also incorporate the interests of the individual.

Hopefully, the framework provided in this chapter will be a helpful tool for readers when deciding when and how to use assistive devices in the school setting. The next chapter takes the reader from theory and goals into the actual design of a device.

Chapter 2
Design

DESIGN

The need for an adaptive strategy or assistive device is identified when a student is unable to perform a desired or necessary task to expectations. When this occurs, the teacher or other school professional who discovers the situation may decide to remediate the problem themselves (if they are qualified to do so) or instead to refer the student to one or more specialists who are deemed to be better qualified in that particular area. Teachers and other staff have a responsibility to educate themselves regarding the roles of all other personnel to ensure that the appropriate referrals will be made.

It is also important for school personnel to be aware of their own professional limitations, not only to ensure that the best solution is obtained, but also to prevent possible injury to a student. For example, some students have fragile medical conditions in which certain positions or movements would have disastrous consequences. For example, a student may have a rod placed in his or her spinal column which would contraindicate any activities involving trunk rotation. Or, a student may suffer frequent shoulder dislocations which may contraindicate any activities in which the arm is raised above a certain height. Possessing a full understanding of a student's medical condition (and related precautions) is absolutely vital before engaging a student in any activity, adapted or not. It is also important to be fully aware of any possible physical effects that mechanical stressors can place on particular body parts.

When and When Not to Perform a "Quick Fix"

Sometimes, when there is a discrepancy between the student's skills and the demands of the immediate task at hand, a "quick fix" (i.e. makeshift adaptive device) needs to be provided by whoever is working with the student at the precise moment. Teachers and teacher assistants, in particular, often find themselves in this situation, since the student spends the majority of time in the classroom. However, other professionals also find themselves providing "quick fixes" from time to time in areas that are officially under another's jurisdiction. If the adult working with the student adheres to the precautions listed in the previous section, he or she should be able to use good judgment to determine whether a "quick fix" solution would be okay or not. For example, adapting a paintbrush for better grasp during a particular art activity or making an impromptu communication board to assist with a class discussion would usually be okay. However, the specialist for that area should ideally be consulted after the activity to ensure that an optimal design is used in the future (to promote better fine motor or communication skills as well as to prevent the loss of skills). In contrast, adapting a student's walker is absolutely not okay, unless you are a physical therapist or a qualified doctor, as it has the potential to affect the student's medical condition or safety.

Performing an Activity Analysis

The careful design of any assistive device begins with an activity analysis. This consists of identifying and analyzing the component parts of the activity, the component skills of the student, as well as the temporal and environmental context within which these two areas intermesh. Questions to be answered include the following:

1. Is the activity one that the student desires, values, or needs to perform at school?

2. Does the student's family support having the student engage in the proposed activity?

3. If the answers to #1 and #2 are yes, what skills does the activity require from the following domains: sensory-integrative, motor, cognitive, intrapersonal, and social?

4. In which of these domain areas is the student either:
   • lacking the skills necessary to perform the task?
   • exhibiting detrimental behaviors when performing the task (e.g. motor; social)?
   • unable to perform the task within necessary time parameters?

5. What developmental level is the student at with regard to the domain(s) in which necessary skills are lacking? (May require administration of specific evaluation tools.)

6. Can a solution (i.e. different set-up, method or device) be found that enables the student to perform the task while simultaneously promoting further development of the specific skill area that is lacking (e.g. hand skills, perceptual skills)?

7. Are there reasons why the solution should not incorporate remediation of this skill (e.g. due to medical contraindications, or would make the task too stressful or difficult to perform)?

8. If remedial goals cannot or should not be incorporated into the solution, at least can a solution be found that enables the student to perform the task without reinforcing inappropriate skills?

Construction Considerations When Designing Devices

After the activity analysis has been completed and an idea for an adaptive device is conceived, the next step is to design the device. There are 4 major construction considerations to take into account when designing an assistive device: aesthetics, durability, time, and cost. Aesthetics and durability often must be weighed against the cost of the materials and the time it takes staff to build the device. Special adaptive design workshops have power tools, expert craftsmen, and the time to make fancy, high quality products out of wood or different plastics. Therapists and teachers often do not have the expertise, tools, and certainly not the luxury of spending an entire school day crafting a beautiful wooden easel or fancy wooden footstool. There are many constraints. However, a good attempt should be made to make the device as attractive as possible and as durable as necessary within these constraints. Simple solutions that are effective, look good and hold up well - that's the ideal goal. When solutions call for expertise or tools beyond those available in the school, adaptive design workshops are a good place to refer a student.

Aesthetics

The appearance of a device can significantly influence the impressions people form of the individual who uses it, especially if the device is worn on the body (such as a headpointer). Just as sloppy or ugly clothing can reflect on the wearer, so can sloppy workmanship or ugly materials reflect on the user of a device. If the device is perceived as unattractive by a student, he or she will either reject the device altogether or only use it within the privacy of the home- certainly not at school in front of peers! Those that use the device only in the privacy of their own home are showing that they do in fact recognize the value of the device for increasing functional performance, but that it does not outweigh the necessity of looking attractive and "normal".

Aesthetics may not arise as an issue for most students until they get older, perhaps during their preteen years, when students become acutely aware of how others perceive them. However, designers should consider aesthetics when developing devices for students of any age. Younger students may not notice the effect robotic-looking devices have on the way they are perceived by others, but the public still does notice, nevertheless. On the other hand, if the device is not typically seen by the public in day-to-day life (such as a button hook) aesthetics need not be a major concern. Finally, remember that the design of the device should incorporate the student's aesthetics, not necessarily the designer's!

Durability

There are two major factors that determine the need for durable materials when making a device: 1) the length of time that the device will be used; and 2) the type of treatment the device will receive (gentle vs. rough). If the device will only be used for one year, in one particular classroom, for one student, then it is usually unnecessary (and unwise) to use expensive materials that require a lot of precious time to assemble. For example, a chair for a young child will be quickly outgrown - might as well adapt one using Triwall material. If the device will travel with the student from classroom to classroom, year to year, or if the device can be used with future students, then durable materials should be used (or a commercially available product should be purchased).

Rough treatment of devices can result from student actions or environmental factors. Examples of student actions are poorly controlled arm movements (which may cause bending or tearing of a device, food spillage, or spillage of craft materials), and constant drooling (which may affect the appearance or the electronics of a device). Examples of environmental factors are the elements of rain and snow (if the device is used outside or is unprotected during transport), splashing of water from a pool, or sand finding its way into the crevices of the device from the beach or a sandbox. Asking where and how the device will be used will help to determine the type of treatment the device will receive, and the type of materials that will be needed to construct the device.

Time

The time it takes to construct an adaptive device is a very important consideration, especially in the school setting. September and October are very busy months for making adaptive devices. Most students have changed classrooms, and as a result, they are sitting in different chairs, using different computers, trying to adjust to different writing paper, etc. The onslaught of requests to therapists can be enormous, and in order to function at their best, the students need the devices now! The following strategies can significantly reduce the time crunch for making devices at the beginning of a school year:

1. Whenever possible, transfer whatever equipment and supplies worked during the previous school year to the new classroom. If a specially adapted chair still fits the student well, it should go to the new classroom. If a certain type of writing paper or pencil grip made the difference between legible and illegible handwriting for a student, then the paper/pencil grip should continue to be made available to the student in the new classroom. And if a therapist spent several months adapting an IBM computer work station for a student until it was finally perfect, and the new classroom has an old model Apple. . . now, there's a problem! Ideally, computers belong to the school and not to individual classrooms, and they should be moved where necessary in order to best meet the needs of the students. If a computer cannot be moved, then a school may have to purchase a new one in order to meet the educational requirements of a particular student.

2. Make sure you have a full inventory of basic supplies at the beginning of each school year. This includes Triwall, hard foam, soft foam, vinyl material, thermoplastic material, Velcro, and any other supplies that might be needed for commonly made devices, e.g., inexpensive packets of hair clips to make sandwich holder splints, 4" wide 3-ring notebooks for angled writing surfaces, metal rods and baseball caps for making head-pointers, commercial finger grips and hollow plastic golf balls for building up pencils and markers, spring-loaded door latches for making cylindrical handles to hold pointers or writing implements, etc. Keeping the adaptive equipment area well-stocked prevents frustration and time delays when trying to meet students' adaptive equipment needs.

3. When a student needs a device immediately that will take some time to build, determine whether an interim solution should be provided. A three-ring binder might suffice as a keyboard stand, an easel can be made out of a cardboard box in about 15 minutes, and a cubby top for a desk can also be made in the same amount of time out of an appliance box. It may still be worth making the more durable device out of Triwall or wood, but at least the quick solution will meet the immediate need.

Cost

Making a device from scratch can be cheaper OR can actually be more expensive than buying a commercially available device from a catalog. It is easy to think of the basic raw materials as inexpensive, but unfortunately, they are not. If you make a measurement error and need to throw out the material, you're throwing out a significant amount of money. Another expense is your time: Remember that the time needed to make the device will reduce the amount of time available to treat. Also please make good decisions regarding where your skills lie. If a device is currently on the commercial market that would suit the student's needs well, then making a homemade device is only cost-effective if the following is true:

> Cost of All Raw Materials (including waste!)
> + Cost of Labor (hourly rate x number of hours needed to make device)
> + Cost of Time Taken Away from Other Professional Duties
> _____
> < Cost of the Ready-Made Product

Availability of Raw Materials

Availability of raw materials is a fifth factor that is often not consciously considered but has a significant impact on which materials are actually chosen for adaptive devices. When teachers and therapists are stumped as to how to design a device, a natural reaction is to survey the immediate surroundings to get ideas for what type of object might serve the purpose needed. When Paulette Binder needed a paper stabilizer for students, she looked around her home economics classroom and soon came up with her cookie sheet paper stabilizer (add adhesive magnetic tape to two flat strips of wood and then sandwich the paper between these magnetic strips and the cookie sheet). Teachers in India have been known to use (small) new potatoes to make enlarged pencil grips. They reportedly work great! [1]

Availability of supplies should always be a consideration when working in different cultures. It does not do nearly as much good to fly to a Third World country with armfuls of supplies (for making devices) that are unavailable in their own country than it does to show them how they can use their own available resources to make the same adaptive devices. As the old adage goes: "If you give a man a fish, you feed him for a day. If you teach a man to fish, you feed him for a lifetime." Bevill Packer, a sociology professor in a Zimbabwean college, exemplifies this philosophy by teaching people from Zimbabwe and other nearby countries how to use Appropriate Paper-Based Technology (APT) to make wheelchairs and other assistive devices [2]. He often uses newsprint, computer paper, cement-bag paper, and thin and thick cards to make these devices, using only a flour-based adhesive to hold the paper together. However, certain rules and procedures have been established to ensure that the device is safe and durable. The resulting product is functional, durable, attractive, and best of all - free!

Chapter 3
Materials & Processes

MATERIALS AND PROCESSES

This chapter discusses a variety of materials that are commonly used to make low tech assistive devices in the school setting, the processes involved in working with these materials, as well as general safety guidelines. The general safety guidelines, as well as the specific information that follows on handling particular materials, are not intended to substitute for proper training by a qualified instructor, but instead should be used as an adjunct to this instruction. The guidelines below do not include specific cautions and safety procedures relating to particular tools. Hands-on lab instruction on the safe use of power tools in particular is strongly recommended. Also read precautions provided by the manufacturers of any tool, material, or other supply that is used.

General Safety Precautions
When Handling Materials and Tools [1,2,3,4]

What to Wear:

- Do not wear loose clothing or jewelry that could get caught in the tools or machinery. Remove ties, roll up sleeves, and tie your hair back.

- Wear an apron to protect clothing from finishes and wood dust.

- Wear safety goggles or safety glasses when operating power tools or when doing any work that creates airborne debris.

- Wear protective gloves when applying wood stains.

- Wear a face mask if you are sensitive to dust or fumes.

How to Act:

- Keep your attention to your work at all times. Do not rush or let your mind wander.

- Do not talk and work at the same time.

The Working Environment:

- Always work in a well-lit and well-ventilated area. Good ventilation is especially critical when using finishes.
- Keep the working area uncluttered:
  - Make sure all tools and materials have a special storage location, and always return them to that location following use.
  - Neatly lay out the tools that will be needed, and make sure there is enough area to work in.
- Always clean and dry tools properly after use, before storing them.
- Always keep a first aid box available, and check it from time to time to make sure it is completely stocked.

Handling Tools:

- Never operate an electric tool in wet conditions.
- Always use a grounded (3-prong) plug, never a 2-pronged plug, to provide power to an electric tool.
- Never carry the tool by the cord or use the cord to pull the plug out of a socket.
- Unplug power tools as soon as you are finished using them, and before making adjustments or changing accessories.
- Check cords and plugs regularly for damage.
- Make sure handles on hand tools are tight.
- Keep tools properly sharpened. Dull tools can slip and cause injury. (Fewer accidents occur with sharp tools.)
- Use each tool only for its intended purpose, and always use the correct size tool for the job.
- Obtain instruction on how to use a tool properly and safely before using it.
- Pay close attention to the position of your body and the position of materials when using tools:
  - Never place your hands in front of the direction of movement of hand tools or in the direct line of power tool blades. When feeding work into a power saw, keep fingers out of the way of the blade, and also make sure thumbs are well out of the way as the blade breaks free at the edge of the work.
  - When cutting with a utility knife or other knife, always position your body and the material so you are cutting away from your body, never toward your body.
  - Make sure power cords are positioned well out of the way of the power tool before turning the tool on.

Handling Materials:

- Always clamp work securely.
- Always use finishes in a well-ventilated area.
- To prevent fires, store oily rags used for finishing in closed metal containers.
- Watch for splinters when dealing with rough lumber.
- Always follow manufacturer's directions when using finishes or any other materials.

MATERIAL: WOOD

Some Uses for Assistive Devices:
Chair inserts (though heavy), footstools, easels, object stabilizers,
working surfaces, keyboard stands, dowel handles, jigs, etc.

HOW TO CUT:

Always clamp wood securely before using a hand saw.

Always sand after sawing, and before attaching pieces together.

Handsaws

RIPSAW: Cuts along the grain. CANNOT cut across the grain.

CROSSCUT SAW: Cuts across the grain and through plywood. CAN cut along the grain. (Therefore, if you have to choose one saw, choose a cross cut saw.)

BACKSAW (MITER SAW): Used for fine work. Often stabilized in a miter box, which is a wooden jig that guides the saw and is used for cutting miter joints and square ends.

COPING SAW: Cuts curves in thin pieces of wood.

- If the blade is inserted with teeth pointing away from the handle, use in a manner similar to a crosscut saw.

- If teeth point toward the handle, support the material to be cut on a "V" shaped board which is held in a vice, hold saw vertically, and cut using vertical rather than horizontal movements [3].

- To make interior cuts with a coping saw:
    a. drill a hole in the wood
    b. detach the blade of the coping saw
    c. thread the blade through the hole and reattach to the coping saw
    d. use the saw to make the interior cut.

Power Saws

There are many types of power saws. The most common types of power saws Include the table or circular saw, band saw, jigsaw, and scroll saw. The electric jigsaw is the most versatile, least expensive, and quietest power saw to use, and can perform most (though not all) wood cutting jobs needed for making low tech assistive devices. Obtain proper training by a qualified instructor before using any power saw, to ensure safe use.

Chisels & Gouges

A gouge is a type of chisel designed for making grooves or shaping edges.

A chisel has a flat blade; a gouge has a concave blade.

- If gouging a groove, use an out-cannel gouge, which has a bevel on the outside of the blade.
- There are many types of chisel blades and handles. Please obtain proper training in choosing and using chisels from a qualified instructor.

Some reminders for proper handling of a chisel:

- Always clamp the wood securely before chiseling it.
- Never place your hand in front of the chisel.
- Usually, the flat side of the chisel is held against the wood with the beveled side up, although there are exceptions (e.g. bevel faces down with out-cannel gouge).
- Hold the chisel with one hand, with index finger extended toward the blade. Guide the blade with the other hand, gripping the blade behind the cutting edge between thumb and index finger, with remaining fingers resting against the work to steady the tool. The guide handle also serves as a brake. [2]
- Always cut with the grain, if possible, to obtain a smooth and controlled cut and avoid splitting the wood.
- If added pressure is needed while chiseling, use a mallet, not a hammer.
- Make "stop cuts" before chiseling out the wood, so if the wood splits, it will do so only in the portion to be removed. To make a stop cut:
  a. Position chisel vertically at the point where the cut should stop, with beveled edge facing the waste wood.
  b. Tap the chisel with a mallet [3].
- Outline the area to be grooved (such as a recess for a hinge) with a series of stop cuts, and also make a series of parallel cuts inside the groove before chiseling out the waste wood.

HOW TO ATTACH/BOND:

Glue

Glue can be used to attach small pieces of wood together without the need for nails or screws, as long as the joint will not receive too much stress. Glue is also sometimes used in addition to metal hardware for reinforcement, although this usually isn't necessary. Always clamp after gluing or immediately attach the screws or nails. Wipe off excess glue with a hot, damp cloth before it dries or else it will seal the wood and reduce absorption of the wood finish. Follow manufacturer's directions when using glues.

Some common types of wood glue:
  a. STANDARD WOODWORKER'S GLUE

  b. HOT GLUE: Applied with a glue gun. This type of glue dries within seconds, so work quickly!

  c. WHITE GLUE (such as Elmer's): Not as durable as woodworker's glue.

Screws

- If the two pieces of wood have different thicknesses, screw all the way through the thinner and into the thicker piece of wood. [1]

- Choose a screw that is about 3 times as long as the thickness of the piece of wood it is to secure (if possible), but make sure it stops at least 1/8" short of the opposite side of the other piece of wood or else it will create a bulge in the wood. [1,2]

- Select the largest screw "gauge" (i.e. diameter) possible without exceeding 1/10 of the width of the wood into which it will be inserted. A good rule of thumb is to use #4 screws when screwing into wood that is 1/2" thick, #6 or #8 screws for wood 3/4" thick and #10 or #12 screws for wood 1 1/2" thick [1].

    FLAT HEAD SCREWS (OR BOLTS) should be countersunk
    (i.e. head is recessed into the wood)

    ROUND HEAD SCREWS (OR BOLTS) should not be countersunk.

    OVAL HEAD SCREWS are used mostly for attaching flat metal to wood, such as hinges, and should be countersunk. [3]

- Screws are also categorized by the type of screwdriver they require. *Always choose a screwdriver that fits the size and shape of the screw slot exactly.* Otherwise, it will strip the screw slot, damage the wood, slip out of the slot and cause injury, or fail to provide enough force to turn the screw.

    PHILLIPS HEAD SCREWS have a cross-shaped groove to fit a Phillips head screwdriver

    SLOTTED SCREWS have a single straight groove to fit a straight-tip screwdriver.

- Always clamp wood securely before using a power drill, or else the drill will tend to spin the wood.

Procedure:

Place the boards to be fastened in their proper position, clamp well, and drill a pilot hole through both, drilling all the way through the first piece of wood. Pilot hole should be slightly smaller than the shank of the screw (and the same size as the root of the screw). When drilling through the second board, pilot hole should be bored about half as deep as the screw enters the wood for soft woods such as pine, and should be bored the same depth as the screw enters the wood for hardwoods [3]. Next, enlarge the hole that was bored all the way through the first board using a drill bit that equals the diameter of the screw shank. This is called a shank hole. Inset screw if flat surface desired - do this by widening the upper end of the shank hole with a countersink bit, which recesses the screw head so it is flush with the surface of the wood. To recess the screw below the surface, use a counterbore bit [3].

Nails

- Nails are quicker and simpler but sometimes loosen and do not produce a well-finished look. They're good for basic box-shapes.
- Nail length should be 3 times the thickness of the first board the nail goes through. Select a nail diameter that is not so large that it will split the wood.

  BOX NAILS and COMMON NAILS have large flat heads.

  FINISHING NAILS have small heads. The head of a finishing nail is often set below the surface of the wood using a nail set, and is then covered with wood putty or wood plastic.

- Drill a small pilot hole through the first board when driving nails through hardwoods.

Procedure:

Hold nail firmly in place with one hand, and tap it lightly a couple of times until it stands unsupported with the tip in the board. Hold hammer handle near the end, and use mostly elbow movements to swing the hammer, not wrist movements. Keep your eye on the nail and strike it firmly square on the head.

To remove nails: Position the claw of the hammer under the nail head and pull on the handle to lever it out. If the nail is too long to remove it with one pull, place the hammer head on a block of wood to increase the leverage.

Dowel Joints

Dowel joints are incorporated in many fabricated devices, especially those that require stabilization yet easy removal, such as an organ keyguard (page 234), keyboard stand attached to lap tray (page 124) or reading stand attached to lap tray (page 172).

Size of dowels: "As a guide, make the length not less than five times the diameter. The longer the dowel, the greater the gluing area will be. The diameter of the dowel can be half the thickness of the wood." [2] Cut with a fine-toothed saw.

Size of hole: Slightly deeper than half the length of the dowel. Drill the hole using a brad-point bit in a power drill, or a brace and auger bit. [2]

Procedure:

1. Cut the dowels and holes to the correct size, as described above.

2. OPTIONAL: Use the fine-toothed saw to cut a lengthwise groove in the dowel to reduce the chances of the wood splitting from the release of hydraulic pressure as it is glued in. Use a pencil sharpener to very slightly angle the end of the dowel to make insertion easier.

3. Apply white glue in the holes and on the ends of the cut dowel. Use a mallet to hammer the dowel in the hole. [2]

Hinge Joints

Hinges are often used when making devices which are designed to increase the surface area of a button or switch. Two examples used at Perkins School for the Blind:

A pay telephone was adapted by attaching a hinged square of hard plastic over the push buttons to serve as an enlarged "operator button". A short dowel was screwed on the underside of the square of plastic at the exact spot where it would contact the real operator button if pressed. The hinge allows the enlarged "operator button" to be moved out of the way for those who use the regular telephone buttons.

A Radio Shack Plug 'n Power environmental control unit was adapted by placing it in a custom-built box with a hinged lid. A short dowel was screwed to the underside of the lid at the exact spot where it would contact the "light on" button if the lid was pressed.

- Hinges are sized by the length and width of each leaf.

- There are many types of hinges. Butt and continuous hinges are recessed into the wood, while many other types of hinges are set flush to the surface. A surface hinge is easiest to attach, although butt hinges are also popular.

- When hinges are used for the lid of a box, they are usually placed at a distance equal to its own length from the edge of the box. [2]

Procedure:

1. Mark the location of the hinge (as described above). If the hinge will be set into the wood: mark the width and the depth of the gain (i.e. recessed area) and use a chisel to outline the gain and chisel out the wood (see Chisel information).

2. Put the hinge in place. Mark the holes for the screws with a pencil.

3. Remove the hinge and drill pilot holes into the wood.

4. Screw the hinge to the box. Fasten only one screw in each hinge leaf at first, so adjustments can be made easily if necessary.[4]

Bolts

Unlike screws, bolts have the same diameter from end to end. They also have more holding power than screws. They are often used when making adaptive devices that need to allow for disassembling or positioning adjustments (such as the height of a book ledge on an easel).

Procedure:

Drill a hole equal to the diameter of the bolt through both pieces of wood, slide the bolt through both pieces of wood, then add a metal washer (optional) and screw on a nut. The washer distributes the pressure of the nut so it doesn't dig into the wood. If the bolt will slide along a slot to adjust positioning of the device, drill two holes that are slightly wider than the diameter of the bolt, one at each end of the desired slot, and use a coping saw to connect the drilled holes.

Hanger Bolts

Hanger bolts have a machine screw thread on one end and a lag screw thread on the other end. Like regular bolts, they allow for disassembly of parts. They are used when the board to be attached is too thick to use a regular nut and bolt attachment, or when one side of the board is inaccessible for attaching a standard nut and bolt (such as when attaching a ceiling light to a ceiling).

Procedure:

1. Drill a pilot hole at the desired location for the hanger bolt that equals the diameter of the root of the lag thread end of the hanger bolt. Drill to the depth that the screw will enter the wood.

2. Screw two nuts on the machine screw end of the hanger bolt until they are locked together.

3. Use a wrench (placed around the locked nuts) to screw the hanger bolt into the pilot hole. Remove the nuts from the hanger bolt.

About using the wrench: Make sure it fits the nut snugly or it will round the corners of the nut. Whenever possible, pull rather than push a wrench to avoid loss of balance and possible injury [3]. If pushing the wrench is necessary, use the base of the palm with fingers open; do not wrap the fingers around the handle.

HOW TO FINISH:

Sanding

Power sanders can be used instead of hand sanding, except for the final light sanding. Please obtain proper training before using them.

Procedure:
1. Before Assembly:
   - Always use a flat sanding block when sanding flat surfaces, to avoid making shallow gullies in the wood.

   - Always sand with the grain.

   - Start with coarse sandpaper, just coarse enough to remove uneven surfaces and flaws. Next use a medium grade sandpaper to remove scratches left from the coarse sandpaper and to further smooth the surface. Finish with a fine sandpaper until wood is as smooth as satin.

2. After Assembling the Pieces:
   Make sure wood is clean and smooth before applying a finish. Dampen the wood with a wet rag to raise the grain and leave to dry. Apply a final light sanding, and remove the wood dust with a cloth dampened with mineral spirits [2].

Finishing Options

Any of the following work well:
   Wood stain, varnish, lacquer, paint, wood-finishing oil, wax

Please follow manufacturer's directions to apply any finish, and observe all safety precautions listed on the label.

MATERIAL: TRIWALL

Some Uses for Assistive Devices:
Chair inserts, cubby tops for desks, raised lap trays/table surfaces,
easels, wrist rests, keyboard and calculator stands, etc.

HOW TO CUT:

Triwall material can be cut with a jigsaw, band saw, or a utility knife.

HOW TO ATTACH/BOND:

Attach triwall pieces together using wooden "nails" and glue, as follows:

To make the wooden nails:
1. Use a fine-toothed saw to cut a 3/16", 1/4", or 5/16" diameter dowel into 3" long pieces. In the projects described in later chapters, 1/4" dowels are used.
☞ There is a difference of opinion regarding the ideal nail size. The 3/16" dowel is more economical and reportedly holds up as well as the larger diameter dowels, but some believe the larger diameter dowels are more effective and durable. The 5/16" diameter nail will form a ridge in the surface of the Triwall when it is hammered unless it is lined up perfectly straight.
2. Sharpen one end of each nail with a pencil sharpener.

Procedure for attaching the pieces:
1. Make pilot holes with an awl in the first board that the nails will go through. Space the holes approximately 3" apart (sometimes up to 6" apart), and 1/3" in from the edge of the board.
2. Fill the pilot holes with woodworker's glue, and dip the ends of the nails in glue as well.
3. Apply hot glue to all contact surfaces of the Triwall, using a carpenter's heavy-duty glue gun. If a heavy-duty glue gun is not available, woodworker's glue may be substituted.
☞ Hot glue dries in seconds, so if you are covering a very large area, it may be necessary to use woodworker's glue instead.
4. Hammer in the nails.

Triwall also can be folded at intervals to form a curved surface. An adapted chair was formed in this manner using only two pieces of Triwall. One flat, horseshoe shaped piece was used for the sitting surface and a second piece curved around the edge of the sitting surface to form the back and side arms. To form folds in Triwall, press the Triwall against the edge of a table, and fold with the flutes.

HOW TO FINISH:

Any of the following work well:
• Cover edges and corners with duct tape or masking tape (former is more heat resistant) and then paint with latex enamel.
• Cover with contact paper.
• Simply cover edges with colored floor tape for an attractive, finished look.

MATERIAL: POLYETHYLENE (HARD) FOAM

Some Uses for Assistive Devices:
To increase the thickness of positioning devices
(such as raised chair seats or raised table surfaces) or to make devices
that require carved-out forms (such as object stabilizers).

☞ 2" thick, 2 lb. density polyethylene foam is recommended. This density is easy to cut, and the thickness serves most purposes that it is used for.

Polyethylene foam is often referred to as styrofoam by therapists, but is in fact a completely different material. (According to the manufacturer, styrofoam refers to the material used inside some coolers.) It can be purchased at a packaging company such as Perry Packaging (see Resource Directory).

HOW TO CUT:
Polyethylene (hard) foam can be cut with an electric carving knife, saw or steak knife. A table saw is recommended for cutting very large pieces.

HOW TO ATTACH/BOND:
Polyethylene foam can be bonded together by melting contact areas until bubbly (using a hot gun) and pressing them together. If the contact areas to be bonded are so large that they cannot stay properly heated before bonding, then place the foam pieces together and use the hot gun around the perimeter to fuse the edges together.

If the desired thickness of hard foam is, say, 1 1/2 times the actual thickness of the foam, then slice one sheet in half using an electric carving knife or a table saw, and bond a 1/2 thickness sheet with a full thickness sheet using the above procedure.

Polyethylene foam can be carved into an endless variety of shapes and forms using the electric carving knife or other cutting tools. You can bond sheets together first (if necessary) using the above procedure, then carve out the shape.

HOW TO FINISH:
Any of the following work well:
• Cover with attractive contact paper.

• Add Triwall as a base, and wrap vinyl material around the whole thing and staple it to the Triwall.

• Cover with vinyl material, and use Barge all purpose cement to bond the vinyl to itself. Cover edges with same-colored floor tape, if desired.

MATERIAL: POLYURETHANE (SOFT) FOAM

Some Uses for Assistive Devices:
To pad positioning devices such as chair inserts or arm/wrist rests;
also occasionally used to increase the thickness of an object for grasp.

HOW TO CUT:

Cut polyurethane (soft) foam with a scissors.

HOW TO ATTACH/BOND:

Polyurethane material is a padding material, and as such, it is usually sandwiched between a base (such as wood or Triwall) and a covering material such as vinyl. The covering material may be stapled to the hard base using a heavy duty staple gun. If a hard base is not used, the covering material is often sewed into a pouch (like a pillow) into which the padding is inserted.

HOW TO FINISH:

Cover with a suitable fabric. Different fabrics have different virtues. Vinyl is durable, waterproof, and very easy to clean, and is a very common covering material. Some students require alternative materials due to sensitive skin, tactile hypersensitivity, tendency for pressure sores, or other reasons. Wheelchair suppliers (including Alimed) are a good source of information on these materials.

MATERIAL: VINYL FABRIC

Some Uses for Assistive Devices:
To cover positioning devices (such as chair inserts, arm/wrist rests)
and other padded devices.

HOW TO CUT:

Vinyl fabric can be cut with a scissors.

HOW TO ATTACH/BOND:

Depending on the type of object being fabricated, any of the following could be appropriate:

Heavy-duty staple gun
Hot glue
Sewing machine
Barge cement (available from North Coast Medical, Inc.)

☞ If using the cement, follow the manufacturer's directions and precautions very carefully, as this is a toxic material.

MATERIAL:
LOW TEMPERATURE THERMOPLASTIC
(SPLINTING MATERIAL)

Some Uses for Assistive Devices:
This material is formulated especially for making hand splints,
but is also used to make low tech assistive devices that require
a curved shape or a formed fit around a body part or device.

Types: There are many types of low temperature thermoplastic materials. The 1997 North Coast Medical Catalog includes an excellent poster that compares the properties (stretch resistance, drape, memory, rigidity, bonding, and surface finish) of the nine North Coast thermoplastics as well as ten other common thermoplastic materials sold by Smith & Nephew Inc. as well as Johnson and Johnson. [5]

HOW TO CUT:

To break off small, hard sections at room temperature:
Score material with a utility knife and then break the material along the scored line.

To cut out the drawn design:
Fill a splinting pan or electric frying pan with water, and preheat the water to the temperature recommended by the manufacturer. Submerge the material until the recommended time/softness is reached, and cut the pattern using heavy-duty or splinting scissors.

HOW TO ATTACH/BOND:

To shape, always make sure the material has cooled sufficiently before shaping to a body part.

Each type of thermoplastic material has different heating temperatures and properties which require different types of handling. Please follow the manufacturer's directions.

To bond two pieces of low temperature thermoplastic material [5]:
Low temperature thermoplastic material can be bonded together with wet heat or dry heat. Dry heat generally results in a firmer bond than wet heat. Some types of material have a special coating to prevent accidental bonding. This coating must be removed with a special solvent or by light surface abrasion before bonding can occur.

Please follow manufacturer's instructions for the particular material being used.

Procedure:

WET HEAT: Soften the two pieces of thermoplastic material in a splinting pan or electric frying pan filled with water and press them together.

DRY HEAT: Use a heat gun to soften the contact surfaces of both pieces, and press them together.

To attach other materials to low temperature thermoplastic materials:
Materials such as hair clips, thin metal rods, etc., can be simply sandwiched between two pieces of thermoplastic material. Sometimes plastic welder glue or other heavy duty glue is used for reinforcement, although this is usually not necessary. Other times, the items are not sandwiched but are instead recessed and glued (using plastic welder glue or other heavy duty glue) into the thermoplastic material.

HOW TO FINISH:

Colored thermoplastic material is recommended when fabricating devices to improve aesthetics.

To finish the exposed edges either of the following work well:
- Use fingers to smooth the edges while heated.

- Use a potato peeler or leather edger to bevel the edges; then dip in hot water and polish with heel of hand. [6]

MATERIAL:
OTHER PLASTIC MATERIALS

Some Uses for Assistive Devices:
To make keyguards, switch mounts, lap trays, mounts
for lap top computers or other communication devices, eye-gaze boards, etc.

Types: Expanded PVC, Acrylics (e.g. Plexiglass, Lexan), Kydex, Others.

HOW TO CUT:

Most hand tools and power tools that are intended for use with wood or metal can also be used with plastic [3]. Since plastic is denser than wood, wood tools dull quickly. Therefore, metal cutting tools and blades are preferable.

Handsaws

Handsaws should have fine-toothed blades. Hacksaws, backsaws, fine-tooth coping saws, and jeweler's saws can be used. Saw with light pressure to avoid cracking the plastic.

Power Saws

A bandsaw or jigsaw may be used, but feed the plastic very slowly to reduce friction and melting. The jigsaw works well with plastic 1/2" thick or less, but thicker pieces will melt. The band saw is less likely to melt the plastic because the blade has a chance to cool.

HOW TO ATTACH/BOND:

Self-tapping, drive, or machine screws can be used to fasten plastic together [3]. Drill a hole slightly smaller than the diameter of the screw shank before inserting it.

When drilling a piece of hard plastic into a piece of wood, use a wood screw, and drill a hole all the way through the plastic using a drill bit equal to the shank (called a shank hole), and drill a pilot hole in the wood equal to the diameter of the root.

Regular twist drills can be used on plastic. When using a drill, use light pressure and slow speed to prevent melting. When drilling into heavier plastic, pull out the drill often to keep the hole cool, so the plastic doesn't melt. If the plastic melts, it will be impossible to remove the drill when it cools again) [3].

Cementing Plastic
It is necessary to use a cohesive (not adhesive) cement with plastic, to allow the contacting surfaces to fuse together [3]. There are many types. Inquire at a hardware store.

Bending Plastic
By definition, any type of plastic can bend if provided with enough heat. High temperature thermoplastic materials can often be heated in a regular kitchen oven. However, they are more dangerous to handle than the low temperature thermoplastic materials, so thorough training should be obtained by a qualified instructor before heating them. Also see manufacturer's directions for the particular plastic to be heated.

Expanded PVC requires only a heat gun to bend the material to the desired shape.

HOW TO FINISH:
Sanding Plastic
The same procedure should be followed for sanding plastic as with wood [3]. Inquire at the hardware store regarding types of sandpaper that are most suitable for the particular material.

Polishing Plastic
If desired, plastic can be polished with a buffing wheel or by hand buffing with a soft cloth and non-scratch household cleaner [3].

MATERIAL: METAL

Some Uses for Assistive Devices:
Flat metal sheets are used for magnetic notebooks and other magnetic surfaces, or to cover an object for protection (such as covering the keyboard of the Macintosh power book to prevent a child who has athetoid movements from damaging it while using the touch screen). Metal rods are used for pointers, as strength reinforcement rods for devices made of low temperature thermoplastic material, or for outriggers to hold sandwich clips, etc.

HOW TO CUT:

Use metal cutters to cut galvanized steel. Cut metal rods with a hack saw. Large metal tubes such as EMT tubing can be cut with a hack saw or metal band saw.

HOW TO ATTACH/BOND:

Galvanized Steel
Thin steel bends easily, resulting in fewer instances in which two separate pieces of steel need to be attached together. When necessary, steel sheets can be attached by gluing, soldering, welding, or brazing. The last two processes usually need to be performed professionally. Gluing can be used to attach small decorative pieces or fittings; inquire at a hardware store regarding types of glues. Please obtain proper training before using a soldering iron.

Metal Rods
These are often attached to other materials, such as low temperature thermoplastic material or wood.

To attach a thin metal rod or wire to low temperature thermoplastic material:
Sandwich the rod or wire between two pieces of very soft, pliable thermoplastic material. If desired, apply plastic welder glue or other heavy duty glue before sandwiching the pieces together. Make a groove in the thermoplastic material, fill with plastic welder glue or other heavy duty glue, and press the wire into the groove. Cover with another piece of thermoplastic material.

To attach a threaded metal rod to wood: Drill a hole that is the same diameter as the threaded metal rod. Screw a nut onto the dowel until it is just past the desired location for the wood. Apply some epoxy glue or hot glue into the drilled hole in the wood and put the metal rod through the hole. Screw a nut onto the part of the rod sticking through the back of the wood piece. Add more glue on both sides of the wood piece and while glue is still wet tighten both nuts against the wood.

HOW TO FINISH:

Metal sheets can be covered with attractive contact paper. However, before attaching the contact paper, remove any rough metal splinters (burrs) from the edges using a metal file and cover edges with a thick material such as duct tape so the student does not become injured from any sharp edges or protrusions.

The rough ends of cut metal rods also need to be deburred with a metal file to reduce the chance of injury. It is also wise to cover the ends of metal rods with another material such as an eraser head, plastic dip (see page 134) or tape, for added protection.

Part II

DEVICES
USED THROUGHOUT
THE SCHOOL ENVIRONMENT

This section of the book describes handmade or modified assistive devices which may be used in a variety of settings throughout the school or to assist with transitions from class to class.

These devices address concerns such as environmental distractions, positioning, mobility, appropriate working surfaces, manipulating objects, and communication with others; concerns which are present no matter what activity is at hand.

It is suggested that the reader review this section first before proceeding to the classroom subject of interest, as many of the solutions to student problems will be found here.

Chapter 4
Positioning

CLASSROOM POSITIONING
FOR POSTURE AND ATTENTION

Whenever setting up an activity for a student, the very first thing to consider is the student's positioning, as this will significantly affect the student's ability to control all parts of his or her body. This includes:

- the use of the arms and hands to perform a task

- control of the neck and oral muscles for eating, talking, using a headpointer or mouthstick

- control of the respiratory muscles for breathing, talking, and coordinating breathing with swallowing

- use of the legs and feet for those students who use thigh or foot pointers or who access switches using their legs or feet.

Good positioning of the body is critical for optimum task performance.

All muscles require a stable base from which to move a body part. Therefore, the trunk of the body must be properly stabilized in order for a person to be able to finely control the direction, speed, and force of limb movements. For example, teachers have long been aware of the direct effect of their students' postures on the quality of their handwriting.

A teacher will often instruct students to sit up straight, with feet flat on the floor, and rest their forearms on the table before beginning a handwriting exercise. However, it is not always recognized that poor posture has an equally negative effect on the successful performance of other tasks as well.

The human body is innately designed to provide a controlled balance between stability and mobility. Those who have physically intact bodies are able to perform most tasks without external supports, unless the task requires a very high level of precision or endurance. It is common for many people to sit on the bed to get dressed or to sit on a backless stool at a breakfast counter to eat a quick breakfast. However, whenever a sitting position needs to be maintained for a greater length of time, such as when eating a full dinner or when sitting in a classroom or movie theater, people usually sit in chairs that have backrests to prevent muscle fatigue. Students who have low or high muscle tone or other physical limitations often lack this balance between stability and mobility, and may need additional external supports when sitting for any length of time.

When a task requires great precision, people usually (often unconsciously) seek out an external support to stabilize the joint or joints that are closest to those used to perform the movements. For example, writing is much easier when the forearms are stabilized on a table surface (which provides a stable base from which to move the wrist and finger muscles). Threading a needle is also simpler when the elbows or forearms are placed on a solid surface or braced against the body. Students who have physical impairments often need adapted working surfaces, wrist rests, and other assistive devices in order to provide this base of stability.

As seen above, the principle that "all muscles require a stable base from which to move" is not only relevant when positioning the trunk and lower extremities in a chair, but also when positioning the arms and hands for object manipulation. For this reason, this chapter is divided into two sections: Seating Solutions and Working Surfaces.

SEATING SOLUTIONS

The first task when setting up any activity for a student is to find an appropriate chair (or sometimes an alternative positioning solution). In fact, many students who look like they may need all sorts of supports to keep them upright may simply be sitting in a chair that is the wrong size! Perhaps the chair is so deep that the student keeps sliding out of it, or so high that the student cannot keep his feet flat on the floor. Providing the right size chair may be the only intervention needed for this student.

The position of the pelvis is the most important determining factor for positioning the body properly in a chair. The pelvis in a neutral position looks like the pelvis in Figure 1. The muscles of the hip flexors and extensors are balanced so that the hip bone is directly above where the head of the femur (upper leg bone) inserts into the pelvis. The pelvis should not fall back into a posterior pelvic tilt shown in Figure 2, (usually due to overactive hip extensors), nor should it be anteriorly tilted as depicted in Figure 3, (which can be due to several causes, including very low tone and severe hip flexion contractures).

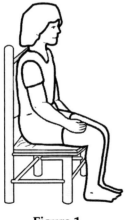

Figure 1
Neutral Position

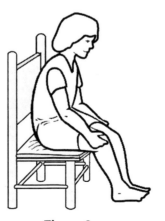

Figure 2
Posterior pelvic tilt

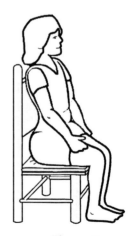

Figure 3
Anterior pelvic tilt

Determining Chair Measurements

The appropriate chair will meet all of these qualifications: The *seat depth* (which is the distance from the backrest to the front of the chair) should allow the pelvis to be positioned in neutral with the back of the buttocks resting against the back support. The knees should still be able to bend at least 90 degrees. The seat itself should reach under the knee as far as possible without limiting knee motion. To measure this, have the student sit on a firm surface. Using a tape measure, measure the distance from the back contact surface (which can simply be a notebook placed against the back of the buttocks) to the crease under the knee. Subtract between half an inch and two inches for knee clearance, depending on the student's size and range-of-motion limitations.

The *height of the chair seat* should be low enough to allow the feet to be fully supported on the floor, but not so low that the thighs are lifted off the chair seat when the feet are flat on the floor. Note also that the pelvis must remain in a neutral position, which is impossible if the thighs are lifted too high.

The *back rest* should provide firm support to the back, at least up to the lower border of the shoulder blades but often higher, especially for students who have fine motor difficulties. The back rest should be at a 90 degree angle to the sitting surface, in most cases. To obtain the height measurement for the back support, first make sure the child is sitting upright on a firm chair with pelvis in neutral and feet supported on a flat surface. Measure from the seat surface of the chair (from behind the buttocks) to the inferior angle of the scapula if the child has good trunk control. When determining measurements for a child with poor trunk control, remember that the height of the back support may also depend on the activity that is to be performed.

Some children will require greater support (to the top of the shoulder, or to the top of the head) when involved in a fine motor activity, and less support when involved in a task that has no upper extremity demands (such as listening to the teacher read a book). This is particularly true if the goal is to increase the child's own trunk control when sitting. [1,2,3]

If a chair of the correct size is unavailable, it may be possible to adapt an available chair by making a Built-Up Seat and/or a Firm Back Support (directions at end of chapter), or a foot stool (see Quick Tip #2). If the chair is too high, a few inches of the chair legs can be cut off. (This suggestion is good only if no other students need to use the chair!) Some students can also benefit from Hip Supports (directions at end of chapter) to stabilize the hips for improved trunk control while sitting. If the student requires additional supports, such as a head support, abductor wedge, pelvic belt, chest harness, etc., the child's physical and/or occupational therapist should be consulted to evaluate exactly what is needed and how it should be designed.

Positioning Duration and Location

*S*ome effective positioning solutions commonly used in the school setting are described in detail at the end of this chapter. It is important to note that students at Cotting School do not remain seated in a school chair, adapted or not, for more than 50 minutes at one stretch. The therapists have found that polyurethane (soft) foam and vinyl are both inexpensive and appropriate materials for this limited use. However, if a student will be sitting in an adapted chair (such as a wheelchair) for longer periods of time, materials will need to be carefully chosen in order to prevent skin breakdown or other problems. Wheelchair suppliers are a good source of information on these alternative materials.

Remember that for most students with physical challenges, prolonged sitting can result in a significantly increased risk for contractures or joint deformities, skin breakdown, osteoporosis, and impaired blood circulation. At Cotting School, most students are positioned out of their wheelchairs at least once a day, usually in some type of stander, and may also be positioned in a side-lyer, posture chair, or bolster chair for certain class periods. Some suppliers of these devices include Rifton, TherAdapt Products, Inc., and Abilations by Sportime.

Finally, don't forget to put some thought into WHERE to locate the student's seat in the classroom:

If the student is *visually distracted,* avoid positioning him or her near the window or door and make sure any bulletin boards placed in view of the student are kept fairly unexciting. If these adjustments are not enough, consider giving the student a cubby desk (i.e. desk with a tall wall around the sides and back) to reduce visual input. Directions for making a cubby-top for an existing desk are given on page 50.

If the student is *hypersensitive to touch,* seat the student away from the pathways leading to cubbies, classroom door, or the teacher's desk, which would put him or her at risk for accidentally getting brushed by students as they pass by. This can make a student hypervigilant (that is, always on the look-out for potential "touchers") which will interfere with the student's ability to concentrate on the task at hand. Make sure the student is sitting in a chair with a comfortable texture as well as appropriate proportions. See Quick Tip #4 for a unique solution that worked well for one individual who is severely hypersensitive to the textures and uneven pressure sensations of most chairs.

If the student is *hypersensitive to sounds,* one great solution is to put tennis balls on the bottoms of all of the legs of the classroom chairs and desks. (See Quick Tip #5) In many school classrooms, every furniture leg is outfitted with a tennis ball, which tremendously reduces the noise levels in those classrooms. Another recommendation is to position the student away from sources of extraneous sounds, (including the door, open windows, any students who make distracting sounds, and perhaps even the teacher's desk). Positioning the teacher's desk at a distance from where he or she usually teaches (i.e. the blackboard) would enable the student to be close to the teaching location, yet separated from students and staff conversing at the teacher's desk.

WORK SURFACES

All students need appropriate work surfaces when engaged in fine motor tasks, since the height and angle of a work surface will significantly affect body positioning and subsequently task performance. This need is most crucial during tasks requiring a high level of precision, such as writing or producing high-detail art work. A general rule that applies to most people is that the table height should be approximately 2" higher than the bent elbow when the student is sitting upright [4,5,6].

This allows the upper arms to be positioned at least 30 degrees forward from the trunk when resting the forearms on the table. However, this measurement may vary

Upper arms positioned 30° forward from trunk of body

depending upon the individual needs of the child. For example, many children who have muscular dystrophy need a higher table to compensate for extreme muscle weakness. Children with cerebral palsy may also need a higher surface to inhibit their tendency to pull into flexion [7]. Whenever possible, be sure that the shoulders are not elevated when the forearms are supported on the table.

One recommended table that is on the commercial market is the adjustable computer table (#26571) sold by Holt, Co. as it is the perfect size for one student, has a large work surface, and requires only a couple of seconds to adjust the height by using the crank. This table is very useful for a wide variety of table-top activities, not just as a computer table. Effective raised table surfaces are also easy to make, and directions are given at the end of this chapter.

Vertical work surfaces are often recommended for many students who have fine motor difficulties in order to improve development of arm and shoulder muscles, wrist extension, thumb opposition, as well as the hand arches [8]. All of the above are prerequisites for the development of precise object grasp, release, and manipulation skills, including the proper holding and use of a pen or pencil.

Vertical work surfaces can be created just by taping the child's work to the classroom wall or having the child write on a chalkboard or a wall-mounted marker board. The child's work can also be set up on a floor easel or table-top easel. One recommended table-top easel is the Activity Tray available through Sammons Preston. It is very big and heavy, which is both an advantage and a disadvantage. It can take a lot of pressure without sliding and has a surface big enough for any type of project. However, it is not as easy to set-up and take down as the lightweight easels. The Table Top Easel by Therapro can be set up at a 60 or a 30 degree angle depending upon how it is positioned on the table, and has a built-in compartment to store art supplies.

The Adjustable Table (#JE27) by Rifton Equipment has always been popular at Cotting School, because it is adjustable in both height and angle (and also has a cut-out design which provides more arm support). However, some students who benefit from an angled surface have switched from using this table to using the Magnetic Notebook and Ruler (see page 190) on a standard desk because the notebook provides the angled surface while still leaving some of the flat desk top surface available for placing pencils and other objects (which roll off the Rifton desk if not caught by the narrow ledge). The notebook can also be used when a group of students are sitting at the same table. Another good vertical working surface for reading materials and some fine motor activities is the Triwall Easel (page 47).

QUICK TIPS *Problems and Possible Solutions*

Following are some solutions which have successfully solved the identified problem for one or more students. Keep in mind that each student has a unique set of abilities and needs and may therefore require an original solution for the problem at hand. If a suggested solution is appropriate for a student, please adapt the design as necessary to best meet his or her needs.

Remember: fit the device to the student, not the student to the device!

1. Student slips and slides on smooth-surfaced chairs.

Place a 12" x 12" rubber-backed, low loop pile carpet square on the seat of the chair. This can have the same effect as Dycem to assist students to remain upright and in one spot so they can focus on their schoolwork instead of worrying about falling off their chair! Outdated samples are available at most carpet stores, or they can sometimes be bought at discount stores.
(Amy A. Houghton, OTR/L, Occupational Therapy Team Leader, Cotting School)

2. Chair is too high to position feet on the floor.

Make a hard foam foot stool: Use an electric knife to carve a block from 2" thick polyethylene (hard) foam sheeting that is big enough to fully support the feet, and then cover it with attractive contact paper. If additional height is needed, layer foam blocks by heating adjacent sides with a heat gun (until bubbly) to bond the layers together. If the child needs an angled surface to fully support the feet, simply use the electric knife to angle the polyethylene foam block.
(Sheryl Zelten, OTR/L, Occupational Therapist, while working at Cotting School)

3. Wheelchair cannot fit under the table.

If it is a standard 4-legged table, make table leg extenders out of polyethylene (hard) foam. Cut four squares of 2" thick polyethylene (hard) foam and carve out a bowl in each one that is big enough to place a table leg into it, using a knife or electric scissors to carve the bowl. If additional height is needed, layer polyethylene foam blocks by heating adjacent sides with a heat gun (until bubbly) to bond the layers together. This has proven to be very stable and is easier and much quicker than building something out of wood.

4. Student is sensitive to the texture or uneven pressure sensations caused by sitting in a typical chair.

Try placing a beaded car seat cover over the chair. (These can be found in the automotive section of large department stores.) This provides consistent pressure input which can be more comfortable for those students who demonstrate this hypersensitivity. Please consult with an occupational therapist who is experienced in treating sensory processing disorders to ensure that this solution does indeed solve the problem and not worsen it.
(Sue Shannon, OTR/L, Occupational Therapist, Perkins School for the Blind)

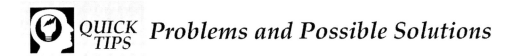

Problems and Possible Solutions

5. The noise of chairs sliding across the floor is distracting to certain students.

Put a tennis ball (old or new) over each leg of the chair. Simply make an X or a wide single slice into the tennis ball using a knife and slip it over the chair leg. This solution can be very helpful for those students who are easily distracted by sounds.

(Michael Talbot, Ed.D., Headmaster, Cotting School)

6. Student is squirmy - has difficulty remaining seated and attentive.

Try the Movin' Sit Cushion, by Ball Dynamics International, Inc., an air-filled, wedge shaped cushion that is placed on a chair seat. The cushion simulates the feeling of sitting on a therapy ball, except that it is much more stable. Recommended by a Cambridge Public School Liaison, this cushion has enabled one student at Cotting to remain seated through entire classroom periods for the first time, and also significantly reduced several inattentive behaviors in another Cotting student, including pushing his chair away from the desk, staring behaviors, and humming.

(Dina Becze, SLP, Team Leader for Related Services, Cambridge Public Schools, Cambridge, Ma.)

7. Student continually tilts chair backwards.

Nail 2 boards (like skis) to the bottoms of the chair legs to stabilize it.

8. Student requires forearm or wrist stabilized when performing fine motor tasks such as painting or using small manipulatives.

The following 2 devices have been found to be very effective for some students who require forearm or wrist stabilization in order to produce their best fine motor work.
They are especially useful for students who have ataxia or tremors:

The Angled Keyboard Stand with Attached Wrist Rest (page 122) can also be very effective when used as a working surface for some vertical-plane fine motor tasks, such as painting.
(Sheryl Zelten, OTR/L, first discovered this alternate use for the device.)

The Forearm/Wrist Rest for Keyboard (page 126) is effective in improving accuracy with object release during flat surface fine motor tasks such as ceramic tile or perler bead projects.

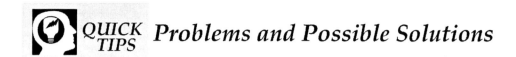
9. Student has difficulty keeping the non-dominant hand relaxed and near midline during sitting tasks, due to abnormal muscle tone (which may also result in asymmetry of the trunk).

💡 Make sure student is positioned in a correctly sized chair with appropriate support.

💡 Attach a dowel to the desk for the student to hold with the non-dominant hand to aid in positioning. (The Single Hand-Held Suction Dowel, available from Therapro Inc., really sticks!) If the student cannot maintain the forearm in a neutral position even with the help of a stabilized vertical dowel, try a stabilized horizontal dowel instead. Observe the student's posture and distribution of muscle tone when using this device to help determine whether or not this solution is appropriate.

(Karen Conrad, Sc.D., OTR/L, Occupational Therapist, Founder and President, Therapro, Inc.)

10. Care has been taken to ensure that the student is sitting in an appropriately sized chair and desk, but the student continues to slouch into a posterior pelvic tilt and/or slump over the desk.

💡 The student may benefit from having a wedge placed on the chair seat. See Modification 1 for the Built-Up Seat for Chairs described later in this chapter. Also remember to choose a chair that will be the correct size for the student once the wedge seat is placed on it.

💡 The Movin' Sit Cushion, by Ball Dynamics International, Inc. is an air-filled wedge that can also improve pelvic alignment and facilitate an upright trunk. See Quick Tip #6.

💡 Have the student try the Posture Chair by TherAdapt. This is also available from Abilitations by Sportime and Flaghouse. TherAdapt also sells an adjustable angle bench which is designed to promote "an anterior pelvic tilt, sitting posture, and increased weight-bearing through the lower extremities".

💡 A more vertically-angled working surface will usually promote better posture.

11. Student sits with one leg hanging off the side of the chair instead of both legs positioned forward, due to excessive hip abduction.

💡 Make a Built-Up Seat with Thigh Guides. See Modification 2 for the Built-Up Seat for Chairs described later in this chapter.

INSTRUCTIONS
FOR FABRICATING
SELECTED DEVICES

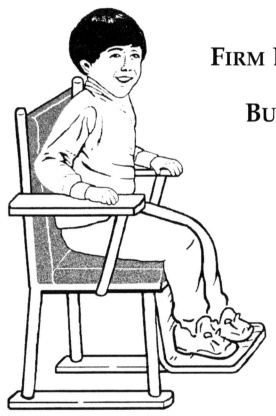

FIRM BACK SUPPORT
AND
BUILT-UP SEAT
FOR CHAIRS

HIP SUPPORTS
FOR CHAIRS THAT
HAVE SIDES

RAISED TABLE
SURFACE

TRIWALL EASEL

TRIWALL CUBBY-TOP FOR DESK

EASY HEIGHT-ADJUSTABLE ARM SLING
(WHEELCHAIR OR CEILING MOUNTED)

FIRM BACK SUPPORT FOR CHAIRS

DESCRIPTION: A sturdy, padded support for use with school chairs. Height and thickness can be customized to suit a particular student's needs.

PURPOSE:

1. To provide firm support for the student's back while in a chair, improving trunk stability and providing a stable base from which to move the arms for functional tasks.

2. To reduce the seat depth of a chair, allowing the student to sit upright with the pelvis in neutral position and feet flat on the floor or a support surface.

☞ Adding a back support to a chair will reduce the seat depth, so be sure to choose a chair that is deep enough to accomodate the planned support.

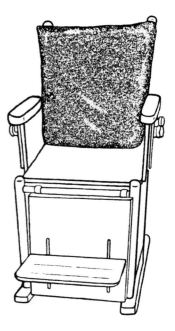

MATERIALS:

1. A chair as close to the dimensions required by the child as possible

2. Triwall material - about 18" by 32"

3. 1" thick polyurethane (soft) foam - about 18" by 32"

4. Vinyl material - about 25" by 40"

5. Optional: Strapping and or Velcro - for straps to attach support to chair

6. Optional: 2" thick polyethylene (hard) foam - for a very thick back support

TOOLS:

Razor knife, band saw, steak knife or jigsaw; heavy-duty scissors; heavy-duty staple gun; metal tape measure; marker

MEASUREMENTS:

1. **HEIGHT:** Make sure the child is sitting upright on the chosen chair with pelvis in neutral and feet supported on a flat surface. Measure from the seat surface of the chair (from behind the buttocks) to the bottom of the shoulder blades (inferior angle of the scapula) if the child has good trunk control. If the child requires full trunk support, measure to the top of the shoulder. If head support is required, measure from the seat surface to the top of the head.

2. **WIDTH:** at least equal to the width of the student's back.

3. **THICKNESS:** subtract the desired seat depth from the actual seat depth of the chair.

☞ Detailed information about determining measurements can be found in the earlier part of this chapter.

ASSEMBLY:

1. First draw a rectangle on the Triwall material using the height and width measurements obtained above. Cut the Triwall, using a razor knife, steak knife, band saw or jig saw.

2. Cut out a rectangle of polyurethane (soft) foam the same size as the Triwall. You can use the Triwall piece you have just made as a pattern, tracing it onto the foam with a marker. Use heavy duty scissors to cut foam.

3. Cut out a rectangle in the vinyl material that is approximately 7" longer and 7" wider than the size of the Triwall, for allowance when folding the vinyl over to the back of the Triwall and foam. If you are adding extra layers of hard foam or Triwall to increase the thickness of the back support (see step 5), add an additional 2" to both the length and the width of the vinyl piece for each added piece of "thickening".

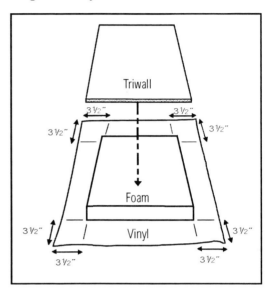

4. If the thickness of the foam and triwall together equal your thickness measurement, then assemble your back support as follows: Lay the vinyl face down on your work surface. Center the foam on the vinyl. Then lay the triwall on top of the foam, so that the edges are aligned with the foam. Now begin stapling the vinyl to the back of the Triwall, using a heavy-duty staple gun. For best results, anchor the center of each side with a few staples to hold all the parts together, and then work outward towards the corners. Overlap corner fabric and staple down. Trim off the excess vinyl material after stapling.

5. If the thickness of the foam and triwall together does not equal your thickness measurement, add an additional piece of Triwall between the Triwall base and the foam. If 2" or more of additional thickness is needed, add a layer of polyethylene (hard) foam between the Triwall and the soft foam. Then cover with vinyl material as described in step #4

6. **OPTIONAL:** Straps can be made of webbing and/or Velcro to attach the back support to the back of the chair. Simply staple the straps to the back of the back support.

7. **OPTIONAL:** Staple another piece of vinyl (same size as the Triwall) to the back of the back support, if it is preferred that the Triwall not be visible at all. Fold the edges in on the vinyl before stapling it to the Triwall.

Designed by
JoAnn Kluzik, M.S., PT., PCS, Physical Therapist,
while working at Cotting School.

BUILT-UP SEAT FOR CHAIRS

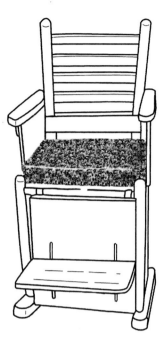

DESCRIPTION: A raised, cushioned seat placed on a chair.

PURPOSE:

1. To build up a seat when a student is sitting too low at the table.

2. To raise the height of the seat surface when the chair is too low to position the hips in neutral with feet fully supported on the floor.

MATERIALS:

1. A chair of appropriate seat width, seat depth, and back support
    Choose a chair with extra seat depth if a back support is also needed

2. Triwall material - same dimensions as seat surface of chair

3. 1" polyurethane (soft) foam - same dimensions as Triwall

4. Vinyl material - see step #2 to calculate amount needed

5. Optional: 2" polyethylene (hard) foam sheeting
    if additional height is needed

TOOLS:

Razor knife, band saw, steak knife or jig saw

Electric knife

Heavy-duty scissors

Heavy-duty staple gun

Metal tape measure

Magic marker

MEASUREMENTS:

1. **WIDTH AND DEPTH:** measure the width and depth of the chair. Use this depth measurement even if the chair is deeper than appropriate. If seat is too deep, a back support (directions included) should be made which will sit on top of the built-up seat and lessen the depth of the chair.

2. **HEIGHT:** subtract the present height of the chair seat from the desired height of the chair seat.

☞ Detailed information about determining measurements can be found
in the earlier part of this chapter.

ASSEMBLY:

1. Cut out rectangles of Triwall and polyurethane (soft) foam that match the width and depth measurements of the chair. Cut the Triwall using a razor knife, steak knife, band saw or jig saw, and the foam with a heavy-duty scissors.

2. Cut out a rectangle of the vinyl material that is approximately 7" longer and 7" wider than the size of the Triwall (or add 3 1/2" to each of the four sides), for allowance in folding the vinyl over to the back of the Triwall. If a layer of polyethylene (hard) foam is to be added (see step # 4 below), the vinyl material should be 12" longer and 12" wider than the Triwall (add 6" to each of the four sides).

3. If the thickness of the Triwall and polyurethane (soft) foam combined raises the chair seat to the desired height, proceed to cover them with the vinyl:

    a. Lay the vinyl face down on your work surface. Center the foam on the vinyl. Then lay the triwall on top of the foam, so that the edges are aligned with the foam.

    b. Now begin stapling the vinyl to the back of the Triwall, using a heavy-duty staple gun. For best results, anchor the center of each side with a few staples to hold all the parts together, and then work outward towards the corners.

    c. Overlap corner fabric and staple down. Trim off the excess vinyl material after stapling.

4. If the thickness of the Triwall and polyurethane (soft) foam combined does *NOT* raise the chair seat to the desired height, then add a piece of polyethylene (hard) foam (same dimensions as the Triwall) or an additional piece of Triwall between the Triwall base and polyurethane (soft) foam. Then cover with vinyl material as described in step #3.

MODIFICATIONS:

1. Wedge-Shaped Built-Up Seat: Use an electric carving knife to carve an angle into the polyethylene (hard) foam described in Step 4. The thickest part of the wedge should be at the front of the seat. Then follow Steps 1 through 3 to assemble and cover the Seat. The size of the polyurethane (soft) foam may need to be adjusted once the wedge shape is cut.

☞ Be sure chair is the correct size for the student WITH the wedge in place.

2. Built-Up Seat with Thigh Guides: Carve the polyethylene (hard) foam described in Step 4 so that it has lateral walls, using the electric carving knife. Then follow Steps 1 through 3 to assemble and cover the Seat. The size of the polyurethane (soft) foam may need to be wider to compensate for the curvature of the seat.

Designed by
JoAnn Kluzik, M.S., PT, PCS, Physical Therapist,
while working at Cotting School.

HIP SUPPORTS FOR CHAIRS THAT HAVE SIDES

DESCRIPTION: Two vinyl covered foam blocks to place between the sides of the chair and the hips while the student is seated.

PURPOSE:
To stabilize the hips and pelvis in the neutral position for improved posture and trunk control while sitting. This device is helpful for some physically challenged students as well as some learning challenged students who have low muscle tone resulting in poor pelvic and trunk alignment when sitting.

MATERIALS FOR A PAIR OF HIP SUPPORTS:

1. A chair of the appropriate size, with arms or sides (e.g. the Arm Chair from Rifton Equipment)

2. Vinyl material - about 1 yard

3. 2" polyethylene (hard) foam (2 lb. density) - about 18" square

4. Floor tape - same color as vinyl, to bind overlapping edges

TOOLS:
Barge Cement (available from North Coast Medical, Inc.)
Marker or pencil
Yardstick and metal tape measure
Electric carving knife or saw
Heavy duty scissors

MEASUREMENTS:

Make sure student is positioned correctly in the chair.

Measure the following:
1. **LENGTH:** the depth of the chair seat

2. **HEIGHT:** the distance from the seat surface to the top of the hips

3. **WIDTH:** the distance from the side of the chair to the hip.

ASSEMBLY:

1. Cut two blocks of polyethylene (hard) foam, each equaling the dimensions determined above. If the 2" foam is too thin or too thick, please refer to the chapter on Materials and Processes for directions on how to adjust the thickness of polyethylene (hard) foam.

2. Draw two rectangles on the vinyl using measurements determined above:

   > **LENGTH:** Length plus twice the height of the foam block.

   > **WIDTH:** Two times the width of the block, plus two times the height of the block, plus one inch.

Cut out vinyl, and note length and width on back if measurements are nearly the same. The rest of the steps will complete one hip support.

3. Wrap the width of the vinyl around the block, centering the overlapping edges on the middle of one long side. Make sure foam is centered with an equal amount of empty space at both ends. Use Barge Cement to glue down the edge of the vinyl where it will overlap, following the manufacturer's instructions. Cut a piece of floor tape the same length as the vinyl and seal your seam.

4. With heavy duty scissors, cut slits in each end of the vinyl from the edge of the vinyl to the corners of the foam inside it, resulting in four square flaps. At one end, fold down the flap containing the overlap. Fold down the other flaps one by one, securing each to the previous flap with Barge Cement, again following the manufacturer's instructions. Repeat for other end using the same sequence, so that both top flaps face the same direction. Be sure to cut off any excess material from second side before gluing flaps.

5. Cut a strip of floor tape the same length as your vinyl width measurement above. Wrap it carefully around the edge of the block, leaving half the width of the tape overhanging the edge of the block. Snip a small "V" out of the overhanging tape at each corner. Press tape down onto the ends of the block, one side at a time, binding and covering all the seams in the vinyl.

6. Repeat steps #3 through #5 for the second block.

Designed by
Amy Houghton, OTR/L, Occupational Therapy
Team Leader at Cotting School.

RAISED TABLE SURFACE

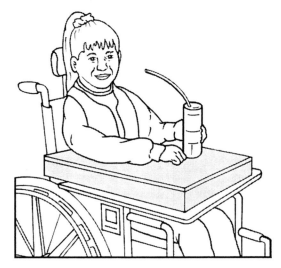

DESCRIPTION: A raised, horizontal work surface, exactly the same size and shape as the lap tray or the cut-out desk that it is placed on.

PURPOSE: To improve sitting posture and arm control during functional table-top tasks, for certain students who have severely increased tone, very low muscle tone, and/or severe muscle weakness. A student who requires a raised table surface often also benefits from using a lap tray or cut-out desk so the arms are fully supported.

MATERIALS:
1. Sheet of 2" thick, 2 lb. density polyethylene (hard) foam, same size as the lap tray or desk top
2. Triwall material same dimensions as the polyethylene (hard) foam
3. Attractive contact paper
4. Pressure-sensitive Velcro hook and loop tape
5. Heavy brown paper to make pattern

TOOLS:
Razor knife, band saw, steak knife or jig saw; electric knife, pencil or marker, heavy-duty scissors

MEASUREMENTS:
Whether a lap tray or cut out desk is used, the easiest measuring procedure is to make a tracing of the desk top or lap tray (including the sides that support the arms) rather than use a measuring tape.

ASSEMBLY:
1. Make a pattern by tracing the cut-out desk top or lap tray onto brown paper and cutting the shape out. Trace the pattern onto the polyethylene foam. Cut out the foam using the electric knife.

2. Using the same pattern, cut out a piece of Triwall.

3. Cover the Triwall with contact paper. If desired, cover the side edges of the polyethylene foam with contact paper, wrapping the contact paper over onto the top and bottom a few inches to keep it from peeling off.

4. Attach the Triwall to the top of the polyethylene foam using pressure-sensitive Velcro hook and loop tape.

Designed by
Sheryl Zelten, OTR/L, Occupational Therapist,
while working at Cotting School.

TRIWALL EASEL

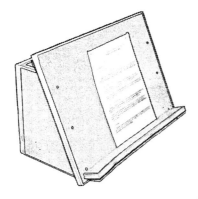

DESCRIPTION: A portable tabletop easel for fine motor activities or to hold a book.

PURPOSES:

1. To position reading materials for better viewing.

2. To improve positioning of the arms and hands for better fine motor performance.

MATERIALS:

1. Triwall material - 18" x 36"
2. 36" Wooden dowel - approximately $1/4$" diameter
3. Woodworker's glue
4. Duct tape, masking tape or colored floor tape to finish edges
5. Optional: Latex enamel paint

TOOLS:

Carpenter's heavy-duty glue gun and glue sticks (if not available, woodworker's glue may be substituted); band saw, jig saw, razor knife or steak knife; pencil sharpener, hammer, awl, yardstick and pencil or marker
Optional: Paintbrush

MEASUREMENTS:

The final measurements for the easel described below are 18" wide by 12" high, which is perfect when serving as a book easel or for a fine motor activity that has a relatively small working area. For students with different needs, alternate measurements are given at the end of these instructions.

Work surface of easel: 18" x 12"
Back of easel: 18" x 10 3/4"
Side panels: $3 1/2$" x $10 3/4$" x $8 1/2$" x 12"
Book ledge: 18" x 2"

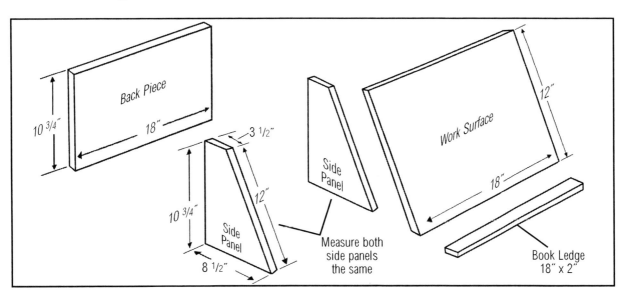

TRIWALL EASEL ASSEMBLY:
1. Draw one work surface, one back, one book ledge, and two side panels onto the Triwall using the measurements above. Cut pieces of Triwall out with the saw or knife.

2. From the wooden dowel, measure and cut three $2\,1/2$" pegs (for attaching book ledge) and eight 3" pegs (for attaching remaining Triwall pieces). Sharpen one end of each peg with the pencil sharpener.

3. Attach book ledge $1/2$" from bottom of the work surface as follows:
   a. Use the awl to make 3 pilot holes in the book ledge and matching ones in the work surface. Make one in the center and one $2\,1/2$" from each end. Fill all the holes with woodworker's glue.

   b. Apply hot glue from the glue gun along the contact surfaces of both pieces of Triwall.

   c. Attach the pieces together by hammering the three shorter wooden pegs into the pilot holes, hammering pegs from the under side of the work surface into the book ledge.

4. Attach the $10\,3/4$" edges of the two side panels flush against the $10\,3/4$" edges of the back piece of the easel:
   a. With the awl, make pilot holes along the $10\,3/4$" edges of the back piece, $1/3$" in from the edges. Put one hole 2" from the top and another $1\,1/2$" from the bottom of each short edge (4 holes total).

   b. Fill the holes on one side with woodworker's glue.

   c. Use the glue gun to make a thick line of hot glue along the two contact surfaces: the $10\,3/4$" cut edge of one side panel and one edge of the back (go right over the pilot holes). Join the glued edges together. Hammer the pegs through the back piece into the edge of the side panel.

   d. Repeat steps b and c to attach the other side panel.

5. Attach the work surface to the now combined "side/back" piece:
   a. With the awl, make two pilot holes in each 12" side of the work surface $1/3$" in from the edge, one 2" from the top and one $1\,1/2$" from the bottom. Fill the holes with woodworker's glue.

   b. Use the glue gun to make a thick line of hot glue along all the contact surfaces: the 12" cut edges of the side panels and the 12" edges of the work surface (right over the pilot holes). This time glue both sides of the work surface at once.

   c. Join the glued edges together. Hammer the pegs in through the work surface of the easel into the side panels.

6. Finish the easel using one of the following methods:

    a. For the greatest durability, cover the edges with masking tape or duct tape and give the easel a coat of latex enamel paint.

    b. Simply bind the edges with duct tape or colorful floor tape to give the easel a finished look. (The duct tape is more durable, but the floor tape looks prettier!)

ALTERNATE MEASUREMENTS:

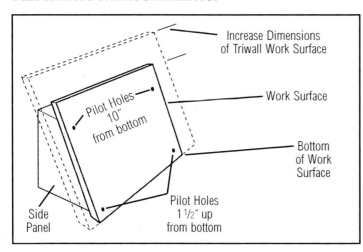

1. If a large range of arm movements is desired (such as for making large paintings), simply increase the dimensions of the large piece of Triwall that forms the work surface of the easel.

When making pilot holes to attach work surface to side panels, make holes 1 1/2" from the bottom and holes 10" from the bottom.

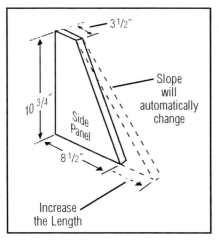

2. If it is desirable for the student to support the forearm on the easel.

    a. Enlarge the work surface as described above (#1).

    b. Adjust the angle of the easel so it is less vertical by increasing the length of the (formerly 8 1/2" long) bottom edge of each side piece as shown in diagram until desired angle is reached.

☞ This will automatically change the slope of the edge that supports the work surface.

    c. Omit the book ledge.

Contributed by
Kathleen D. Hickey, M.Ed., Special Needs Teacher at Cotting School.

TRIWALL CUBBY-TOP FOR DESK

DESCRIPTION: A three-sided enclosure, placed on top of a student's desk.

PURPOSE: To reduce the amount of visual stimuli in the student's environment so the student can focus more easily on his or her work.

MATERIALS:
1. An extra wide student desk such as the Adjustable Table from Rifton Equipment
2. Triwall material: Two 2' x 4' sheets
3. Two aproximately $1/4$" thick wooden dowels
4. Woodworker's glue
5. Duct tape to reinforce the corners and finish the edges
6. Optional: Latex enamel paint or non-distracting contact paper

TOOLS:
Bandsaw, jigsaw, utility knife or steak knife
Pencil sharpener
Awl
Hammer
Carpenter's heavy-duty glue gun and glue sticks
 (if not available, woodworker's glue may be substituted)
Yardstick and pencil or marker

MEASUREMENTS:
The finished Triwall cubby top will rest flush with the edge of the desk (or flush with the inside edge of the perimeter ledge if it has one) and be a bit higher than the top of the seated student's head.

 BACK: Seat student close to desk. Measure from desk surface to top of head. Add 4" to get your height measurement. Width should equal width of desk top (or inside of perimeter ledge).

 SIDES: Height measurement calculated above. Width should equal the depth of the desk minus 1" (or depth of inside edge of perimeter ledge minus 1").

ASSEMBLY:
1. Draw one back piece and two side pieces on the Triwall using the dimensions calculated above. Also draw a rectangular piece of Triwall that is 5" x the width of the desk top. This piece will fit across the top of the cubby as a reinforcement brace.

2. Cut out the four pieces of Triwall, using a saw or knife.

3. Make 3" wooden pegs by cutting up the wooden dowels into 3" pieces and sharpening one end of each peg using a pencil sharpener.

4. Attach the two side pieces to the back piece of Triwall:

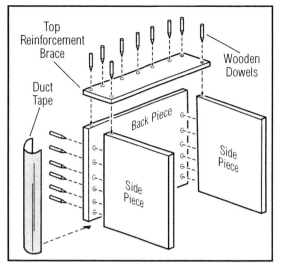

   a. Use an awl to make a vertical row of pilot holes along both side edges of the back piece of Triwall, approximately 4 inches apart and $1/3$" in from the edges of the back piece. Start your line of holes four inches from the top edge, and put your last hole an inch from the bottom.

   b. Fill each of the pilot holes on one side of the back piece with woodworker's glue.

   c. Use the glue gun to apply a thick line of hot glue along the contact surfaces: on the cut edge of one side piece, and along the edge of the back piece right over the pilot holes (on the side the white glue was just applied).

   d. Press the contact surfaces together, and then hammer a wooden peg in each pilot hole.

   e. Repeat steps b through d to attach the other side piece.

5. Cover each of the two corners of the cubby with a long length of duct tape on the outside surface. Make each length of duct tape extend about 2" past the Triwall both top and bottom. Cut a vertical slit down the middle of the 2" extensions of duct tape and fold around over the edges of the Triwall. Repeat on the inside surface of both corners.

6. Attach the 5" wide reinforcing brace to the top back of the cubby:

   a. Use the awl to make pilot holes in the reinforcement piece $1/3$" in from one long edge, approximately 4" apart, starting 3" from the short ends. Make two pilot holes in each short edge of the reinforcement piece, $1/3$" in from the cut edge.

   b. Fill the pilot holes with woodworker's glue.

   c. Use the glue gun to apply a thick line of hot glue along the contact surfaces of the reinforcement piece and the cubby top.

   d. Press the contact surfaces together, and then hammer a wooden peg in each pilot hole.

7. Cover all raw edges of Triwall with long lengths of Duct tape.

OPTIONAL: Finish your cubby by painting it (including the duct tape) with latex enamel paint OR cover it with non-distracting contact paper.

☞ If the desk does not have a perimeter ledge to hold the cubby top on, use hot glue to attach narrow Triwall pieces on the outside of each wall of the cubby that extend below the bottom of the cubby top.

This design incorporated advice from
Kathleen D. Hickey, M.Ed., Special Needs Teacher
and
Val Greene, B.S. Ed., Industrial Arts Teacher at Cotting School.

EASY HEIGHT-ADJUSTABLE ARM SLING
(WHEELCHAIR OR CEILING MOUNTED)

DESCRIPTION: An arm sling which is easily adjustable in height via a rope pulley system and which is mounted with heavy cord or wire to a sturdy ceiling hook or a secure ceiling pipe; or mounted to a large, inverted L-shaped metal pole which fits into the arm rest hole of the wheelchair when the arm rest is removed.

PURPOSE:
To enable greater ease of arm movements for students who have significant muscle weakness. A head-injured teenager used this sling pulley system very successfully to perform a variety of tasks throughout the school, including operating a computer and performing a variety of Industrial Arts activities, such as sanding and painting wood projects.

☞ When deciding between a ceiling mount or a wheelchair-attached sling pole, keep in mind the following:

- Increasing the distance between the pulley and the student's arm will allow for wider arm excursions, which may increase the ease and range of arm movements, but at the possible expense of arm stability and control.

- Reducing the distance between pulley and the student's arm will narrow the possible range of arm excursion; however in some cases this may be desired in order to increase arm stability and control.

MATERIALS:
1. Electrical mechanical tubing (EMT) 8 feet long for sling pole (if sling will be attached to the wheelchair).
2. Metal pulley device strong enough to bear human weight.
3. Strong nylon cord or other unbreakable cord such as window sash cord.
4. 1" thick wooden dowel - approximately 6 inches long
5. 6" square piece of thick polyurethane foam or other suitable material for padding between the wrist and the cord loop.

TOOLS:
Electric drill; table vise; hack saw or metal band saw; tubing bender.

☞ Borrow a tube bender from an electrician or plumber or ask to have the tubing bent when you purchase it.

MEASUREMENTS:

1. The height of the metal pole should clear the student's head, but should also be low enough to fit through a doorway. See note above for further considerations.

2. The length of the string will vary depending upon the distance between the student and the pulley as well as the arm height at which the student produces his or her best functional performance.

ASSEMBLY:

1. To make the sling pole (if needed):

   a. Determine desired height of the sling pole as well as the desired length of the cross bar of the pole. The final length of the electrical mechanical tubing should equal the sum of these two measurements, but cut it longer at first (in case it "bends" at the wrong spot) and trim it later. Use a hack saw or a metal band saw to cut the EMT.

   b. Mark the spot where the EMT should be bent (to form the inverted L-shape). Use a tubing bender to bend the tube at the appropriate spot.

   c. Drill a small hole approximately 1-2" from the top end of the EMT. Hole should be just big enough to thread the nylon cord through. (A smaller hole will maintain the strength of the metal pole). Drill all the way through the tube and out the opposite side.

2. To attach the pulley:
Tie the pulley to the sling pole (through the drilled hole). If sling will be ceiling mounted, tie it to a secure ceiling hook or secure exhaust pipe (get O.K. from the building maintenance dept.) using heavy-duty nylon cord, heavy insulated wire, or other suitable tying material strong enough to support body weight. *Tie multiple knots, making sure they are very secure as the student may get injured if the pulley falls off!!*

3. To assemble the pulley sling:

   a. Drill a hole near each end of the 6 inches long dowel. Holes should be just wide enough in diameter to thread the cord through, but not wide enough for the thick cord knot to slip through.

   b. Make a reinforced knot in the end of the cord (it must hold body weight), and thread the cord through one of the holes in the dowel. Then thread it through the pulley device and back through the other hole in the dowel.

   c. Make a loop in the remaining cord and knot it. The loop is the sling, and should be covered with foam, vinyl and/or other material to provide comfort and maintain good blood circulation. The sling is positioned under the student's wrist.

   d. To adjust the height of the sling, simply raise or lower the wooden dowel.

Designed and fabricated by
Val Greene, B.S. Ed., Industrial Arts Teacher at Cotting School.

Chapter 5
Mobility

DEVICES TO ASSIST WITH MOBILITY
IN THE SCHOOL SETTING

For students who have perceptual, cognitive, or motor deficits, moving from class to class within the school building is often not the simple task that it is for most students, and can in fact be quite stressful. Students with motoric limitations may feel that same sense of urgency and frustration that commuters feel when stuck in a traffic jam on the way to work. They know they should just relax since their legs or wheelchair can only move so fast, but they also know they are expected to be in class on time and feel badly if they are not. Add a few additional environmental barriers, such as finally arriving at the elevator only to find the elevator operator (if there was one to begin with) nowhere in sight, and before you know it the student's stress level is off the charts. Some of these students wouldn't need an elevator operator if the elevator buttons were adapted for them, or if they had an "elevator wand". Instructions for making these devices are provided later in this chapter.

Another mobility dilemma for those who are physically challenged is how to transport books and other school supplies from class to class. Students who use wheelchairs or walkers do not have their hands free to carry anything. There are a number of bags and baskets designed for users of wheelchairs, walkers, or crutches which are available through wheelchair and adaptive equipment suppliers. However, many of the wheelchair bags on the commercial market are intended for the back of the wheelchair and are inaccessible for those who have severe motor impairments. Many students also cannot access storage bags that fit under the wheelchair seat. Sue Shannon, OTR/L, at Perkins School for the Blind, told the author about the Advantage Bag Company. The catalog shows a wide variety of gorgeous bags of different types and sizes, including a few that can be strapped to the arm rest of a power chair.

It is also possible to make items yourself that enable students to be independent in storing, accessing, and transporting their school books and supplies. These are generally less expensive than devices on the commercial market. Melissa Litton's Quick Tip (#2) provided a power wheelchair user with severe quadriplegia independent access to his school supplies. Walker bags (page 63) are also easy to make. As Paulette Binder (the designer) points out, a homemade bag can be easily adapted to suit the particular needs of the student.

Students who are not mobility impaired may nevertheless experience their own set of frustrations when traveling through the school building. There are quite a number of students who, due to perceptual or cognitive impairments, have great difficulty finding their way from one place to another. Some get quite fearful at the prospect of having to walk to a particular location by themselves, almost as though they think they might get lost for good. Various successful strategies can be used with these students, which can be found in the Quick Tips section of this chapter.

There are also students who know exactly how to get from one place to another, have no mobility problems, and yet cannot arrive at their destination without stopping to chat with every person that passes by them, looking out the window to check out the scenery, and stopping to look inside each classroom they pass. Some of these students can benefit from wearing an FM listening device, wearing a headset that covers the ears (and blocks out a lot of auditory distractions). Through this the student receives verbal reminders such as "Keep going" or "Don't stop to chat". The instructions are given through a small microphone clipped to the shirt of the teacher or specialist and are transmitted to the student through FM radio waves so there are no wires between student and teacher. This enables the teacher to walk several yards behind the student, thus promoting an increased level of independence with this task of "walking without stopping".

Finally, there is the challenge of trying to shepherd a group of easily distracted students from one part of the school building to another without having them scatter in different directions. In this case, a rope may be useful. No, not a lasso, simply a rope long enough for all the students to hold onto so they form a single line down the hallway. Eventually, once the students get the "standing in line" concept, the rope can be eliminated.

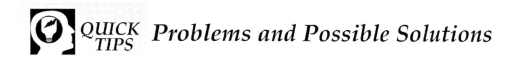

QUICK TIPS *Problems and Possible Solutions*

Following are some solutions which have successfully solved the identified problem for one or more students. Keep in mind that each student has a unique set of abilities and needs and may therefore require an original solution for the problem at hand. If a suggested solution is appropriate for a student, please adapt the design as necessary to best meet his or her needs.

Remember: fit the device to the student, not the student to the device!

1. Student with decreased strength has difficulty opening some of the doors in the school building, such as the door to a classroom or door to the school bathroom.

Remove the tension rods on the doors.

(David Creesy, MBA, Director of Buildings and Grounds, Cotting School)

2. Student in power chair is unable to access school books and supplies from the wheelchair bag.

Try mounting a Sammons Preston Economy Walker Basket to one of the arms of the power chair using two velcro straps threaded through holes in the wire-welded basket and around the wheelchair arm.

(Melissa Litton, OTR/L, Occupational Therapist, Cotting School)

3. Student is unable to carry an unused crutch in the traditional manner while ascending or descending stairs, due to poor hand grasp.

Make a loop strap for the unused crutch, which the student can slip his or her hand through before grasping the crutch that is being used to assist with ascending or descending the stairs. To make the loop strap, place pressure-sensitive (adhesive back) Velcro hook tape on the unused crutch and attach a 12 - 14" strip of non-adhesive Velcro loop tape to the hook tape so it forms a strap large enough for the student's hand to go through. Before sticking the hook tape to the crutch, play around with the location of the loop strap on the crutch shaft, until a spot is found that allows the crutch to "hang well".

(JoAnn Kluzik, M.S., PT., PCS, Physical Therapist, Cotting School)

4. Student leaves his or her crutches sprawled on the floor for others to trip over.

At a hardware store buy metal brackets that screw into the wall and are designed to hold brooms and mops. Attach these to the side of the student's cubby desk (or other suitable desk) to hold the crutches.

(Virginia Birmingham, P.T., Physical Therapist, Cotting School)

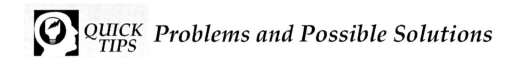

5. Ambulatory student has difficulty carrying heavy books and supplies from class to class due to decreased muscle strength, and may drag his or her bookbag along the floor.

Try a lightweight wheeled luggage carrier which allows the user to either push or pull the cart. These are available at large department stores.

(Marcie A. Theriault, Program Assistant, Cotting School)

6. Student has bruises on hands from propelling a manual wheelchair.

Try having student wear gloves. Weight lifting gloves, available at sporting goods stores, offer good hand protection. Wheelchair gloves are available from adaptive equipment suppliers including Sammons Preston.

7. Student has quadriplegia and tends to get his or her hands caught in doorways when wheeling through them.

Try attaching arm guards to the student's lap tray. One easy way to do this is to add a raised ledge along the back and side edges of the lap tray. The arm guards should be the minimum height and length needed to help prevent the arms from falling off of the tray (perhaps 5"). Cover the raised edge with thin polyurethane (soft) foam and vinyl material to prevent arm bruising.

8. Student has difficulty finding classrooms or other rooms in the school building.

Color-code the hallways so students know what section of the school they are in, either by painting the hallway doors certain colors or painting a line along the walls using colors that represent certain sections of the building. This has been done at Cotting School and is also a common hospital strategy at Cotting School.

Place laminated signs at strategic intersections.

If student needs written or pictorial directions, have the student choose landmarks that are relevant to them, and incorporate these personal references into the written instructions.

9. Student has poor attending skills and stops to chat with (or stare at) everyone he or she passes in the hallways or to look out the window, etc.; and arrives at destination late or forgets it altogether.

Try an FM listening device, in which the teacher gives instructions to the student through a wireless headset to "keep walking", while staying many yards behind the student. See text of this section for more details.

INSTRUCTIONS
FOR FABRICATING
SELECTED DEVICES

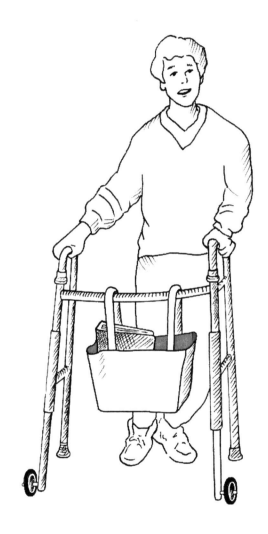

ADAPTED ELEVATOR BUTTON

ELEVATOR WAND

WALKER/WHEELCHAIR BAG

ADAPTED ELEVATOR BUTTON

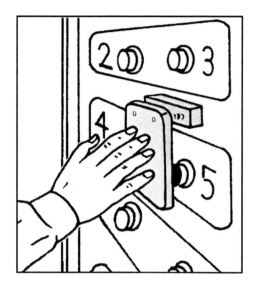

DESCRIPTION: An enlarged plastic elevator button shield which depresses the existing elevator button when pushed.

PURPOSE:
To enable a student who has only gross arm movements to press the elevator button easily.

MATERIALS:
1. 1/8" clear Lexan - 7" long x 3" wide, for shield
2. ABS plastic, or wood - 3/4" x 3/4" x 3" bar, for support block
3. Two 1" x 5/8" light pressure compression springs
4. Two 1" wood screws
5. Two brass finish washers
6. Pressure-sensitive Velcro hook and loop tape - 3" of each one
7. 1" round self-stick rubber foot

TOOLS:
Band saw, drill, sandpaper

MEASUREMENTS:
The measurements given above will produce a 'pressing surface' 3" wide and 7" high. The size of this device can be varied depending upon the location of the elevator buttons and the particular needs of the student.

ASSEMBLY:

1. Cut the Lexan and the ABS plastic pieces or wood pieces to the desired sizes. Sand all edges and corners.

2. Attach the Lexan shield to the support bar as follows:

    a. Drill two holes at one 3" end of the shield, one inch from the top and one inch in from the left and right sides. Drill bit should equal the diameter of the screw shank.

    b. Drill shallow holes in the support block, 1" from each end, to prepare for inserting the wood screws. Drill bit should equal the diameter of the screw root. To make sure the holes correspond with the holes in the shield, line the block up under the shield and mark with a pencil through the holes already drilled.

    c. Place the finish washers over the holes in the Lexan and insert the wood screws. Slide one compression spring over each wood screw. Place the screws against the support bar and tighten.

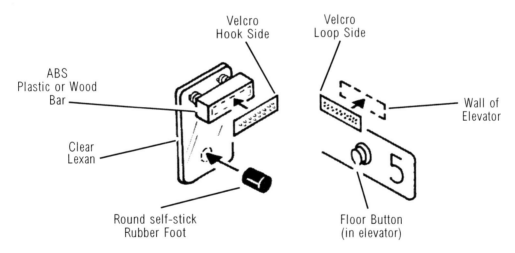

3. Affix the rubber foot at the exact spot on the back of the shield where the floor button will be engaged when the shield is pressed.

4. Mount the unit on the wall of the elevator by attaching the pressure-sensitive Velcro hook tape to the back of the support bar and the Velcro loop tape to the wall of the elevator.

Designed by
Alex Truesdell, M.Ed., Adaptive Design Specialist,
Perkins School for the Blind in Watertown, Ma.

ELEVATOR WAND

DESCRIPTION: A long thermoplastic pointer with a loop handle.

PURPOSE:

1. To enable a power wheelchair user to independently depress elevator buttons.

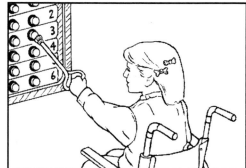

2. The loop handle allows more grasping options, an important consideration for those who have poor grasp skills and need to perform the task in a time-efficient manner.

MATERIALS:

1. A sheet of low temperature thermoplastic material, about 10" x 12"

2. Optional: 1/2" piece of pressure-sensitive Velcro loop tape or a rubber tip for the end of the wand

☞ Some types of low temperature thermoplastic materials require special solvent or light abrasion before bonding can occur. Please follow manufacturer's directions.

TOOLS:

Splinting pan or electric frying pan and water, heavy duty scissors

MEASUREMENTS:

The thermoplastic material is cut in an L-shape. The width of the material should be 2 inches.

For the long side of the "L" shape: Position student as close to elevator buttons as convenient, and have student extend arm as much as possible. Measure from student's M.P. joints (knuckles) to furthest elevator button.

For the short side of the "L" shape: Measure around student's hand, starting and ending at knuckle of middle finger and add 2".

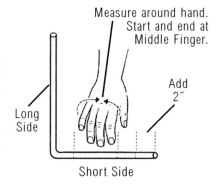

ASSEMBLY:

1. Heat the thermoplastic material in splinting pan and water, following the manufacturer's instructions, until pliable and cut out an L-shape using the measurements determined above.

2. Roll the short end of the L shape into a snake-shape and form it into a loop big enough to fit around the student's hand. Bond the ends of the loop together.

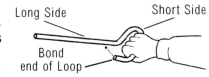

3. Roll the long end of the L shape so it is a long snake shape. Keep this straight to form the pointer that presses the elevator button.

4. **OPTIONAL:** Attach the piece of Velcro or a rubber tip to the end of the wand to prevent the wand from slipping off the button.

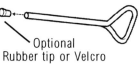

Optional
Rubber tip or Velcro

Designed by Melissa Litton, OTR/L, Occupational Therapist, Cotting School.

WALKER/WHEELCHAIR BAG

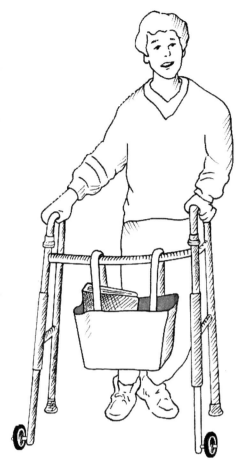

DESCRIPTION: A shallow, square-bottom cloth tote bag that can be fastened to a walker.

For students with impaired tactile discrimination skills, see-through material or netting can be used.

PURPOSE:

1. To store books and other school supplies, so the student's hands are free to maneuver the walker.

2. To balance the weight being carried in the middle of the walker, making it easier to ambulate.

3. The shallow, square-bottom shape of this bag helps to keep the sides of the bag spread apart. This is very useful for those who have impaired reaching skills and/or fine motor coordination.

MATERIALS:
1. Cotton/polyester blend fabric or netting, 21" x 15"
2. Heavy cardboard - 10" x 4"
3. 1 " wide cotton belting material - 4 pieces, each 10" long
4. 1/2" wide Velcro hook and loop tape - two 4" long strips of each
5. Optional: Iron-on letters

TOOLS:
Sewing machine, thread, and scissors

MEASUREMENTS:
The final measurements of this bag are 10" wide by 4" deep by 8" high.
If the student needs a bag of different dimensions, adjust the size of your fabric accordingly. Consider range and ease of trunk and arm movement, hand dexterity, as well as the student's kinesthetic sense. If the latter is a problem, consider using a see-through material and/or make the bag shallow and wide enough so the student can use his or her vision to locate items in the bag. To make bag sides higher or lower, adjust 21" measurement 2" for every 1" desired. To make bag wider or narrower, adjust 15" measurement 1" for every inch desired.

ASSEMBLY:

1. Stitch along the cut edges of the fabric and the belting material to prevent fraying of the material, using zigzag stitch if available.

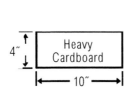

Heavy Cardboard
4″
10″

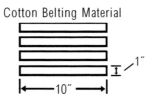

Cotton Belting Material
1″
10″

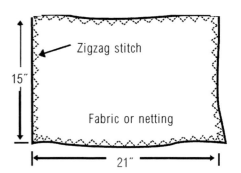

Zigzag stitch

15″

Fabric or netting

21″

2. Fold the fabric in half so right sides are together and it measures $10^{1}/2$" high by 15" wide. Press fold in with an iron or your fingers.

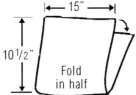

15″
$10^{1}/2$″
Fold in half

The folded side will be the bottom of the walker bag. With raw edges even, sew a 1/2" seam through both layers along the two 10 1/2" sides, leaving the side that is opposite the fold open.

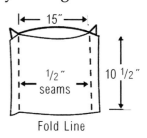

15″
1/2″ seams
10 1/2″
Fold Line

This remaining unsewn side will be the top of the walker bag. It now looks like a pouch.

3. Keep the pouch inside out. Form the corners as follows:

    a. Spread the sides of the bag apart, and flatten one of the sides against the bottom of the bag, lining the side seam up against the pressed-in fold. Smooth fabric outwards, forming a triangular point with the seam running up the center.

    b. Measure 2" up from the point, and sew across perpendicular to the existing seam, opening seam allowance before sewing over it.

    c. Repeat with other side seam.

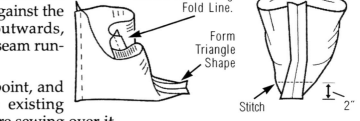

Flatten Sewn Side inward to lie along Fold Line.

Form Triangle Shape

Stitch

2″

4. Trim off the triangles of fabric, leaving $1/2$" of fabric next to stitch line. Turned right-side out, the pouch will now have a square bottom.

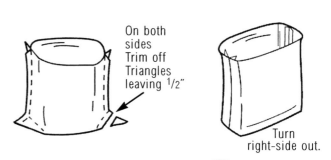

On both sides Trim off Triangles leaving 1/2″

Turn right-side out.

5. Fold the top edge of the pouch inward 1/2" (wrong sides together) and sew it down.

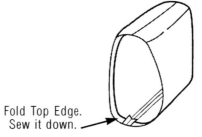

Fold Top Edge. Sew it down.

6. Form the straps: Sew one 4" strip of Velcro on top of each 10" piece of belting material near one end, so that each piece of belting has a piece of either hook or loop Velcro sewn onto it.

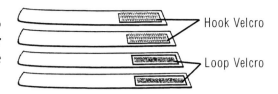

7. Sew straps to bag:

a.   Position both pieces of belting material that have the hook on them on the inside surface on the same side of the pouch, about 3" from the side seams of the bag, so that the hook is facing towards the open pouch. Sew straps to the inside surface of the bag with two or more straight seams (for reinforcement), near the top edge of the bag. Strap should overlap bag edge at least 1".

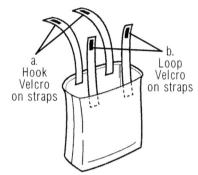

b. On the other side of the pouch, repeat the above procedure using both pieces of belting material that have the loop on them. This time, make sure the loop surface is facing away from the opening of the pouch.

☞ To attach bag to wheelchair, see modification below.

8. **OPTIONAL:**

If desired, add iron-on letters to personalize the bag.

9. Finally, place the piece of cardboard in the bottom of the bag so it will have a nice square bottom.

MODIFICATION: WHEELCHAIR BAG
Attach straps "backpack style" as follows:
a.   Attach both straps with loop tape onto the outside surface on the same side of the pouch, 1" from the top and about 3" from the side seams of the bag. with the loop tape facing toward the open pouch.

b. Attach the bottom of each hook tape strap 6" below a loop strap, so that it is 3" from the bottom of the bag. Hook tape should be facing away from the bag.

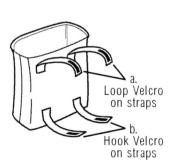

Designed by Paulette E. Binder, Home Economics Teacher, Cotting School.

Chapter 6
Communication Aids

COMMUNICATION AIDS

Communication is the glue that connects an individual with family, friends, the community, and the world at large. It is so essential to the growth and well-being of individuals that it is recognized as a basic human right. This right is often taken for granted by those who do not need to rely on communication devices. After all, the human voice is a connected part of the body and cannot be accidentally "left" somewhere or be removed by another person if inconvenient.

However, this does happen with communication devices, and when it does, it can make an individual feel suddenly isolated and powerless. It is therefore important to analyze the reasons for removing a communication device from a student. Does it take up so much space that it prevents the student from performing a particular activity? In that case, perhaps another type of communication device can be provided that does not conflict with the activity at hand. If this is not workable, than maybe a small sign (or voice-output switch) is needed on the wheelchair lap tray for the student to point to (or activate) that says "Please get my communication board (or other device)", so he or she can still have access to the communication device at any time while participating in the activity.

Types of Communication Devices

Communication systems generally fall into two categories - aided and unaided. Unaided systems include speech, sign language, gestures, vocalizations and facial expressions. Aided systems involve the use of physical, mechanical or electronic devices [1,2,3]. Following are some examples of aided systems.

Written Output Devices

PAPER AND PENCIL

COMPUTERS, including alternative keyboards and other computer access devices

ELECTRONIC TYPEWRITERS, such as Typemate and Brother

DEDICATED AUGMENTATIVE COMMUNICATION DEVICES such as the Canon Communicator, as well as synthesized speech systems that can be attached to a printer to produce written output.

Voice Output Devices

SYNTHESIZED SPEECH SYSTEMS: The most common type of voice output device. Messages are programmed into the computer system. Systems usually offer a choice of voices (adult, child, male, female). A notable example is the DynaVox from Sentient Systems Technology Inc., which has a dynamic touch screen display which can also be accessed by joystick, auditory, and visual scanning modes. These systems are available from Innocomp, Prentke Romich Co., Words+, Inc., Zygo, Phonic Ear, ADAMLAB, Microsystems and Texas Instruments. [2,4]

DIGITIZED SPEECH SYSTEMS: With digitized systems, messages are recorded onto each key of the device by speaking into an attached microphone. The message is repeated whenever the key is pressed (by body part, pointer or switch access). Popular models include MessageMate from Words+, Inc. and the MACAW from Zygo. Other systems are available from Innocomp, Prentke Romich Co., Adaptivation Inc., Attainment, TASH and AbleNet. [2,4]

TAPED SPEECH SYSTEMS: Switch systems that activate a built-in tape player. An example is the "Say It" Switch Plates from Enabling Devices, a division of Toys for Special Children.

Devices with No Written or Voice Output

COMMUNICATION BOARD OR BOOK: A board or book containing communication symbols such as words, pictures, Bliss Symbols or Picture Communication Symbols. To use, the student points to the desired symbol using a body part or pointing device.

EYE GAZE BOARD OR BOOK: A transparent communication board or book usually positioned vertically at eye level between the communicating partners. The transparency and position of the board enable the receiver to interpret messages delivered when the student "points" with his or her eyes at the desired symbols. Eye-gaze systems can sometimes be trickier to read than other pointing systems, and often require "double checking" by the receiver of the message, as in "I think you were looking at the E, is that correct?". However, eye-gaze boards are very successfully used with many students who are unable to adequately control any other body movements for communication.

SIMPLE ELECTROMECHANICAL COMMUNICATION BOARD: A low-tech, switch-activated communication board with simple mechanical parts which enables the user to make choices. Examples are Dial Scan from Don Johnston, Inc. which has a clock-like rotary dial; and the Sequential Scanners from Enabling Devices (a division of Toys for Special Children) which light up the choice compartments in sequence.

Personal Amplification Devices

HEARING AID: A device worn in the ear which amplifies all sound, both relevant sounds and background noises.

FM LISTENING DEVICE: Resembles hearing aids or a headset. This device blocks out most background noise while receiving speech input from an individual wearing a special wireless microphone which transmits sound via FM radio waves.

VOICE AMPLIFIER: A special microphone, usually worn on the chest, which amplifies the voice of an individual who has an especially soft voice.

☞ Most of the companies listed above will be around for years to come, but their devices change frequently as new technology is developed. The best thing to do is to contact all of the companies for brochures, and to check back every year or so for updated information. Most of these companies also belong to the Communication Aid Manufacturers Association (CAMA), which sponsors educational workshops for clinicians and parents throughout the country.

Choosing a Communications Device: *Student Factors*

When choosing an appropriate communication system for a student, it is important to consult with a communication specialist, and often other members of the student's TEAM as well. Many student factors need to be taken into account, including:

- positioning (which, as explained in an earlier chapter, significantly affects the quality of all muscle movements)

- oral-motor skills for producing verbal speech

- arm and hand control for pointing to communication boards or operating high tech devices

- visual acuity and control of the eye muscles for looking at eye-gaze or other communication boards

- visual-perceptual skills for scanning and discriminating among options on a communication board

- the complexity of language skills that the student possesses.

The combination of human factors provides a unique set of requirements for each student. Some combinations create special challenges. For example, there are many students who have a very large vocabulary yet have no functional speech as well as poor arm and hand control. Enlarging communication symbols and spacing them farther apart might address the student's impaired ability to isolate arm movements for pointing, but then only a few communication symbols could fit on the board. A very effective solution was found, to enable one such individual to have access to a very large vocabulary, which is described on page 80.

Other students have a limited range of movement but are highly accurate pointers within this limited range. A miniature communication board may be a very effective solution for these students. An example of this is a student who uses a thigh-mounted penlight pointer to access a small letterboard (see page 88). If a student has impaired visual-perceptual skills as well, then a miniature communication board may not be a workable solution. Alternative body movements might then be considered that utilize a greater range of motion (perhaps the student has adequate ocular control for using an eye gaze board). The student may need to try a high-tech solution such as using a trackball to access an onscreen communication board that can be modified to accommodate the impaired perceptual skills.

Choosing a Communications Device: *Device Characteristics*

In addition to these student factors, there are several device characteristics that must be considered when choosing from the multitude of options that are available. These include:

INDEPENDENT ACCESS: Does the device require another person to set it up each time, or can the student access the device without assistance? Sometimes the answer to this question depends less on the type of device and more on how the device is positioned or mounted for the student. For example, a student might have independent access to a communication book if it is attached to the wheelchair lap tray (see page 78) or the wheelchair arm rest (see page 82), but not if it is loose on top of the tray or in a backpack.

Using an eye gaze board may require the communication partner to hold the board at eye level for the communicator to use. Often, however, it is possible to mount an eye gaze board on a student's wheelchair (see page 85). If the student is using a computerized system or an electronic device, consider whether or not the student can perform the steps necessary to turn it on.

PORTABILITY: Can the device travel with the student from classroom to classroom, and from lunch to recess? Desk-top computers work well when the student is hooked up to it, but are no help when the student wants to communicate with someone while in the hallway or the cafeteria. At least one effective portable device should be made available to the student for those numerous times during the school day when the student is on the move.

EXPENSE: Is the device the most cost-effective solution? Sometimes an expensive device is necessary in order to effectively meet a student's needs, but other times a less costly solution will work just as well or even better.

ACTIVITY COMPATIBILITY: What activities can the student perform while having access to the device? Can the student retain access to the communication device while propelling a power wheelchair? While eating? While performing school work? Unfortunately, very few communication devices are usable during all activities, which is the next topic to be addressed.

Utilizing Multiple Communication Devices: *An Example*

Students often benefit from using a combination of low-tech and high-tech communication devices to accomodate the many situations and activities encountered during a school day. For example, Kevin, a student at Cotting School, has a total of four communication devices. The first, and simplest, is a yes/no system which consists of two small pieces of paper with these words on them, which are taped to his clear plastic lap tray, one over each knee. Kevin uses hip flexion of the appropriate leg to indicate his answers to yes/no questions using this system. This system accommodates any activity, so long as he is positioned in his wheelchair with his lap tray. However, this passive system does not enable him to initiate conversations, allowing him only to answer when spoken to.

In order to enable Kevin to initiate conversations with others and engage in the usual social greetings, he was provided with a second communication device, a MACAW (by Zygo), which is set on a scanning mode with pre-programmed sentences, such as "Hi, How are you", "Fine", etc. The MACAW is especially effective for grabbing the attention of other students walking down the hall or for communicating with a group of students in the classroom. Kevin is limited to these preprogrammed sentences; however, one of the preprogrammed sentences directs the person he is communicating with to get a third communication device, which is an eye-gaze communication board.

The eye gaze letterboard is Kevin's most accurate and quickest method of communication. It is the most accurate because the words he uses are truly his words as opposed to preprogrammed words or the words of another person who is playing 20 questions with him. It is his quickest method because he can quickly point to each letter or word with his eyes instead of waiting for a scanning program to get to the correct row and column. The eye-gaze board enables the conversation to progress to a more personal level after Kevin is finished engaging in the usual social pleasantries with the MACAW or yes/no system.

Kevin also has a fourth communication device, which is an IBM computer set on a row-column scanning mode. Kevin uses this system to write phrases and copy sentences to complete his schoolwork. If Kevin has something to say while in the midst of his work, he clicks into the SideTalk window of the EZ Keys Software Program (Words+, Inc.), which enables him to communicate messages "on the side" without having those messages incorporated into his written work. Providing SideTalk to Kevin as a communication option while performing his classroom work is an excellent example of enabling a student to keep his "voice" while engaged in another task. A major disadvantage of this method is that it can only be used while he is hooked up to the classroom computer. The row-column scanning system is also more time consuming than the direct selection system (his eye-gaze board). However, row-column scanning is the only system available that Kevin can physically operate to generate the written output required in school.

"Which commercially-available devices have been found to be most useful in the school setting for promoting communication skills?"

This question was posed to Kate Moore, M.S., CCC-SLP, Elizabeth Miller, M.S., CCC-SLP, and Deena Gulezian, M.S., CCC-SLP, at Cotting School. One device that is invaluable to this team is a desktop Macintosh computer with ample memory that is adapted using Ke:nx (a keyboard emulator available from Don Johnston Inc., a touch screen, and a variety of switches and other input devices, such as adapted keyboards, a trackball, or a joystick. This is used as both a classroom tool and as an evaluation tool. It can also be used to make low-tech communication boards with software such as Boardmaker (from Mayer-Johnson Co.), which eliminates all the cutting and pasting and time spent at the copier machine.

Portable communication equipment and portable assistive devices such as digitized voice output communication aids (e.g. MACAW by Zygo, BIGmack by AbleNet, MessageMate by Words+, Inc.) and personal amplifiers are also very useful, according to this team. Please see the Resource Guide for names and addresses of commercial suppliers.

Included in this chapter are instructions for making some successful low tech devices to improve a student's ability to communicate with others in the school setting. Other low-tech aids that may assist with communication can be found in the chapters on Switches & Switch Mounts, Pointers & Mouthsticks, and Computers.

QUICK TIPS *Problems and Possible Solutions*

Following are some solutions which have successfully solved the identified problem for one or more students. Keep in mind that each student has a unique set of abilities and needs and may therefore require an original solution for the problem at hand. If a suggested solution is appropriate for a student, please adapt the design as necessary to best meet his or her needs.

Remember: fit the device to the student, not the student to the device!

1. The student's finger slides from one letter (or symbol) to another when using a communication board, leaving the receiver of the message confused as to which letter or symbol the student is trying to indicate.

Make raised separators between letters and numbers on simple communication boards using easily found materials such as rubber bands, yarn, string, or cardboard strips.
(Kate Moore, M.S., CCC-SLP, Speech-Language Pathologist, Cotting School)

2. Student has difficulty turning pages of a communication book.

Glue small sponge pieces, formboard, or other lightweight, thick materials to the pages of the communication book to keep the pages apart.
(Deena Gulezian, M.S., CCC-SLP, Speech-Language Pathologist, Cotting School)

3. Student has difficulty articulating some letter sounds, resulting in speech that is not always understood.

On a cloth watchband, print (with permanent marker) the letters of the alphabet which the student has difficulty articulating. Have the student wear the 'letter cue watchband' at all times, so he or she can simply point to the missing letter(s) whenever a word is not understood.
(Kate Moore, M.S., CCC-SLP, Speech-Language Pathologist, Cotting School)

4. Student speaks so fast that it is difficult to comprehend what he or she is saying.

Make a 'word pacing board' to help the student pace each word so he or she can be understood by others. Simply glue 3" long wooden strips (such as popsicle sticks or coffee stirrers) across a 3" x 12" rectangular board, with spaces in-between, and paint each strip a different color. Have the student touch the strips in sequence as he or she speaks, touching one strip per word spoken. These boards are available commercially as well.
(Kate Moore, M.S., CCC-SLP, Speech-Language Pathologist, Cotting School)

5. Student has no functional speech and cannot participate in routine oral classroom activities.

Q Use loop tapes with a cassette player that is adapted with a switch, to enable the student to participate with the rest of the class in daily routines such as reciting the pledge of allegiance or 'reading' sentences during oral reading tasks.
(Deena Gulezian, M.S., CCC-SLP, Speech-Language Pathologist, Cotting School)

6. There is no room for the student's communication book at the lunch table because of food, plates, and other mealtime paraphernalia.

Q Make a special placemat for the student that includes a communication board. Choose words, symbols, and/or pictures that relate to the task of eating as well as those that would facilitate social interaction with others. See page 296 for directions on how to make one.
(Beth Jackson, M.S., OTR/L, Occupational Therapist, and
Deena Gulezian, M.S., CCC-SLP, Speech-Language Pathologist, both at Cotting School)

7. Student has no functional speech and needs to capture the teacher's attention.

Q Give the student a BIGmack by AbleNet, which is a special switch that repeats a programmed statement when activated, such as "Mrs. Jones, I need help!"
(Kate Moore, M.S., CCC-SLP, Speech-Language Pathologist, Cotting School)

8. Student has extreme difficulty attending to the teacher's instructions due to auditory distractions.

Q First try to reduce the auditory distractions with enviroment modifications. See chapter on Positioning for more information. If these do not adequately resolve the problem, consider an FM listening device. Please consult with student's communication specialist first, as this device should only be used in extreme cases.

INSTRUCTIONS
FOR FABRICATING
SELECTED DEVICES

COMMUNICATION BOOK

CORK-TABBED
MULTI-PAGE
COMMUNICATION BOOK
SECURED TO LAP TRAY

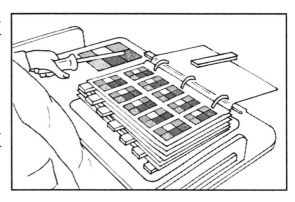

2-STEP COLOR-CODED POINTING SYSTEM
FOR COMMUNICATION BOARDS

(REMOVABLE) ARMREST MOUNTED
COMMUNICATION BOARD HOLDER

PLEXIGLASS EYE-GAZE BOARD

WHEELCHAIR-MOUNTED
EYE GAZE COMMUNICATION BOARD

CHEST MOUNT FOR VOICE AMPLIFIER

THIGH-MOUNTED PENLIGHT POINTER
FOR COMMINICATION BOARDS

COMMUNICATION BOOK

DESCRIPTION: A multipage book of communication symbols, made using a presentation book which has plastic page protectors.

PURPOSE:
To provide a means of communication for a student who has no functional speech but has accurate pointing skills and the ability to turn pages.

MATERIALS:
1. A presentation book can be obtained at an office supply store.
   The Mayer-Johnson Co. (see Resource Guide) offers a selection of binders, books, and folders specifically designed to display communication symbols.
2. Sheets of paper

DESIGNING THE PAGES:
By far the easiest and quickest method for designing a communication book is to use software such as Boardmaker (Mayer-Johnson Co.). Otherwise, draw or copy symbols from a book (such as the Picture Communication Symbols Books, also obtainable through the Mayer-Johnson Co.) and then cut and paste them to make the board. The communication symbols may include letters, words, Picture Communication Symbols, Blissymbols, and/or other types of symbols.

The Communication Book works well when organized thematically. Each page of the book can be set up with vocabulary suited to a particular activity or subject, such as Circle Time, Journal Time, the student's family, etc. It may also include a letterboard (which can be used for any activity).

Every communication book is unique, since no two students have identical needs or identical personal information. The student's communication specialist should be consulted when designing a communication book so that it can be set up to meet the student's current skill level and also foster further development of appropriate communication skills and patterns.

ASSEMBLY:

1. Create the pages for the communication book, using regular paper.

2. Slip each page into a protective sleeve of the presentation book.

Contributed by
Kate Moore, M.S., CCC-SLP, Speech-Language Pathologist, Cotting School

CORK-TABBED MULTI-PAGE COMMUNICATION BOOK SECURED TO LAP TRAY

DESCRIPTION: A vinyl communication book attached to the wheelchair lap tray with U-bolts. Staggered corkboard strips separate the pages. The user flips each page over the front edge of the lap tray until the desired page is found.

PURPOSE:
To stabilize and facilitate easy page selection and page-turning of a communication book for individuals who have poor arm and hand coordination. The system described here is very durable, to accommodate a particular individual who has severe incoordination due to athetosis. She uses the system in conjunction with a two-step color-coded system and a special pointer for turning the pages, both described on page 80.

MATERIALS:
1. Sheets of vinyl of desired page size (such as 11 1/2" x 8 1/2"), one per page of communication symbols
2. Sheets of paper with communication symbols (e.g. letters, words, Blissymbols, Picture Communication Symbols) carefully laid out on them, designed by the student's Communication Specialist
3. Two sheets of thin, hard plastic, same dimensions as the vinyl, to form the front and back book covers. Other materials can be substituted but may not be as durable.
4. Glue or tape
5. Clear contact paper
6. Corkboard strips, approximately 1" x 5", of appropriate thickness one per page. Quick Tip #2 offers alternate materials.
7. Heavy duty glue such as hot glue
8. Three large U-bolts, approximately 2" deep
9. Strip of metal, approximately 9 1/2" long x 1" wide, (U bolts are soldered to this strip of metal)
10. 2 wood screws, no longer than the thickness of the laptray

TOOLS:
Hand drill, heavy-duty hole puncher, screwdriver, welding supplies

IMPORTANT CONSTRUCTION NOTES:
1. A welder will be needed to attach the U-Bolts. For some students, large metal rings (obtainable at a stationary store) can be substituted.
2. Some factors to consider when designing a lap-tray attached communication book are:
- other purposes of the tray it is used on
- whether pages can be more easily turned when positioned horizontally or vertically
- whether separation between the pages is required, and if so, how much
  - use the least amount of separation needed in order to keep the size of the book manageable
- whether the pages need to be made of thick, stiff material or not.
Please adjust materials and design accordingly.

ASSEMBLY:
1. Make Communication Sheets
   a. Glue or tape the communication sheets to the sheets of vinyl, and cover with clear contact paper.

   b. Hot glue one 5" x 1" long cork tab (vertically) onto the back of each page of the communication book, allowing approximately 1" of the tab to extend from the front edge of the book. Stagger the positions of the cork tabs to resemble tabbed dividers in a cookbook. Cover the cork tabs with clear contact paper.

2. Make Metal Lap Tray Attachment:
   a. Position the U-bolts so they look like upside-down U's, and weld the back end of each of the U-bolts onto the metal strip, approximately 4 inches apart from each other.

   b. Drill two holes through the metal strip large enough to fit the screws, placing each hole between two of the U-bolts.

   c. Drill two pilot holes in the lap tray to correspond with the holes drilled in the metal strip. Drill the holes so the metal strip will be parallel to the far edge of the lap tray and will also be the desired distance from the student's body.

3. Punch Communication Sheets and place on U-bots:
   a. Drill three holes along the top of each of the two hard pieces of plastic to correspond with the locations of the U-bolts.

   b. Punch three holes along the top of each of the communication board pages to correspond with the locations of the U-bolts.

   c. Place the front plastic cover of the communication book, then the vinyl pages, then the back cover of the communication book, onto the U-bolts.

4. Attachment to Metal Tray:
Position the holes of the metal strip over the pilot holes previously drilled in the lap tray and then screw the communication board to the lap tray.

This particular version was designed by
staff and therapists at the United Cerebral Palsy Association, Watertown, MA.,
with the help of Design-Able, Inc., 65 Ryan Drive, Unit 2F, Raynham, MA 02767.

2-STEP COLOR-CODED POINTING SYSTEM
FOR COMMUNICATION BOARDS

DESCRIPTION: A communication book with clusters of color coded symbols which correlate with an enlarged (e.g. 4" x 6") color grid taped to the wheelchair lap tray.

In order to choose a communication symbol, the student first points to the specific cluster in the communication book, and then to the specific color on the enlarged color grid to indicate the specific symbol within the chosen cluster.

☞ Communication sheets should be designed by the student's communication specialist, who is trained in the complex process of choosing vocabulary, content, type of symbols, etc.

PURPOSE:

To allow access to a greater vocabulary (i.e. greater number of communication symbols) when using a communication book, for those who have limitations in pointing range or accuracy. This system may accomodate different motor impairments depending upon how the pointing locations are arranged. For example:

• A student who has difficulty grading the speed and direction of arm movements due to involuntary movements (such as athetosis) may need to have the pointing locations widely separated from each other.

• A student who has a limited range of motion with good pointing accuracy within this range may need to have the color-coded pointing locations positioned in close proximity to one another.

☞ Some students may need to use a pointer with this system. A woman who has athetosis very successfully uses this color-coded system with a pointer made from an old golf club (for the extra weight), cut to the right length, with the end dipped in Plastisol (a plastic dip) which can be purchased at an electrical or building supply store.
Chapter 9 contains descriptions of other pointers.

MATERIALS:

1. Software program for designing communication sheets or a book of communication symbols to copy

2. A communication book - in which to place the communication sheets

☞ This color-coded system may be used successfully in conjunction with the Cork-Tabbed Communication Book Attached to Lap Tray, described previously.

3. Colored pencils

4. Sheet of paper

5. Sealing tape or clear contact paper

MEASUREMENTS:

The measurements of the communication book may be 11 $^1/2$" wide x 8 $^1/2$" high and the measurements of the color-coded grid taped to the wheelchair lap tray may be 4" wide by 6" high. However, the ideal measurements for this device will vary from student to student depending upon motor, visual-perceptual, and cognitive skills.

ASSEMBLY:

1. Construct the communication sheets using a software program such as Boardmaker (Mayer-Johnson Co.) Or, copy the symbols from a book (such as the Picture Communication Symbols Books, also obtainable from the Mayer-Johnson Co.) and cut and paste them to construct the sheets. Design the sheets so the symbols are grouped into appropriate-sized clusters, such as groups of 6 in a 2 x 3 grid. Up to 10 clusters may fit on an 8 $^1/2$" x 11 $^1/2$" page, if desired.

2. Assign a different color to each position on the grid. Use colored pencils to lightly shade each of the symbols in each group, depending upon the symbol's location within the grid. For example, the top left symbol might always be shaded yellow; the top right symbol might always be shaded blue, and so on.

3. On a separate piece of paper, draw an enlarged version (such as 4″ x 6″) of the color-coded grid. Color the squares with the appropriate colored pencil. Use sealing tape or clear contact paper to attach the grid to an easily-accessed pointing location on the wheelchair lap tray.

☞ If the student has limited range of motion combined with precise pointing accuracy, the color-coded grid may need to be reduced in size rather than enlarged. In addition, rather than pointing directly to the cluster group in the communication book, this student may need to use the color-coded grid to choose both the cluster group as well as the precise symbol within the group. Simply outline each cluster group with a different color to correspond with a color on the color-grid. If using this variation, only six cluster groups can be placed on each page of the communication book.

Contributed by
staff and therapists at the United Cerebral Palsy Association, Watertown, MA.

ARMREST MOUNTED COMMUNICATION BOARD HOLDER
(REMOVABLE)

DESCRIPTION: An angled flat surface which easily slides on and off a wheelchair armrest, which can hold a letterboard or other communication board.

PURPOSE:
To stabilize a communication board on a wheelchair for students who prefer not to use a lap tray or find one to be ineffective for this purpose.

MATERIALS:
1. Low-temperature thermoplastic material: 12 x 18 sheet
2. A 12" long x 1 1/2" wide strip of thermoplastic material which will encase the wire reinforcer and provide additional stability of its own
3. A 10" long stiff wire, such as coat hanger wire
4. 12" of pressure-sensitive Velcro hook and loop tape
5. 6" of non-adhesive Velcro loop tape

☞ Some types of low temperature thermoplastic materials require special solvent or light abrasion before bonding can occur. Please follow manu facturer's directions.

TOOLS:
Splinting pan and water, heat gun, heavy-duty scissors, heavy duty glue (e.g. superglue or plastic welder glue)

MEASUREMENTS:
DIMENSIONS: 6" wide x 8 1/2" high rectangle (supporting surface for letterboard), at the bottom of which is a 2" wide and 1" long neck, which then expands into a 7" wide x 3 1/2" long rectangle (which molds around the arm rest).

The dimensions given here create a relatively small surface, which may work well for many students as it is small enough not to interfere with wheelchair mobility. However, these dimensions may need to be altered depending upon the size of the letterboard, range and ease of arm movements, and type of arm rest.

ASSEMBLY:

1. Heat the thermoplastic material following manufacturer's directions, until pliable and cut it into the shape shown in the diagram. Curve all edges when cutting out the shape.

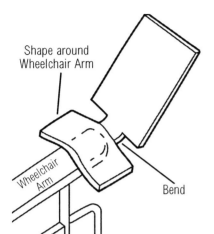

Shape around
Wheelchair Arm

Wheelchair
Arm

Bend

2. Heat and mold the 7" x 3 1/2" section of material around the arm rest, centering the heated material over the arm rest and bending it around the sides and an inch or so under the armrest.

3. Heat the narrow "neck" of the material and curve it to form the desired angle for the communication board support surface.

4. Position the wire down the center of the underside of the device as shown in the diagram. Bend it so it hugs all surfaces of the device. Surround the wire shaft with heavy-duty glue and place the wire into its correct position. Immediately melt the long, narrow strip of thermoplastic material and press it firmly over the wire to help keep the wire in place.

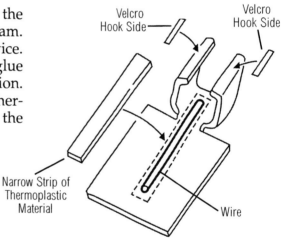

Velcro
Hook Side

Velcro
Hook Side

Narrow Strip of
Thermoplastic
Material

Wire

5. Attach pressure-sensitive Velcro hook to the section molded around the arm rest section (along underneath edges)

6. Slide holder onto armrest. Use Velcro loop strap to hold it securely.

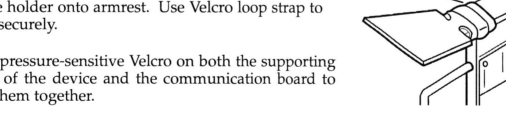

Velcro
Loop Side

7. Use pressure-sensitive Velcro on both the supporting surface of the device and the communication board to attach them together.

☞ Heat up thermoplastic material before adhering Velcro.

Designed by
Sheryl Zelten, OTR/L, Occupational Therapist
while working at Cotting School

PLEXIGLASS EYE-GAZE BOARD

DESCRIPTION: A rectangular piece of clear plastic upon which is taped the student's communication symbols. Sufficient space is left between each of the squares for the receiver of the message to "read" the student's eye movements from the other side of the communication board.

PURPOSE:
To provide a means of communication for a nonverbal student who has poor arm and hand control and is unable to access communication aids which rely on finger-pointing or other pointing devices. Eye-gaze systems can sometimes be trickier to read than other pointing systems, and often require "double checking" by the receiver of the message, as in "I think you were looking at the E, is that correct?". This is particularly true with inexperienced eye-gaze readers. However, eye-gaze boards are very successfully used with many students who are unable to adequately control any other body movements for communication.

MATERIALS:
1. 1/8" thick plexiglass or other suitable clear hard plastic material, cut to desired size, such as 12" x 18". (Many hardware stores will cut the plexiglass to size, or else it can be cut with a bandsaw.)
2. Sandpaper for sanding edges of plexiglass
3. Small white squares of paper with black symbols on them (e.g. letters, words, picture symbols), or conversely, small black squares with white symbols on them, depending upon which color contrast style works best for the student. These may be 1" squares but will vary depending upon the skills of the student and "reader".
4. Clear sealing tape

MEASUREMENTS:
The measurements of the eye-gaze board, symbols, and distance between symbols will depend upon the skills of the student (eye control, complexity of language skills) as well as the skill of the reader in discriminating between closely-spaced eye-gaze points. Eye-gaze boards can range from the size of a sheet of paper to the size of a large posterboard.

ASSEMBLY:
1. Sand all edges of the plexiglass.
2. Use the clear sealing tape to tape the paper symbol squares onto the plexiglass.

MODIFICATION:
A 2-step, color-coded eye gaze system can be used instead of this "direct selection" system, if caregivers continue to have difficulty reading closely-spaced eye-gaze locations. Please see page 80 for an example of how this might be setup with a communication book, and simply transfer this approach to an eye-gaze board.

Contributed by
Kate Moore, M.S., CCC-SLP, Speech-Language Pathologist, Cotting School

WHEELCHAIR-MOUNTED EYE GAZE BOARD

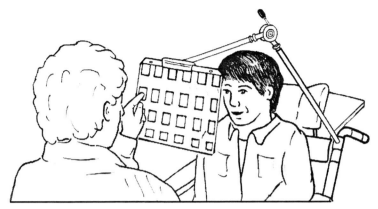

DESCRIPTION: A single-page eye-gaze board, mounted on the student's wheelchair using a universal mount.

PURPOSE:

To provide a portable, student-accessible and inexpensive communication system for those who rely on eye gaze for communication. A commercially available mount such as the Bogen arm allows optimal, hands-free positioning of the communication board and can swing away when not in use.

MATERIALS:

1. Plastic photo sleeve - 8" x 11", or other standard size.
2. 1"-2" squares of paper with the student's communication symbols on them, such as letters, words, Blissymbols, or Picture Communication Symbols (one symbol per paper square).
3. Clear tape
4. Universal mount, such as the Bogen Arm (available through AbleNet)
5. Pressure-sensitive Velcro hook and loop to attach the communication board to the mount.

ASSEMBLY:

1. Tape the paper communication symbol squares inside the plastic photo sleeve, making sure to leave enough space between each one so the receiver of the message can "read" the eye movements from the other side of the communication board.

2. Attach the universal mount to the student's wheelchair high enough on the bar of the wheelchair back support so it can be positioned at eye level in front of the student. Arrange it so it can easily swing away when not in use.

3. Attach the communication board to the universal mount using pressure-sensitive Velcro hook and loop.

MULTIPAGE EYE-GAZE COMMUNICATION BOARD: If the student has complex language skills and requires a multi-page eye gaze communication book, each page can be constructed as described above and then be connected together using metal binder rings which can be bought at an office supply store. This multi-page communication book will need to be held at the student's eye level by the receiver of the message, who will also need to be responsible for turning the pages of the book as directed by the speaker.

Contributed by
Kate Moore, M.S., CCC-SLP, Speech-Language Pathologist, Cotting School

CHEST MOUNT FOR VOICE AMPLIFIER

DESCRIPTION: A voice amplifier holder, made out of thermoplastic material, that is worn over the chest.

PURPOSE: To position a voice amplifier closer to the student's mouth than would be achieved by clipping the amplifier to the shirt, for those who have an especially soft voice.

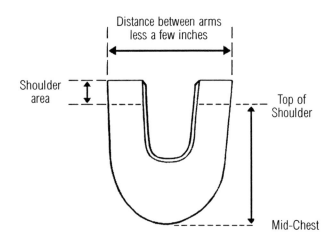

MATERIALS:
1. Low temperature thermoplastic material: 18" x 18" sheet
2. Pressure-sensitive Velcro hook tape, 1" wide x 6" long, cut into 3 equal pieces
3. Pressure-sensitive Velcro loop tape, 1" wide x 2" long
4. Velcro loop tape (non-adhesive), 1" wide x 12" long

☞ Some types of low temperature thermoplastic materials require special solvent or light abrasion before bonding can occur. Please follow manufacturer's directions.

TOOLS:
Splinting pan and water, heat gun, heavy-duty scissors

MEASUREMENTS:

The bib-shaped vest should extend down to the mid-chest. The shoulder extensions should be long enough to completely curve over the top of the shoulders.

ASSEMBLY:
1. Draw and cut out a flat panel of thermoplastic material shaped like a bib with two shoulder extensions, following proportions above. (See diagram).

2. Heat the material in the splinting pan and water, following manufacturer's instructions, until it is soft, let cool until it is comfortable to the touch, and form the bib to the student, folding the extensions over the shoulders.

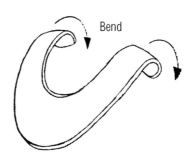

Bend

3. Attach one 2" pressure-sensitive Velcro hook strip to the end of each shoulder extension and use the non-adhesive Velcro loop strip to connect the extensions.

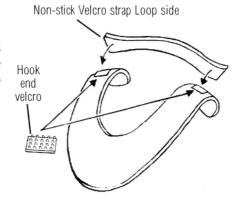

Non-stick Velcro strap Loop side

Hook end velcro

4. Heat and cut out a 1" by 5" piece of thermoplastic material and form it into a "C"- shape.

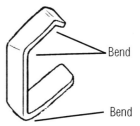

Bend

Bend

5. Attach the "C"-shape plastic to the bib panel using adhesive or a heat gun to bond the pieces together.

"C"-Shaped Plastic

6. Add remaining pieces of pressure-sensitive Velcro to the outside of the C and to the voice amplifier to attach the voice amplifier to the holder.

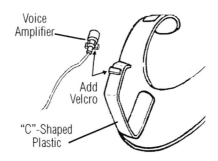

Voice Amplifier

Add Velcro

"C"-Shaped Plastic

Designed by
Sheryl Zelten, OTR/L, Occupational Therapist,
while working at Cotting School

THIGH-MOUNTED PENLIGHT POINTER
FOR COMMUNICATION BOARDS

DESCRIPTION: A laser light or penlight, strapped to the thigh, which is used to high-light letters on a small communication board mounted on the front of the wheelchair. The student uses hip movements to position the light beam on the appropriate letters or communication symbols to communicate.

PURPOSES:

1. To enable a severely physically challenged student (who is only able to isolate and control movements at the hip) to communicate with others. This is a direct selection system and is therefore quicker than relying on a computer scanning system. It is also very inexpensive and highly portable.

2. It can also be used to play games such as tic-tac-toe, Bingo, or checkers on a reduced-size board.

> **MATERIALS:**
> 1. Laser pointer (obtainable at office supply stores) or standard penlight
> 2. 1" wide strip of Velcro loop tape measuring the circumference of the student's thigh plus 2"
> 3. 1" wide Velcro hook tape - 8" long strip
> 4. A universal mount, such as the Bogen Arm (available from AbleNet)
> 5. A small letterboard or communication board made out of cardboard or any other suitable material
> 6. A few inches of pressure-sensitive Velcro hook and loop tape to attach the letterboard to the universal mount.

☞ A laser pointer has a very sharp, pinpoint light beam allowing for more precise "pointing". This enables the student to use a communication board with smaller symbols, which means more symbols can fit on the board.

> *CAUTION: A laser light should never be pointed toward anyone's face as it is very dangerous for the eyes. If use of a laser pointer cannot be closely supervised, a standard penlight may be the better choice.*

ASSEMBLY:

1. To make thigh strap, attach the Velcro hook tape onto the end of the Velcro loop tape, wrap joined tapes around student's thigh, and sandwich the penlight between the hook and loop tapes before pressing it together.

2. Make a cardboard or other suitable letterboard in a size small enough to enable the student to reach all letters or symbols using thigh movements.

3. Attach the universal mount to the front of the wheelchair (perhaps on the bar of a footrest) positioning the letterboard in line with the penlight.

4. Attach the letterboard to the universal mount using pressure-sensitive Velcro hook and loop tape.

☞ The penlight or laser pointer may be attached to a thigh pointer (page 142) instead of a thigh strap, if desired.

Designed by
Robin Levy, OTR/L, Occupational Therapist, while working at Cotting School

---

Chapter 7
Switches

ADAPTIVE SWITCHES AND SWITCH MOUNTS

Adaptive switches play an important role in helping students who have severe physical limitations participate more fully in the various activities that school offers. Switches can be used to operate power wheelchairs, computers, toys, environmental control units, as well as various appliances and machinery throughout the school setting, from electric blenders in Home Economics to electric power tools in Industrial Arts. In fact, many students with severe physical challenges have made their most dramatic improvements in functional performance and level of independence with the use of adaptive switches.

Before choosing among the various switch options for operating a power wheelchair or computer, please consider the following:

1. The fastest and most efficient system for operating a power wheelchair is usually one that is coordinated (can combine directions, such as forward/left) and proportional (can vary speed depending upon how hard you push), such as is offered with most joystick systems [1]. So before considering an alternative system for operating a power wheelchair, carefully evaluate whether or not the student has enough graded control over any part of their body to use a joystick system. Joysticks can be operated not only by movement of an arm, hand, or finger, but also can be operated by other parts of the body, such as the head or foot.

2. The fastest and most efficient system for operating a computer is usually one that allows direct selection, which means the student directly hits the keys of the keyboard (which can also be an onscreen keyboard) using a finger or some type of pointer such as a typing stick, headpointer, mouthstick, or eye-pointing system. The student should be carefully evaluated to determine whether or not there is a feasible direct selection system available before considering a single switch system for the computer.

If it has been determined that the student does not have good potential for using one of the above systems, then an alternate switch system must be considered.

Methods for Activating Switches

Adaptive switches may be activated by a variety of methods, including the following, with examples listed:

PHYSICAL CONTACT - buttons, joysticks, switch plates, and levers.
MUSCLE CONTRACTIONS - electromyographic (EMG) switch.
LIGHT RECEPTION - infrared light switch.

AIR PRESSURE - sip and puff switch, squeeze ball switch, air cushion switch.
SOUND - voice activated computer programs.
GRAVITY CHANGES - mercury switch.
MAGNETIC FIELDS - magnetic switch.

(Adapted from Mann and Lane [2])

Multiple Switch Systems

There are both single and multiple switch systems available. A multiple switch system consists of two or more switches used together to operate a device, with each switch performing a different function. The switches may either be connected together within a single device, such as the keys in a computer keyboard, or they may be completely separated from each other. Separated switches may all be activated by the same body part (e.g. the hand) or may each be activated by a different body part (e.g. one by the hand and one by each knee). If the purpose of the system is to operate a power wheelchair, each switch might be set up to control a different direction, such as forward, right, and left.

In a more complex multiple switch system, each combination of on/off switch positions could provide a different function, thereby increasing the number of commands available to the user. Pressing the "Caps Lock" key on a keyboard to change the function of a letter key from lower case to upper case is an example of this concept. An increase in the number of switches provides more command combinations to the user. [2]

Single Switch Scanning Systems

Unfortunately, most students who need to rely on switch access find multiple switch systems too cumbersome to use - both motorically and cognitively. These students must rely on single switch systems. Simple single switch systems provide the student with very limited options in controlling a device, such as turning a device on and off. For this reason, they are often paired with scanning programs which allow an almost unlimited number of options.

Single switch scanning systems are commonly used to enable students with severe physical challenges to operate power wheelchairs, computer software programs (including word processing programs), and environmental control devices.

Operating a scanning program is a multistep process. The student hits the switch to activate the scanner, which then sequentially scans from an array of choices. To provide a couple of examples, choices might be forward, backward, right, and left directions if the system is used to operate a power chair, or they may be the letters of the alphabet if the system is used to operate a computer. The student then must hit the switch again when the scanner highlights the desired choice.

There are different types of scanning modes that can be used. Row-column scanning is very common for choosing letters of the alphabet during word processing tasks. However it requires a total of three switch closures to choose each letter, if the student hits the switch at the right time each time the desired choices are highlighted. For this reason, using a scanning program is often a time-consuming process.

Students who must rely on single switch scanning systems have very poor motor skills. Finding a point of control on a student's body that has the qualities necessary to operate a switch for a certain type of function can therefore be a laborious process. For example, in order to use a scanning system on a computer or a power wheelchair, a student must be able to move the designated body part in a quick and timely manner. Most power wheelchair systems require the student to maintain contact with the switch for long periods of time in order to travel any distance, and also be able to remove their body part from the switch easily to avoid accidents. A latched switch system is useful for students who are unable to maintain contact with a switch for extended periods (hitting the switch "latches" it on); however, the student must be able to consistently hit the switch when necessary to stop the chair, or else using the chair can become a safety hazard.

Commercial Suppliers of Switches and Switch Mounts

Switches and switch mounts are readily available on the commercial market, but some can be quite expensive. Some companies that sell switches include Zygo Industries Inc., TASH Inc., Prentke Romich Company, AbleNet Inc., Innocomp and Don Johnston Inc. Many of these companies also sell switch mounts. Two adjustable mounting systems currently on the market include Sammons Universal Switch Mounting System (Sammons Preston) and the Bogen Arm (AbleNet Inc.).

Making Switches and Switch Mounts

Effective switches and switch mounts can be easily fabricated for a small fraction of the cost of commercially available products. Another benefit of making a switch is the ability to incorporate the therapeutic needs of the student into the design. Instructions for making the more basic switches using project boxes can often be found at large electronic supply warehouses. Directions for making some of the more creative switches, designed by teachers and therapists to meet specific students' needs, are presented at the end of this chapter. Some fabricated switch mounts that have been successful for particular students are also presented.

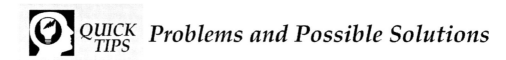 **QUICK TIPS** *Problems and Possible Solutions*

Following are some solutions which have successfully solved the identified problem for one or more students. Keep in mind that each student has a unique set of abilities and needs and may therefore require an original solution for the problem at hand. If a suggested solution is appropriate for a student, please adapt the design as necessary to best meet his or her needs.

Remember: fit the device to the student, not the student to the device!

1. Switch needs to be mounted so that it can be activated by using hip flexion.

Mount the switch to the undersurface of a lap tray using Velcro.

2. Switch needs to be mounted so that it can be activated by using tongue protrusion.

Attach a fiberoptic switch to the mouthpiece of a microphone headset.
(Rucker Ashmore, CEO/Applications Engineering Director, Adaptive Switch Labs, Austin, TX)

3. Student uses hip abduction movements to activate a switch, but leg changes resting position which compromises accuracy.

Foot stabilization is often necessary to insure precise movements using hip abduction. A foot stabilizer can be purchased commercially or can be made by forming a 2-3" wide strip of thermoplastic material against the sides and back of a wooden base that is the same size and shape as the student's shoe sole, and then screwing it into the base. The foot stabilizer can be mounted to the wheelchair foot rest using Velcro.
(Faith Safler, P.T., Val Greene, B.S. Ed., Industrial Arts Teacher, and the author, Cotting School)

4. Student needs a vertical cylindrical handle for a toggle switch.

Place a short piece of cylindrical foam over the toggle switch just thick enough to push a cylindrical toothbrush holder (used for travel) over it.
(Sue Shannon, OTR/L, Occupational Therapist, Perkins School for the Blind)

5. Student can only move using a total extension pattern of the arms, and needs to have switch access.

Make an arm extension switch mount. Screw two pieces of wood together at an obtuse angle (so the side piece is vertical and the top piece angles like the roof of a house) and screw this into a wooden base. C-clamp the wooden base to the wheelchair lap tray. Attach a switch to the underside of the overhanging piece of wood using pressure-sensitive Velcro. See Materials and Processes for directions on how to cut and screw wood together.
(Kate Moore, M.S., CCC-SLP, Speech-Language Pathologist, Cotting School)

INSTRUCTIONS
FOR FABRICATING
SELECTED DEVICES

BATTERY ADAPTER

CASSETTE TAPE COVER SWITCH

NERF BALL SWITCH

EASEL SWITCH

CHIN SWITCH HARNESS

HEAD-MOUNT FOR CHIN SWITCH

HEAD SWITCH MOUNTED
TO
EXISTING HEAD SUPPORT

BATTERY ADAPTER

DESCRIPTION: A cable that has a standard make jack on one end and a 1/2" square copper plate on the other end.

PURPOSE:
To adapt virtually any battery-operated toy or battery-operated appliance so that it can be operated using a switch.

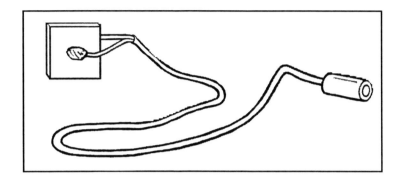

MATERIALS:
1. 1/2" x 1/2" Dual-Sided PC Board

2. 24 Gauge Speaker Wire, 18" long.

3. 1/4" female jack

TOOLS:
Soldering gun or liquid solder, utility knife

ASSEMBLY:
1. Cut a 1/2" x 1/2" piece of dual-sided PC board. To cut this material, score both sides of the board with a utility knife and then snap along cut lines.

2. Cut an 18" length of speaker wire. Strip 1/8" of insulation off all four ends.

3. Solder two of the ends to the PC board (one on each side), and the other two ends to the jack.

4. Place the wafer (PC board) into the battery housing of the toy or appliance so that it interrupts the circuit. Turn the toy or appliance on. Plug a switch into the jack.

Contributed by
Karen Conrad, ScD, OTR/L, Occupational Therapist,
Founder and President, Therapro, Inc.

CASSETTE TAPE COVER SWITCH

DESCRIPTION: A switch made using a plastic cassette tape cover. Pushing down on the lid of the cassette tape cover activates the switch.

PURPOSE:
To enable a student to operate a battery-operated toy or battery-operated appliance using a single switch.

☞ A battery adaptor is necessary if the appliance is not designed to accept a switch - see page 95 for directions on how to make one. To be used with a plug-in electrical appliance, this switch must be used in conjunction with an electrical appliance converter such as the AbleNet Power Link.

> **MATERIALS:**
> 1. Cassette tape cover
> 2. Insulated electrical wire, about 48"
> 3. Switch - such as a GC Snap Action (Momentary) Switch, part number 35-834, Single Pole, Double Throw, 5 AMPs, 250 Volts AC. (Many other types of switches can be substituted. A salesman at large electronics store can recommend one.)
> 4. 3/8" rubber plug
> 5. 1/4" plug (male phone jack)
> 6. Two 3/8" long screws
>
> **TOOLS:** Drill, soldering gun

ASSEMBLY:
1. Position the switch inside the "box" side of the cassette cover, against the long edge that opens (opposite the hinge), so the small button is facing up toward the lid. Position the switch where it will be activated by pressing the cassette cover, but will not be activated when the lid is positioned lightly closed without pressure. Mark where the screw holes of the switch contact the cassette cover. Set switch aside. Drill the holes for the screws.

2. Drill a hole 1/4" in diameter approximately an inch to the right of the screw holes for the switch, and position the 3/8" rubber plug in this hole.

3. Use a utility knife to scrape off 1/2" of wire covering on each end of the wire to reveal red and black insulated wire. Solder one end of the wire to the metal protrusions at the bottom of the switch. Position the switch in the cassette cover and push the wire through the hole that has the rubber plug on it. Screw the switch onto the cassette cover.

4. Solder the other end of the wire onto the 1/4" plug (male jack).

Contributed by
Suzanne Collins, M.S., OTR/L, Clinical Supervisor at Franciscan
Children's Hospital, Brighton, Ma. (Designer unknown)

NERF BALL SWITCH

DESCRIPTION: A pressure activated switch embedded in half a nerf ball.

PURPOSE:
To enable a student to operate a battery-operated toy or battery-operated appliance using a single switch. Some students prefer the textured surface of the nerf ball, and it requires only gross movements of the arm or hand to activate it.

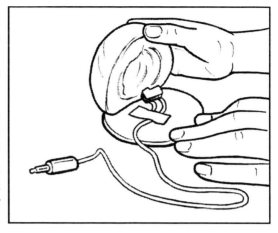

☞ A battery adaptor is necessary if the appliance is not designed to accept a switch - see page 95 for directions on how to make one. To be used with a plug-in electrical appliance, this switch must be used in conjunction with an electrical appliance converter such as the AbleNet Power Link.

MATERIALS:
1. A switch, such as a GC Electronics Snap Action (Momentary) Switch, part number 35-838, Single Pole, Double Throw, 5 Amps, 250 Volts AC. (Many other types of switches can be substituted. A salesman at a large electronics store can recommend one.)
2. 24 Ga. Speaker wire, 30 inches long
3. 1/4" plug (male jack)
4. Round piece of formboard or heavy cardboard, 4" in diameter.
5. 4" Nerf Ball

TOOLS:
Electrical tape, sharp knife, scissors, soldering gun, glue

ASSEMBLY:
1. Cut a Nerf ball in half.
2. Scrape off 1/2" of insulation off of each of the four ends of the speaker wire. (The speaker wire splits at each end into 2 sections - scrape off all 4 sections.)
3. Using a soldering gun, solder the two sections of one end of speaker wire onto the first two metal extensions which extend under the switch and solder the two sections of the other end of the speaker wire onto the 1/4" plug.
3. Tape the switch to the center of the round piece of formboard/cardboard using electrician's tape.
4. Scoop out the center of one of the Nerf ball halves, leaving approximately 1" of Nerf ball remaining around the edges of the hollow. (Scoop out enough so it only takes a little touch of the Nerf ball to turn on the switch.)
5. Glue the scooped out Nerf ball over the switch on the piece of board.

Designed by
Kristen Taylor Rooney, M.S., Classroom Teacher,
Franciscan Children's Hospital, Brighton Ma.

EASEL SWITCH

DESCRIPTION: A switch mounted in the front surface of a Triwall easel and covered by a square plate of expanded PVC material to enlarge the switch surface.

PURPOSES:
1. To position a switch so that shoulder flexion and elbow extension are encouraged.
2. To enable a student to operate a computer, battery-operated toy or battery-operated appliance using shoulder flexion and elbow extension. These movements are often desirable for those who exhibit the opposite motor pattern (i.e. flexor motor pattern) due to a neurological disorder.

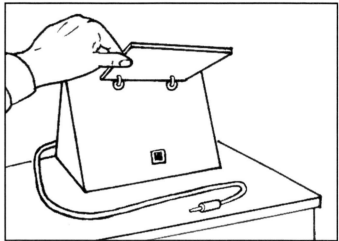

☞ A battery adaptor is necessary if the appliance is not designed to accept a switch - see page 95 for directions on how to make one. To be used with a plug-in electrical appliance, this switch must be used in conjunction with an electrical appliance converter such as the AbleNet Power Link.

MATERIALS:
1. Triwall material, 2' x 4' sheet
2. One 1/4" thick wooden dowel
3. Woodworker's glue
4. Expanded PVC material, 6" x 6" square
5. Speaker wire, long enough to reach from the easel switch to the computer or appliance
6. Pressure-sensitive Velcro hook and loop tape.
7. Switch such as a GC Snap Action (Momentary) Switch, part number 35-834, Single Pole, Double Throw, 5 AMPs, 250 Volts AC. (This switch can be purchased from an electronics store. Many other types of switches can also be used.)
8. 1/4" plug (male phone jack)
9. Two beads - approximately 1/2" in diameter.
10. String or ribbon, about 12" long
11. Cloth tape or electrical tape
12. Optional: Latex Enamel - to paint the Triwall

TOOLS:
Bandsaw, jigsaw, utility knife or steak knife; pencil sharpener, soldering iron; carpenter's heavy duty glue gun and glue sticks. (If not available, woodworker's glue may be substituted.)

MEASUREMENTS:
The Triwall easel is about 12" wide by 9" tall. These measurements can be easily altered to suit the needs of the student and situation.

ASSEMBLY:

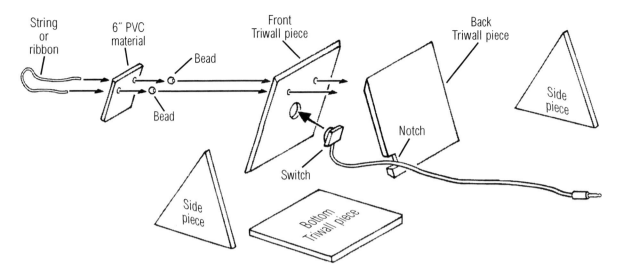

1. Cut out 3 rectangles of identical dimensions, such as 12" x 9". Cut out a notch in one of the sides of one of the rectangles (the wire will fit through this). The notched rectangle should form the back piece of the "tent shape" when assembled.

2. Attach the rectangles together to form the tent shape using the procedure for attaching Triwall described in the chapter on Materials and Processes. Angle the raw edges first so the contact edges are flush together.

3. Trace the end of the assembled "tent" twice on the remaining piece of Triwall. Cut these two triangles out. These will cover the ends of the "tent" in step 9.

4. If desired (for added stability), use hot glue to glue the above "tent shape" onto a larger (e.g. 9" x 18") Triwall base.

5. Cover all corners and edges of the Triwall with duct tape or masking tape and then paint all outside surfaces of the Triwall, if desired. Paint triangular pieces as well.

6. Strip an 1/8" of insulation from each of the four ends of the speaker wire. Solder two of the ends to a switch and the other two ends to the jack.

7. Cut a hole in the center of the front surface of the Triwall easel just big enough to fit the switch through. Tape the switch in the hole using cloth tape or electrical tape so only the button juts out beyond the front surface of the Triwall.

8. To attach the 6" square of PVC over the switch to serve as the switch plate, punch two holes in the easel and two holes in the top of the PVC. Thread each end of a string or ribbon first through the PVC, then through a small bead, and finally through the Triwall. Tie the two ends of the string together inside the easel. It is essential that a small bead be placed between the PVC and the Triwall so that the switch is not activated accidentally due to pressure from the PVC.

9. Use pressure-sensitive Velcro to attach the triangular ends to the easel.

Designed and fabricated by
Subhashini Balagopal, M.Ed., Preschool/Primary Cluster Coordinator,
Franciscan Children's Hospital, Brighton, Ma.

CHIN SWITCH HARNESS

DESCRIPTION: A thermoplastic chin switch holder worn on the chest. The switch is held on to the harness with Velcro and can be easily removed.

PURPOSE:
To stabilize a switch for chin activation.

MATERIALS:
1. Low temperature thermoplastic material, - 18" x 18" sheet
2. Pressure-sensitive Velcro hook, 1" x 16"
3. Pressure-sensitive Velcro loop material, 1" x 6"
4. Two 12" lengths of Beta pile or Velcro loop tape (non-adhesive), 1" wide

☞ Some types of low temperature thermoplastic materials require special solvent or light abrasion before bonding can occur. Please follow manufacturer's directions.

TOOLS: Splinting pan and water, heat gun, heavy duty scissors

MEASUREMENTS:
The butterfly-shaped chest mount tapers toward midline from the shoulders until it is only about 4" wide at the midchest, and then extends laterally a couple of inches on each side. The top shoulder extensions should be long enough to completely curve over the top of the shoulders.

ASSEMBLY:

1. Draw and cut out a butterfly shape from the thermoplastic material to form the harness, using the measurement guidelines above and diagram.

2. Heat the material in the splinting pan and water until it is soft, let cool until it is comfortable to the touch, and form the harness to the student, folding the extensions over the shoulders.

3. Attach one 2" long pressure-sensitive Velcro hook strip to the end of each of the four extensions. Attach beta pile or Velcro loop straps in an "X" formation across the back connecting the 4 extensions.

Mid-Chest area ——————

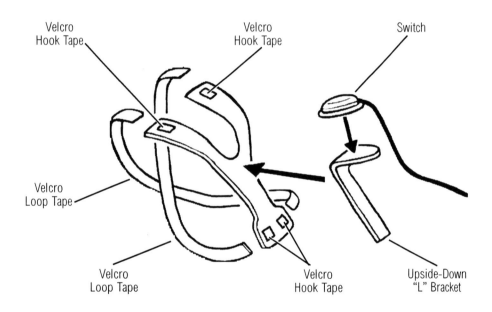

Velcro Hook Tape

Velcro Hook Tape

Switch

Velcro Loop Tape

Velcro Loop Tape

Velcro Hook Tape

Upside-Down "L" Bracket

4. Cut out a strip of thermoplastic material to make the upside-down "L" bracket. This flat strip should be wide enough to hold the switch and approximately 8" in length. Heat the strip and form an inverted "L" shape. Attach this to the harness with pressure sensitive Velcro as indicated in diagram.

5. Mount the switch to the top of the inverted "L" shape using pressure-sensitive Velcro.

OPTION: If less stabilization is required, omit the bottom extensions and attach one strap across the back of the neck, connecting both top extensions.

Designed by
Sheryl Zelten, OTR/L, Occupational Therapist,
while working at Cotting School.

HEAD-MOUNT FOR CHIN SWITCH

DESCRIPTION: A thermoplastic "hat" with an attached wire which is bent down around the face and under the chin. The switch is attached with Velcro to a small thermoplastic square at the end of the wire under the chin.

PURPOSE:
To stabilize a switch for activation using jaw movements.

MATERIALS:
1. Low temperature thermoplastic material, 18" x 6" sheet, preferably colored
2. Stiff wire, such as a hanger wire, about 20" long
3. Plastic welder glue
4. Pressure-sensitive Velcro hook and loop tape, 1" x 4" strip
5. TASH Cap Switch or other appropriate switch

☞ Some types of low temperature thermoplastic materials require special solvent or light abrasion before bonding can occur. Please follow manufacturer's directions.

TOOLS:
Splinting pan and water, heavy duty scissors, small clamps

MEASUREMENTS:
The perpendicular strip of thermoplastic material should be long enough to form around the top of the head and rest just above the ears. The horizontal strip of thermoplastic material should be long enough to be molded around the back of the head, from ear to ear, and will bond to the perpendicular piece just above the ears.

ASSEMBLY:

1. Draw and cut out two strips of thermoplastic material using the measurement guidelines above. If unsure of needed dimensions, make strips of paper the size which seems right and check for fit.

2. In the splinting pan and water, heat the strip that will be formed over the top of the head until it is soft, following manufacturer's instructions. Let cool until it is comfortable to the touch, and form it over the head. Cut off excess material so it rests just above the ears.

3. Heat the second strip of material until soft, let cool until comfortable to the touch, and form it horizontally around the head from ear to ear. Cut off excess material. Bond this strip over the first strip according to manufacturer's instructions.

4. Form a deep longitudinal groove in the center of the vertical strip by spot-heating the thermoplastic material with a heat gun and pressing the wire into it. Continue the groove downward into the horizontal piece of thermoplastic material where it is bonded with the vertical piece. Remove the wire.

5. Shape the wire so it fits snugly into the groove with an extension long enough to curve under the chin. Apply plastic welder glue into the groove, and then press the wire back into the groove. Clamp.

6. When dry, form the free wire extension into the desired position under the chin. Sandwich the end of the wire between two same-sized squares of thermoplastic material large enough to support the switch. Do this by softening the thermoplastic material in the splinting pan, applying plastic welder glue to the wire and then bonding the squares of thermoplastic material together over the wire.

7. Attach pressure-sensitive Velcro hook tape to the underside of the switch, and pressure-sensitive Velcro loop tape to the top surface of the switch support. Mount the switch.

8. **OPTIONAL:** If saliva is a problem, protect the switch with a plastic cover (a plastic baggie will do).

☞ To improve the aesthetics of this design, attach a baseball cap over it using a rivet gun; or glue an additional strip of thermoplastic material over the wire that is attached to the head piece.

Designed by
Sheryl Zelten, OTR/L, Occupational Therapist,
while working at Cotting School.

HEAD SWITCH MOUNTED TO EXISTING HEAD SUPPORT

DESCRIPTION: A head-switch mount which consists of a strip of expanded PVC that is formed so that it hooks around a head support. A Velcro strap connects the ends of the head-switch mount. The switch is bolted to the mount.

☞ This is just one of several styles of head switch mounts, and is only compatible with some types of switches and head supports. Please consult with an occupational therapist to be sure this design is the best solution and does not promote undesirable movements.

PURPOSE:
To stabilize a switch for activation by head movements.

MATERIALS:
1. Expanded PVC material, 12" x 4"

2. Velcro loop tape (non-adhesive), 1" x 6" strip

3. Velcro pressure-sensitive hook tape, 1" x 4" strip

4. Three 1/2" long bolts with matching nuts

5. A switch appropriate for head activation,
   such as an AbleNet Jelly Bean switch

TOOLS:
Jigsaw
Heatgun
Scissors

ASSEMBLY:

1. On the PVC material, trace the outline of the switch, and then draw 1 1/4" wide extensions from opposite sides of the tracing as follows: the extension on one side can be approximately 1 3/4" long, and the extension on the other side needs to be long enough to wrap over the top of head support (perhaps 6" long).

2. Cut out the drawn shape on the PVC material using a jig saw.

3. Heat the PVC with a heat gun to bend it around the head support at the desired location, with the switch surface facing the back of the student's head.

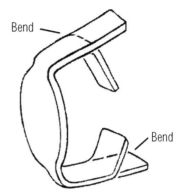

4. Attach the switch to the head mount using three 1/2" long bolts and nuts, as shown in the diagram. (See the chapter on Materials and Processes for directions on applying bolts.)

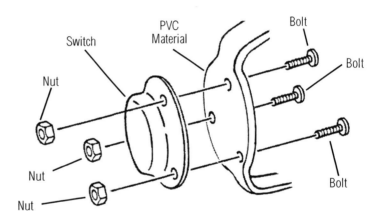

5. Attach pressure-sensitive Velcro hook to the ends of the extensions and add a Velcro loop strap to secure it to the head support.

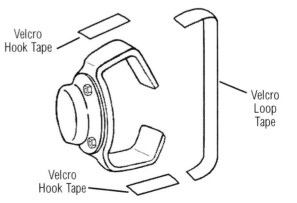

Contributed by
Staff and therapists
at the United Cerebral Palsy Association in Watertown, Ma.

Chapter 8
Computers

ASSISTIVE DEVICES FOR COMPUTER TASKS

Many students who have special needs rely heavily on computers to complete academic work, due to inadequate writing skills. Since the quality of work produced on the computer will significantly affect the student's academic performance, the primary goal when designing a computer work station is to enable the student to perform computer tasks with as much ease, accuracy, and speed as possible. Since computer use also requires repetitive movements, a secondary goal is to set up the task to encourage desirable movement patterns or at least discourage the use of detrimental movement patterns (e.g. those that may accentuate any significant muscle imbalances or that may cause significant stress to the muscles or joints). Usually both goals can be met without much difficulty. For certain students who have severe motoric limitations, the secondary goal cannot be met without sacrificing the primary goal, in which case some compromise is needed.

In order to meet the above goals, it is important to carefully assess the student in the following areas: positioning; upper extremity motor control (especially range and accuracy of hand placement, motor endurance, motor planning, and hand skill development); visual and perceptual skills; and cognitive skills.

If it is determined that the student's arm and hand control is inadequate for operating the computer, other body movements should also be assessed. Usually, all of the above factors are assessed simultaneously within a functional context (that is, while the student is actually using a computer), beginning with an educated guess as to what adaptations may be needed, and then making adjustments as new information is obtained.

Positioning the Student for Computer Tasks

Good positioning is critical when evaluating the student's motor control for computer access, as it will have a significant effect on the student's performance. In the case of some students who have severely limited movement, it may be necessary to evaluate the student's motor control in more than one position to determine the best one for using the computer. The method of computer access that is chosen (e.g. standard keyboarding, mouthstick, foot-operated switch, or other method) may also influence the decision as to how to position the student. For example, it may be ultimately determined that a headpointer is the best method for operating the computer for a particular student, and that the student's best head control occurs while positioned in a prone stander.

Once an appropriate method of computer access is determined, select the position in which the child is most stable and muscle tone is most normal when producing the movement. Please refer to Chapter 4 for a more in-depth discussion on positioning, including how to choose an appropriate chair and how to adapt one if necessary.

Keyboard Height

The best height for a keyboard will vary depending upon individual factors as well as the type of adaptations used. The standard ergonomic principles that are applied in corporate offices across America (including positioning the keyboard slightly below elbow level) are not applicable for many students with special needs. These ergonomic principles were designed for typical adults who do not have neurological, visual, or perceptual impairments, and who will be performing word processing tasks for many hours per day, using all fingers of both hands.

For many students who have impaired hand function, there are several reasons positioning the keyboard below elbow level is not recommended. First, it encourages the use of wrist flexion (even if a wrist support is available), which reverses all therapeutic efforts to help improve wrist stability. Second, it increases the static load on the arms, that is, the arms are hanging freely off the shoulder joints as opposed to being supported on a surface. This can be an unstable and fatiguing position for those who have low or fluctuating muscle tone. Those who have high flexor tone often can not reach a low keyboard to begin with, which makes this issue a mute point! Finally, many students with special needs are unable to use the standard method of keyboarding and need to "hunt and peck". This is difficult to do when the keyboard is positioned very low, and can often contribute to and even encourage poor posture.

On the other hand, there are students who do benefit from having the keyboard supported at a lower height. For example, one student who uses a wheelchair experienced back pain whenever she used the keyboard, which was positioned on a table high enough so her wheelchair could fit under it. She now uses a lap desk to support the keyboard, which has eliminated the back pain. Some older students who have intact perceptual and motor function and who have mastered standard keyboarding may also benefit from adhering to standard ergonomic principles: both positioning the keyboard at a lower height (to allow optimal blood flow and reduce muscle strain) and using a wrist support.

In a school setting, the best place to position a computer is on a computer table that is adjustable in height (see Quick Tip #1 for a specific recommendation). These can be easily adjusted to accommodate the needs of most students who will be using the keyboard, including those who use wheelchairs. Having a lap desk also on hand will accommodate those students who are positioned in wheelchairs but need a keyboard that is lower than any table their wheelchair fits under. Other students may find it easier to set the keyboard on their wheelchair lap trays.

Adaptations for Students Who Have Impaired Motor Control

Students who have impaired range of motion, muscle tone, muscle strength, or motor planning skills often demonstrate movement abnormalities when using a keyboard, which compromise performance. Following are some common types of movement abnormalities that have been observed in these students, along with some suggested adaptations to eliminate these patterns:

Shoulder Fixing

One common movement pattern that is seen in some children who have abnormal muscle tone is "fixing" the upper arm out to the side, elbow at shoulder level, in an attempt to improve stability at the shoulder. This is a very fatiguing posture and is also detrimental to the muscles and to further development of motor control. One solution is to provide a well-positioned support for the forearm and/or wrist. The Angled Keyboard Stand with Attached Wrist Rest has been particularly successful in eliminating this problem for some students. Directions for making this keyboard stand are provided later in this chapter.

Wrist Flexion and/or Finger Hyperextension

An inappropriate movement pattern that is commonly observed in students who have increased flexor tone or who are generally low-toned is the use of repetitive wrist flexion to hit the keys which may result in hyperextension at the finger M.P. joints (at the base of the fingers). Hyperextension of the M.P. joints is usually a compensation for weak wrist extensors or hypertonic wrist flexors. Wrist flexion can also be a sign that the student is attempting a hand grasp or manipulative task that is beyond his or her present developmental level. For example, students who have difficulty isolating the index finger from other fingers will often exhibit increased wrist flexion.

☞ It is common for able-bodied students who are at the "hunt & peck" stage of keyboarding to keep their remaining fingers extended rather than flexed; however, this is usually not accompanied by wrist flexion or hyperextension of the finger M.P. joints. It is only when these detrimental movement patterns occur that remedial strategies are necessary.

Some possible solutions for these inappropriate movement patterns are presented in the following developmental flow-chart. The guidelines presented assume that the student has adequate range and accuracy of hand placement to use a standard keyboard. These guidelines are definitely not written in stone, since every student is unique, and since the author is not aware of every successful strategy that has been used with students.

GUIDELINES TO ASSIST IN KEYBOARD SET-UP FOR STUDENTS WHO HAVE IMPAIRED HAND FUNCTION:
A Developmental Approach

The purpose of this chart is to help professionals develop their clinical decision-making skills, based on a developmental approach, for solving commonly observed hand function problems as they relate to computer use. These solutions have been known to work successfully with some students. These guidelines are not intended to imply that these are the only solutions that may be appropriate.

1	**Does the student demonstrate isolated movement of the index finger with the wrist in neutral or extension?**	**If yes:** ☞No adaptations are needed to assist with pointing. Further questions to ask are: Can the student isolate all of the fingers of both hands sufficiently to perform standard keyboarding? If not, can (or should) the student use both index fingers on each side of the keyboard?	*If no:* ☞ Go on to questions 2 and 3.
2	**Does the student exhibit wrist flexion when isolating the index finger?**	**If yes:** ☞ Try using a firm wrist rest or the combination of firm wrist rest and angled keyboard.	*If the tendency still exists:* ☞ Go on to Question 3.
3	**Does the student have difficulty isolating movements of an index finger from other fingers?**	**If yes:** ☞ Try having the student hold a small object in the palm during keyboarding, such as a piece of sponge, a small plastic koosh ball, or a short dowel. The object should be held against the palm by the remaining fingers while the index finger is used for depressing the computer keys. This technique increases the stability of the ulnar (little finger) side of the hand, which provides a more stable base from which to isolate the index finger.	*If the student cannot maintain a neutral or extended wrist position while using this approach:* ☞ Go on to Question 4.
4	**Is the student unable to hold an object in the palm to keep remaining fingers flexed, or does the student exhibit wrist flexion when doing so?**	**If yes, one of the following solutions may work:** ☞Some students are able to isolate their index finger while curling their remaining fingers over the top of the angled wrist rest of the Angled Keyboard Stand with Attached Wrist Rest (page 122). ☞ Using a pincer mitt (Quick Tip #3) may reduce the stress in attempting to isolate the index finger so that they no longer exhibit wrist flexion when doing so [1]. An old tube sock with a hole in it for the index finger to poke through is a good modern-day substitute for a pincer mitt [2]. If wrist flexion is exhibited when using these aids, they are probably developmentally inappropriate.	*If neither of these solutions work:* ☞ Go on to Question 5.
5	**Is the student unable to extend the index finger even with a pincer mitt and also unable to maintain the wrist in neutral unless the fisted hand is placed on a firm surface?**	**One of the following solutions may work:** ☞Have the student hold a pointer (such as the T-shaped pointer, page 138) in the fisted hand and drag the fisted hand over a keyguard, using the keyguard to facilitate keeping the wrist positioned in neutral. This has worked well in conjunction with an expanded keyboard, and is remedial (i.e. helps to improve wrist stability) as opposed to splinting the wrist, which is purely compensatory. ☞ Try the Keyguard Slider, which is also used in conjunction with a keyguard. This device is described in *Assistive Technology for Rehabilitation Professionals*, by Jennifer Angelo [3]. **If the student has very high flexor tone:** ☞ This student will most likely not be able to use a forearm or wrist support but may possibly benefit from a support placed under the elbow or against the inside or outside of the elbow (such as a 3" high, well-padded edge on a lap tray to press the elbow against) to improve stability and pointing accuracy. This student may also need a wrist splint (see Question 6) and/or a pointer.	*If the these methods do not work:* ☞ Go on to Question 6.
6	**Do all of the above methods fail to eliminate wrist flexion?**	**If yes:** ☞ A wrist immobilization splint (such as a cock-up splint or soft wrist brace) may be necessary to prevent the reinforcement of this undesirable movement pattern when performing keyboarding tasks. A typing stick can be made to attach to the wrist splint using Velcro (see Quick Tip #8). If a soft splint is chosen, a pointer with a horizontal cylindrical handle is often preferable to a typing stick because it has qualities that promote hand development (page 136).	

Developed by Lynn Ciampa Stoller, M.S., OTR/L, BCP.

Limited Range of Motion Due to Muscle Weakness:

Some students lack sufficient range of motion to use a standard keyboard, due to muscle weakness. One cause of severe muscle weakness is muscular dystrophy. Students who have Duchenne's Muscular Dystrophy, for example, lose their proximal motor control before losing their distal control. They often reach a point when they cannot lift their arms off a surface and therefore cannot reach all of the computer keys on a standard keyboard. At this stage, a mini-keyboard (e.g. TASH, Inc.; ComputAbility Corporation) can be a very effective solution. Alternatively, a trackball or special membrane pad such as the Un-Mouse (MicroTouch) can be used to access an on-screen keyboard. A trackball is essentially a mouse placed upside down, but, unlike a mouse, it requires only finger or thumb movement. The Un-Mouse is a small touch tablet surface that performs the functions of a mouse.

Limited Range of Motion Due to Increased Muscle Tone/Spasticity:

When range of motion in the upper extremities is severely limited due to increased muscle tone, hand function is usually also severely compromised. Occasionally, the student can be fitted with a special pointer to operate a mini-keyboard, but more often than not the student will need to find an alternative body part to operate a computer, such as a headpointer, mouthstick, other pointer system, or a switch system.

Poorly Graded Movements

Other students have sufficient range of motion but have difficulty isolating arm or wrist movements due to fluctuating muscle tone (athetosis and/or ataxia), which results in many errors when using the computer. For some of these students, a forearm/wrist rest has helped stabilize their arms and isolate wrist and finger movements more precisely. Experimentation will determine whether the student benefits most by using a flat or an angled forearm/wrist rest. The Angled Keyboard Stand with Attached Wrist Rest has been very successful in eliminating this problem for at least three students at Cotting School who have athetosis and/or ataxia. Directions for both of these devices are provided later in this chapter.

A keyguard (hard plastic template with holes that is placed over the keyboard) is sometimes necessary for some students if they are unable to use a forearm or wrist rest or do not have enough precision when using one. A keyguard can be purchased through most major computer suppliers; however, if choosing to make one, see Quick Tip # 9 for some suggestions. A benefit of using a forearm support instead of a keyguard (when possible) is that it doesn't obstruct the vision when locating keys and also eliminates the problem of fingers getting stuck in the holes. A keyguard can slow typing speed as well.

If placing a keyguard on a standard computer is insufficient for improving the student's pointing accuracy, an expanded keyboard may be necessary. This is an extra-large keyboard with extra-large keys. Most models consist of a matrix of touch-sensitive membrane squares that can be combined to form larger key surface areas. For the student who has poorly graded movements, it will probably need to be used with a special keyguard, so the student can move the hand to the appropriate spot without activating other keys. A pointer, such as the thermoplastic T-shaped pointer described on page 138, may also be necessary with this set-up. Some manufacturers of expanded keyboards include: TASH Inc., Innocomp, IntelliTools, Inc., Unicorn Engineering, Inc., Don Johnston, Inc., and EKEG Electronics Co., Ltd.

Touch screens have also been used successfully by some students who have poorly graded arm movements. This is a special panel which is placed over the screen of a computer monitor and can sense the position of a finger or pointer. Examples are the EZ Touch by Words+, Inc. or Touch Window by Edmark.

In addition to the above hardware adaptations, many of these students also benefit from using software programs that require fewer keystrokes. An example is the use of word prediction programs such as Co-Writer (Don Johnston Inc.).

Motor Perseveration

Some students who have severe motor planning impairments tend to arbitrarily hit computer keys. The initial key stroke may be correct but the student continues to perseverate, hitting random strokes, without stopping to plan his or her actions. Use of the Angled Keyboard Stand with Attached Forearm/Wrist Rest eliminated the perseveration tendency in one boy. The boy was taught to rest his hand on the forearm/wrist rest after each keystroke, which allowed him to "stop and plan" his next destination, significantly increasing his stroke accuracy. It worked significantly better than using this strategy with a typical flat wrist rest, because the angled design facilitates automatic use of the forearm/wrist rest (it's almost hard not to rest the hand while using this device).

Non-Functional Use of the Upper Extremities

Some students who are unable to use their hands to operate a standard keyboard may be able to operate one using a headpointer. These are commercially available through suppliers such as Sammons Preston, Maddak, Inc., and Zygo Industries. Complete directions for a Baseball Cap Headpointer are provided on page 140, which some students find to be more "cool-looking" and less robotic than the commercially available models. The biggest advantage of using a headpointer or other pointing device as opposed to a switch system is speed. This is discussed in more detail in Chapter 7. A raised keyboard stand that fits onto a lap tray can be very useful for some students who use a headpointer to access the computer. This stand is described later in this chapter.

Mouthsticks are also frequently used to access computers, especially by those who have suffered spinal cord injuries. These are discussed on page 130. Some alternative pointing systems have also been developed for the computer, such as the HeadMouse (Don Johnston, Inc.), HeadMaster Plus (Prentke Romich Company), and the Eye Gaze Computer System (LC Technologies), which expand the options for those who are unable to access a keyboard.

Voice recognition programs, such as Dragon Dictate (Dragon Systems, Inc.), are considered the Mercedes Benz of computer access methods. However, they are not as easy to use as one might imagine. These programs require a lot of training as well as good visual, cognitive, language, and sequencing skills, but it is worth it for the right candidates.

If the student does not have potential to use any speedier methods and needs to use a switch system to activate a scanning program, there are numerous types of switches to choose from, including eye-blink switches; sip and puff switches; elaborate tongue switches that are inserted in the mouth like a retainer, such as the TongueTouch Keypad (New-Abilities); switches that can pick up the slightest movement of a muscle (such as when crinkling the forehead); as well as the more typical switches, many of which are discussed in Chapter 7.

Very detailed information on all of the high-tech devices discussed in this chapter, as well as others that were not mentioned, can be found in *The Handbook of Assistive Technology* by Gregory Church and Sharon Glennen [4]. Another good reference on high-tech devices is *Assistive Technology for Persons with Disabilities - The Role of Occupational Therapy*, by William C. Mann and Joseph P. Lane [5].

Adaptations for Students
Who Have Visual and/or Perceptual Deficits

Copy material, the keyboard, and the computer monitor can all be adapted to improve performance with computer tasks for students who have visual and/or perceptual deficits. Copy material refers to any printed material (e.g. written dictation, workbook) that the student is copying from or referring to during computer work. Some common strategies are described below.

Visual Adaptations When Setting Up the Copy Material

Many classroom computer tasks require shifting eye focus from the copy material to the keyboard to the monitor and then back to the copy material, which can be a very difficult task for some students. For some students, it is more difficult to shift eye focus side to side, especially if it involves crossing the midline of the body. Many of these students perform best when the copy material is lined up between the keyboard and monitor so that the eye travels vertically instead of horizontally. However, there are many exceptions to this generalization, so it is best to consult a vision specialist if there is any question about a student's ability to switch eye focus.

The print on the copy material can be enlarged and/or you can limit the amount of print on the paper to make it easier for the student to keep his or her place. One effective approach that teachers often use is to skip a line between rows of print when writing down the student's oral dictation. Then, if any grammatical corrections need to be made before the student types it onto the computer, there is enough space to write them in so they can be easily read. A copy easel with a visual cue bar (moveable bar positioned just under the line being copied) can also be bought commercially at office supply stores to help the student locate where he or she left off when switching focus back to the copy material. For those students who could benefit from using a hands-free magnifier to read copy material, a large selection is available from Maxi-Aids.

Another approach is to first underline each line of print on the copy material with a different colored marker to make it easier for the student to relocate his or her place during keyboarding. For students who have very poor ability to scan material in a left to right manner, it is sometimes necessary to print single words on index cards and have them flip it over when they are done typing the word. However, for students who have too much difficulty switching eye focus (and attention) from the copy material to the keyboard, monitor, and mouse, it is often best to avoid situations that involve copying work. Touch screens are especially beneficial for these students because eye focus always remains on the monitor [2]. Two examples are the Edmark Touch Window and the KeyTech touch screen, both available from Don Johnston, Inc.

Visual Adaptations for the Keyboard

Visual adaptations are also available for the keyboard. Angling the keyboard can make a significant difference in enabling a student to see the letters on the letter keys. Enlarged key labels (such as Zoom Caps by Don Johnston, Inc.) are very useful for many students who have visual impairments as well as some who have figure-ground impairments. There is a choice of black letters on a beige background or white letters on a black background. Students who have figure-ground impairments sometimes benefit from color-coding certain keys or using a template that exposes only certain keys. Other students may benefit from having the teacher hold a 3" diameter bubble wand (or facsimile) over the section of keys in which the correct key is located. This reduces the figure-ground requirements while keeping surrounding keys exposed so that the student can learn the positional relationships between the letters. Word prediction programs such as Co-Writer (Don Johnston, Inc.) can also be helpful in reducing the visual demands of word processing tasks.

If the above solutions don't effectively compensate for the figure-ground difficulties, then an expanded keyboard or special on-screen keyboard may be preferable to using a standard keyboard. Expanded membrane keyboards allow the user to enlarge the keys and/or reduce the number of "keys" used on the keyboard. This increases the distance (or white space) between the symbols on the keys, reducing the figure-ground requirements. Likewise, on-screen keyboards frequently allow the user to create custom-made on-screen grids to accommodate visual needs.

The Big Keys Keyboard, by Greystone Digital (available from Don Johnston, Inc.), worked like a charm for one boy who has figure-ground difficulties compounded by shaky letter recognition skills. The letters on this keyboard are arranged in alphabetical order (not Qwerty-style) and each letter is colored one of 5 different primary colors. A template was first used over the board which only exposed the letters of the boy's first name, but after a month of practice, this template was removed and the boy began copying other short words.

Visual Adaptations for the Monitor

Monitors have built-in functions that allow them to be easily adapted for students who have visual impairments. The type can be enlarged to any size desired, and the style and thickness of the letters can also be changed (usually, the thicker the better). Virtually any background color can be chosen. Choose a type color and background color that have as much contrast as possible, while taking into account any color-blindness that the student may have. Some students who have visual impairments work best with white type on a black background, but this varies depending upon the individual. Experimentation will determine which combination works best for the student. A vision specialist can also provide specific recommendations.

The tool bar and icons on the computer monitor can also be adapted to better accommodate students who have visual or perceptual impairments (refer to the computer's instruction manual).

The auditory feedback option that comes with some word processing programs (such as Write:Outloud by Don Johnson, Inc.) makes it easier to identify keyboarding mistakes so they can be corrected. For those who have difficulty finding the cursor on the monitor screen, try Biggy Cursors by R.J. Cooper (also available from Don Johnston, Inc.) which are compatible with Macintosh computers.

Another factor to consider when accommodating visual impairments is the position of the monitor. The monitor should be positioned directly in front of the user, approximately 18"-28" away from the eyes. In most cases, the top line of characters on the monitor screen should be at eye level. Looking slightly downward is much more comfortable for the eye muscles than looking upward, for most people [6]. However, many students with special needs have ocular-motor, visual-field, or other visual impairments which make it necessary to alter the height or position of the monitor. For example, some students have severe neurological impairments which include paralysis of the eye muscles, resulting in the inability to look in certain directions, such as down or to the left. Students who have visual field neglect can move their eyes in all directions but neglect to register visual information that occurs in the right or left visual fields. The computer monitor needs to be positioned in a manner to compensate for these impairments; that is, the computer should be positioned where the student can best see it. Do not decide to use the monitor as a remedial device to treat these disorders by positioning it in a "difficult" spot.

Adaptations for Students Who Have Cognitive Impairments

Cognitive and academic skills are also important to consider when setting up computer keyboard tasks. It is a waste of time adapting a standard keyboard for a student if the student is not yet able to discriminate between the letters of the alphabet, except perhaps to color-code or otherwise highlight a few keys such as the arrow keys or enter key. Many students at this level will be using primarily the mouse to operate simple, preschool level software programs. However, some alternative keyboards can be very effective learning tools for these students because the letters can be replaced with pictures or other symbols. For example, the IntelliKeys Overlay Maker enables users to create custom overlays for the Intellikeys keyboard (IntelliTools, Inc.). Some of the adaptations discussed for visual perceptual impairments (above) are also useful for those with impaired cognitive skills, such as setting up and adapting the tool bar and icons on the computer monitor so they are easier for the student to comprehend and use.

Finally, the most important compensation for impaired cognitive skills is to carefully choose software programs that correspond with the developmental age level of the student. Many companies produce software suitable (and often especially designed) for students who have impaired cognitive skills, including the following: IntelliTools, Inc., Don Johnston, Inc., Laureate Learning Systems, Inc., R.J. Cooper and Associates, SoftTouch/kidTech, Sunburst Communications, and Edmark Corporation. Call them for catalogs or brochures.

I would like to thank Eileen Kiernan, M.Ed., Remedial Specialist at Cotting School, who, over the past 14 years, took the time to patiently explain to me (usually more than once!) how various computer systems and related high technology devices work.

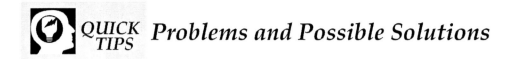 **QUICK TIPS** *Problems and Possible Solutions*

Following are some solutions which have successfully solved the identified problem for one or more students. Keep in mind that each student has a unique set of abilities and needs and may therefore require an original solution for the problem at hand. If a suggested solution is appropriate for a student, please adapt the design as necessary to best meet his or her needs.

Remember: fit the device to the student, not the student to the device!

1. Student's wheelchair cannot fit under the computer table (and it is known that this student can benefit from a high keyboard position).

The 30" x 36" adjustable computer table sold by Holt, Co. is highly recommended and is used throughout Cotting School.

If a table is too low and there are no other suitable tables for supporting the computer, a cheap, effective, and quick solution is to cut a 1" deep hole in each of four blocks of 2" (or thicker) polyethylene foam to fit the table legs into. If this does not raise the table high enough, use a hot gun to heat bond two pieces of polyethylene foam together. This solution is quite stable as the polyethylene foam provides enough friction to prevent sliding on the floor.

2. Student is unable to line up a diskette to fit into a disk drive.

If the floppy disk drive is only a few inches from the table surface (such as with the old Apples), simply cut out a rectangular block of polyethylene foam that is as high as opening of the disk drive, cover it with contact paper, and place it in front of the disk drive so it can be used as a disk guide. Disk guides are also available from TASH, Prentke Romich, Co. and other commercial suppliers.

3. After considering various options, it has been determined that the student would probably best benefit from using a pincer mitt to assist in isolating the index finger when using the keyboard. How can this be made?

Sew a cloth mitten that has holes cut out for the thumb and index finger. Sew Velcro onto the pincer mitt at both the fingertip end (palmar surface) and the base of the palm in order to "stick" the middle, ring, and little fingers against the palm.

Use an old tube sock with a hole cut out of it for the index finger.

(Barbara Berberian, MA, OTR/L, Adaptive Computer Specialist, Assabet Collaborative, Marlboro, MA.)

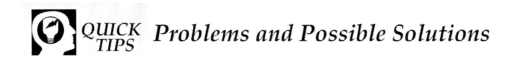

4.   Student is learning keyboarding and has difficulty remembering which finger to use for which keys, and is also frequently looking at the keyboard to visually monitor her finger movements.

Make a color-coded keyboard chart and attach it to the monitor so the student can refer to this chart instead of looking at the keyboard. First find a good illustration of a keyboard in a typing text, enlarge it on a copy machine, and then color-code the letter keys according to which finger is used to access it. For example, all little finger keys may be colored blue, all ring finger keys may be green, and so on. If the student is also using a software typing program, make sure the color-coded system used for the keyboard chart is consistent with the color-coded system used in the software program, to avoid confusion.

5. Several students use the same keyboard, but they each need different keys highlighted with colored stickers. Putting the stickers needed for all of these students on the same keyboard is too confusing for the students!

Give each student his or her own personal moisture guard, and place the stickers (and Zoom Caps) on top of the moisture guard. Simply switch moisture guards when a different student uses the keyboard. Moisture guards are available from Don Johnston, Inc., Prentke Romich Co., as well as several other computer product companies.

(Barbara Berberian, MA, OTR/L, Adaptive Computer Specialist,
Assabet Collaborative, Marlboro, MA.)

6. Student's fingers shift off the home row keys.

Place tiny squares of pressure-sensitive Velcro loop on the F and J keys to provide tactile cues that the fingers are positioned correctly, so the student does not have to monitor this visually.

Locator dots provide tactile cues to assist in positioning the fingers on particular keys. Different types are available from Maxi-Aids. State Commissions for the Blind will usually provide these for free to any student that is legally blind.

(Barbara Berberian, MA, OTR/L, Adaptive Computer Specialist,
Assabet Collaborative, Marlboro, MA.)

7. Student has no functional hand use and needs a method for accessing the mouse (for typical mouse functions or to operate an onscreen keyboard).

Some suggestions for those who use headpointers or mouthsticks:

🕭 For Macintosh users, use the Easy Access keys option that is installed in every Macintosh computer.

🕭 For IBM PC users, buy WinAccess (available from Microsoft; Maxi-Aids carries it) which operates on Windows. Every Windows 95 software allows use of the number pad arrow keys for moving the mouse, but WinAccess is necessary to use:

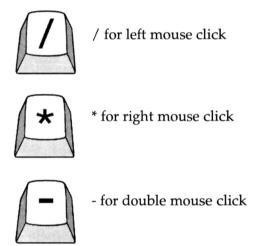

/ for left mouse click

* for right mouse click

- for double mouse click

🕭 Some alternatives to using a headpointer or mouthstick:

EZ Keys for Windows (available from Words+): enables fast and convenient mouse operations via keyboard, switch scanning, or Morse Code, for those who are unable to efficiently use a mouse-type device [7]. EZ Keys provides all of the access methods that formerly required separate programs (Scanning WSKE and Morse Code WSKE).

HeadMouse (Origin Instruments Corporation; also available from Don Johnston, Inc.): a headcontrolled pointing device consisting of a small reflective dot sticker placed on the forehead or glasses which controls the cursor. Available for Macintosh or Windows, desktops or laptops.

HeadMaster Plus (Prentke Romich Company): another device controlled by head movements which "are captured by ultrasound imaging and converted to electrical signals identical to those produced by a normal mouse" (company brochure).

8. Student needs to wear a thermoplastic (volar) wrist splint while keyboarding, but is unable to extend the fingers while wearing the splint in order to punch the computer keys.

There are several possible solutions as well as variations to these solutions. Here are a couple:

Make a typing stick out of thermoplastic material and attach it to the base of the splint using pressure-sensitive Velcro. To do this, melt and cut out a thin, long rectangular shape out of low temperature thermoplastic material that is approximately 1 1/2" wide and a few inches longer than the length that is desired for the typing stick. Form one end against the palmar surface of the wrist splint (do not bond) allowing the rest of the strip to protrude through the web space, and use scissors to trim and curve the edges of the palmar section. Roll the rest of the strip so it is shaped like a pencil, curve it downward to the desired angle, and attach an eraser head to the bottom of it.

Combine the Sandwich Holder Splint (page 288) with the Spring-Grip Cylindrical Handle for Pointers and Drawing Implements (page 136), by following steps 1 through 3 for the Sandwich Splint-Design 1 and adding a spring-operated door latch to the radial end of the dowel section to hold a dowel pointer or writing implement.

9. The student needs to use a keyguard but it is difficult to locate a commercially available one for the particular keyboard.

Keyguards are now commercially available for most keyboards, through computer manufacturers, computer supply companies, or adaptive equipment catalogs. However, if an appropriate one can not be located, here are a couple of solutions:

Have one made by Tech-Able, Inc. They can make a keyguard for anything, including lap tops. The Prentke Romich Company also makes custom keyguards.

Make your own as follows: First make a "rubbing" of the keyboard using a piece of thin paper and a dull pencil. Place a piece of clear hard plastic (e.g. Plexiglas, Lexan, acrylic) over the rubbing and mark the spots for each of the keys. Use a drill press to drill the holes. Glue miniature wooden dowels along the edges of the keyguard and attach small bits of pressure-sensitive Velcro to the bottom of the dowels and to the computer keyboard to attach the keyguard to the keyboard.

(Eileen Kiernan, M.Ed., Remedial Specialist, Cotting School)

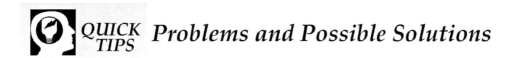

10. Student needs a spherical handle for a computer joystick.

Make a hole in a racket ball just big enough to stick the joystick through it. Stick it over the joystick and secure it in place by wrapping Coban tape over the entire ball and around the base of the joystick.
(Amy A. Houghton, OTR/L, Occupational Therapy Team Leader, Cotting School)

11. Student needs a built-up, vertical cylindrical handle for a joystick.

Place a short piece of cylindrical foam over the joystick and cover with a cylindrical toothbrush holder (made to hold a toothbrush while traveling).
(Sue Shannon, OTR/L, Occupational Therapist, Perkins School for the Blind)

12. Student needs to access a joystick using the index finger due to impaired hand function.

Make a hollow-tube joystick handle. Remove the existing handle of the joystick if possible. Wrap thermoplastic material around the joystick base to form a hollow, vertical tube. The student places a finger inside the tube to operate the joystick. This joystick surrounds the finger, thus providing the student with optimal directional control.
(Suzi Collins, M.S., OTR/L, Clinical Supervisor, Franciscan Children's Hospital, Brighton, Ma.)

13. Student needs a horizontal cylindrical handle for a joystick with lateral supports to the hand to provide increased joystick control.

Make a goal-post joystick out of low temperature thermoplastic material. Form the thermoplastic material into the shape of a football goal-post. This looks like a capital T shape with vertical extensions on each end of the horizontal bar. Follow the directions for the hollow tube joystick (see previous Quick Tip) and fit the "goal-post" into the hollow tube. This design encourages a very stable hand grasp and increases lateral directional control of the joystick.
(Suzi Collins, M.S., OTR/L, Clinical Supervisor, Franciscan Children's Hospital, Brighton, Ma.)

INSTRUCTIONS
FOR FABRICATING
SELECTED DEVICES

ANGLED KEYBOARD STAND
WITH ATTACHED WRIST REST

RAISED KEYBOARD STAND
FOR HEADPOINTER USE

FOREARM/WRIST REST FOR KEYBOARD

ANGLED KEYBOARD STAND WITH ATTACHED WRIST REST

DESCRIPTION: Two angled boards mounted on a flat wooden base. The front board is padded with foam and vinyl and is used as a wrist rest. The back angled board holds a computer keyboard.

PURPOSE:

To improve a student's ability to exhibit controlled hand movements. This device has been especially helpful for students who have ataxic and/or athetoid movements. The wrist rest reduces involuntary movements. Both the wrist rest and keyboard are angled to encourage wrist extension and eliminate abnormal movement patterns.

MATERIALS:
1. 5/8" thick plywood, 24" x 36" will be more than enough
2. 14" x 1" x 1/4" thick wood strip for the keyboard support ledge
3. 1" polyurethane (soft) foam, 14" x 5 1/2"
4. Vinyl material, 20" x 12"
5. Sixteen 1 1/4" flathead wood screws
6. Three very thin (1/16" thick) 5/8" nails
7. Two 14" strips of pressure-sensitive Velcro hook tape and loop tape

TOOLS:

Circular saw or band saw, drill press or hand-held power drill, electric sander and/or sandpaper, heavy-duty staple gun

MEASUREMENTS:

The measurements provided support a keyboard that is 14 inches in width. The measurements for this device can be altered to accommodate the size of the keyboard that will be placed on the support. However, a larger keyboard is probably undesirable for someone who has ataxia or athetosis (if used in conjunction with this device) because it requires a wider range of arm movements which usually increases the involuntary movements.

BASE:
rectangle: 15″ x 11″

KEYBOARD SUPPORT:
rectangle: 14″ x 7″
two triangles: 3 1/2″ x 3 1/2″ x 5″
wood strip: 14″ x 1″ x 1/4″

WRIST REST:
rectangle: 14″ x 5 1/2″
two triangles: 1 1/2″ x 4 1/2″ x 4 3/4″

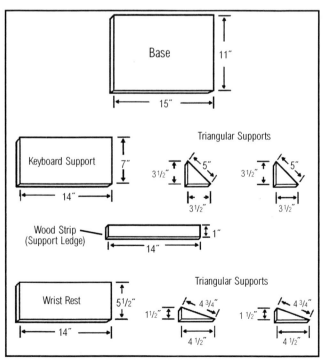

ASSEMBLY:
1. Sand all pieces of wood.

2. Attach triangular supports to keyboard support and wrist rest:
  a. Attach the two 3 1/2" high triangular supports two inches from each end of the keyboard support using two screws for each triangle. First drill pilot holes in the triangles and keyboard support at the appropriate locations. Then use a countersink to inset the screws into the piece supporting the keyboard. Drill the countersink holes 1/4" deep into the keyboard support over the already drilled pilot holes. These holes must be wider than the head of the screw. Then screw the screws from the front of the keyboard support into the wooden triangles.
  b. Repeat this procedure to attach the 1 1/2" high triangular supports for the wrist rest into the wrist rest.

3. Padding the wrist rest:
Lay the vinyl material face down on your work surface. Center the polyurethane (soft) foam on the vinyl, and place the plywood wrist rest on top of the foam. Fold the vinyl material up over the plywood and staple it in place using a heavy-duty staple gun. For best results, put a few staples at the center of each side to anchor the layers together, and then work outward to the corners. Trim off excess vinyl if desired.

4. Form a ledge for the keyboard by nailing the long narrow piece of wood to the bottom of the keyboard support using the 3 thin nails.

5. Attach the keyboard stand and wrist rest to the base:
  a. Before screwing the keyboard stand or wrist rest to the base, set the whole contraption up (including the actual keyboard that is going to be used) and have the student experiment to determine the optimal distance between the keyboard stand and the wrist rest.
  b. With the pieces positioned correctly, trace the triangular supports where they contact the base.
  c. Mark where the screws should go within the tracings of the triangular supports, then countersink two screws from the underside of the base into the triangular supports - two screws per triangular support. To do this, drill the pilot hole from the top surface all the way through to the bottom, then turn the wooden base upside down and widen these holes using a countersink (drilling approximately 1/4" deep). Screw in the screws.

6. Attach two long horizontal strips of Velcro hook to the keyboard support and the Velcro loop to the back of the keyboard itself to help secure it in place. The easiest way to line this up is to adhere the loop tape to the keyboard, press the hook tape onto the loop tape, peel the paper backing off the hook tape (exposing adhesive) and last, press the keyboard and Velcro together onto the wooden keyboard support.

OPTIONAL: This can also be made out of Triwall. See the chapter on Materials and Processes for directions on cutting and attaching Triwall, and modify the steps accordingly. Omit the bottom ledge to support the keyboard - the Velcro is sufficient.

Originally designed and built using Triwall by the author.
Joseph E. Trickett, Carpenter, built this wood version while working at Cotting School.

RAISED KEYBOARD STAND FOR HEADPOINTER USE

DESCRIPTION: A raised wooden platform with pegs on the bottom that fit into holes drilled in the student's lap tray. The "plunk it into the slots" design ensures that it will always be positioned in exactly the same spot on the lap tray, so time isn't wasted with set-up. It takes a split second to set up and remove.

PURPOSE:
To raise the keyboard to an appropriate height for a student using a headpointer.

MATERIALS:
1. 1" x 8" board, about three feet long (see Measurements)
2. Four 1" pieces of 3/16" dowel
3. Woodworker's glue
4. Six #6 Dry Wall Screws (1 5/8" long)

TOOLS:
Saw, drill, sand paper or electric sander, hammer, screwdriver

MEASUREMENTS:
The measurements of the platform will vary depending upon the size of the keyboard and the distance between the lap tray and the tip of the head pointer. The dimensions of one student's keyboard stand are 20" wide by 7 1/2" deep by 3 1/4" high; however, these measurements are unique to this student.

Keyboard stand: should equal the dimensions of the keyboard
Two "legs": should each be (depth of keyboard) x (desired height of keyboard stand minus 3/4")

ASSEMBLY:

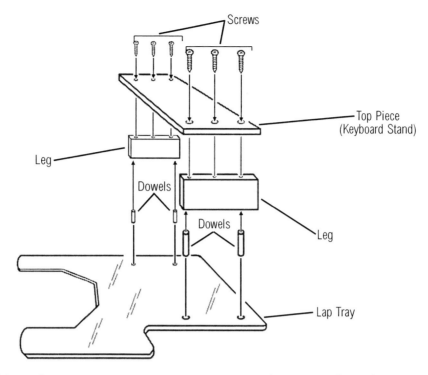

1. Cut the wood into three pieces using measurements determined on the previous page. Sand all pieces of wood.

2. Attach "legs" to keyboard stand:

a. Drill three pilot holes 3/8" in along both of the short edges of the keyboard stand. One hole should be placed 1" from the front edge, one 1" from the back edge and a third in the middle. Drill the holes all the way through the keyboard support. Do not drill pilot holes in the "legs".

b. Screw the "legs" onto the keyboard stand.

3. Put dowel pegs into bottom of "legs":

a. Turn the keyboard stand upside down, and drill holes 1/2" in from each end of both "legs". Drill the holes 1/2" deep and exactly 3/16" wide. (The diameter of the holes should equal the width of the dowels.)

b. Fill holes half way with woodworker's glue and tap the dowels into the holes with a hammer.

4. Installing keyboard stand on lap tray:

a. Place the keyboard stand in the desired position on the lap tray and mark the spots where the dowels contact the lap tray.

b. Drill holes in the lap tray slightly larger than the dowels. Make sure the holes are big enough to allow the dowels to slide in and out..

Designed by
Val Greene, B.S. Ed., Industrial Arts Teacher, Cotting School.

FOREARM/WRIST REST FOR KEYBOARD

DESCRIPTION: A padded arm rest that is both wider and more supportive than commercially available wrist rests. The forearm rest is placed along the front of the keyboard and can be used with the keyboard flat or slightly angled.

PURPOSE:
To reduce tremoring or other involuntary arm movements while using the computer keyboard.

MATERIALS:
1. Triwall material, approximately 5" wide and as long as the keyboard
2. 1/2" thick polyurethane (soft) foam, the same size as the Triwall material
3. Vinyl material, 5" longer and wider than the Triwall material
4. Optional: polyethylene (hard) foam, the same size as the Triwall material
5. Optional: Two 14" strips of pressure-sensitive Velcro hook tape and loop tape

TOOLS:
Heavy-duty staple gun

MEASUREMENTS:
The width of the forearm bar may need to be adjusted according to the size of the student. Generally speaking, it should be almost half the length of the student's forearm (from wrist to elbow).

ASSEMBLY:
Lay the vinyl material face down on your work surface. Center the polyurethane (soft) foam on the vinyl, and place the Triwall rectangle on top of the foam. Fold the vinyl material up over the Triwall and staple it down using a heavy-duty staple gun. For best results, put a few staples at the center of each side to anchor the layers together, and then work outward to the corners. Trim off excess vinyl if desired.

MODIFICATION: ANGLED FOREARM/WRIST REST
This variation is especially useful for old computers which do not have a detached keyboard. Cut a wedge out of polyethylene (hard) foam, using an electric carving knife or steak knife. Attach the forearm rest to the wedge using pressure-sensitive Velcro.

Chapter 9
Pointers & Mouthsticks

POINTERS AND MOUTHSTICKS

The previous chapter included guidelines on how to choose an appropriate method for pointing when accessing a computer keyboard. However, pointers (including mouthsticks) can be used to perform numerous other tasks such as pushing elevator buttons, accessing calculators, communication boards, and other mechanical appliances, and even stabilizing objects. Pointers have even been used successfully to play musical instruments (autoharp, one-string bass guitar, percussion and keyboard instruments). Various tools and utensils, such as pencils, paintbrushes, and gardening tools, can be attached to pointers, enabling students to enjoy a greater variety of activities. This chapter will discuss the use of pointers and mouthsticks as they relate to non-computer activities.

Using Pointers to Assist the Dominant Hand

One often overlooked use for a pointer is to assist the dominant hand in performing a manipulative task. Many students have full use of only one hand and are unable to use their non-dominant hand even to stabilize objects. Often these students resort to using clamps, Dycem, or jigs to stabilize objects. Although helpful, these devices are not very versatile and may require another person's help to set up. One student discovered that using a mouthstick enabled him to perform a variety of bimanual prevocational tasks independently, such as applying gluestick to labels, folding paper, stuffing envelopes, and using paper clips. The student was also able to use scissors independently for the first time by operating stabilized loop scissors and cordless electric scissors with the mouthstick while using the dominant hand to hold and turn the paper. In Music Class, this same student also learned to play an autoharp by using the mouthstick to press the chord buttons while strumming the strings with his dominant hand.

Hand Held Pointers

For those who need to use a hand-held pointer, the style that is chosen depends upon several factors:

- the task to be accomplished
- the student's hand skills
- the student's age.

For tasks such as pushing an elevator button or buttons on a pay phone, independence and expedience are top priorities. These are very quick, non-repetitive tasks, so it is usually not critical what the hand looks like when it performs the task. Melissa Litton's thermoplastic Elevator Wand (described in Mobility chapter) has a simple loop handle which can be perfect for these types of tasks. The loop handle allows a variety of grasps and is easy to grip no matter how it is positioned. Other push button tasks, such as hitting computer keys or buttons on augmentative communication devices, are very repetitive and require more attention to hand position, to promote better hand function.

When designing hand-held pointers for frequently performed tasks, carefully assess the student's developmental level of hand skills and note any inappropriate hand patterns. The ideal design will eliminate the inappropriate hand patterns and help to develop the missing components of hand development.

Erhardt discusses three key grasp patterns which are often missing in many neurologically impaired students [1,2]. These grasp patterns are important because they help to develop critical pattern components necessary for the development of more mature grasps. These key grasp patterns are the *radial-palmar grasp*, the *palmar-supinate grasp*, and the *scissors grasp* .

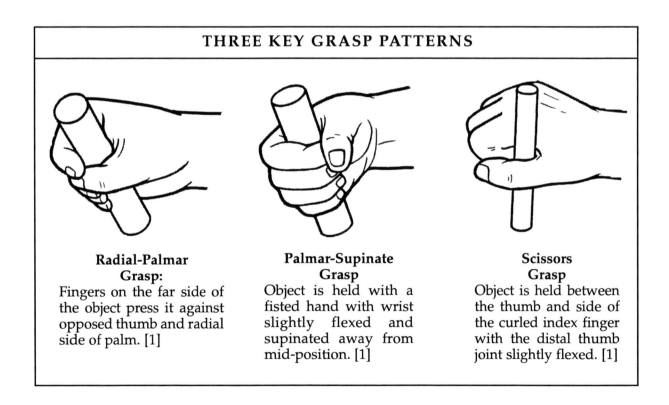

THREE KEY GRASP PATTERNS

Radial-Palmar Grasp:
Fingers on the far side of the object press it against opposed thumb and radial side of palm. [1]

Palmar-Supinate Grasp
Object is held with a fisted hand with wrist slightly flexed and supinated away from mid-position. [1]

Scissors Grasp
Object is held between the thumb and side of the curled index finger with the distal thumb joint slightly flexed. [1]

When object grasp is accompanied by wrist flexion and thumb adduction, aids such as hand-held pointers and special marker holders could be designed to require use of the *radial-palmar grasp.* The Spring Grip Cylindrical Handle for Pointers or Drawing Implements (page 136) and the Bicycle Handle Grip to Hold Pointer (Quick Tip #1) are examples of designs that require this grasp. These devices are positioned horizontally to compensate for the inability to supinate the forearm to neutral. Erhardt states that the radial-palmar grasp "is one of the most stable of all grasps, because the palm, all fingers, and thumb are shaped securely around the object. Because of this stability, less effort is required. The wrist no longer needs to flex to reinforce finger flexion, and the web space begins to enlarge as the thumb comes out of the palm and fully participates in grasp." [1]

If the student is able to supinate to neutral, even with some effort, a pointer that encourages use of the *palmar supinate grasp* is often preferable. A pointer of this type can be made by simply placing cylindrical foam over a wooden dowel. This grasp can be fatiguing for those who have impaired supination and may need to be alternated with another type of pointer or used only for short tasks, like a computer game using only arrow keys or math problems on a calculator.

For those that need to develop the *scissors grasp,* a thin wooden dowel can be placed between the thumb and the side of the curled index finger with the hand fisted. If hyper-extension is present in the thumb at the base of the web space, position the dowel deep into the web space to eliminate this. The student can be asked to extend the thumb so the dowel can be positioned correctly at the beginning of the task, and extend the thumb again when it is time to remove the pointer. The student won't be ready for this until he or she is able to actively extend the thumb while the fist is supported on a table surface. Until then, an adult may securely support the student's fist and wrist to provide a stable base from which the student can better attempt thumb extension.

None of the solutions discussed above may work for a student who has involuntary movements caused by severely fluctuating muscle tone. These students often need a pointer which allows them to press the hand or the pointer against a surface for increased stability and control. Two pointers designed with this intent in mind are the Hand-Gripping Thermoplastic T-Shaped Pointer (page 138) and the Dolphin Pointer (which resembles a primitive iron with a horizontal dowel handle. The Dolphin Pointer was developed at the TRACE Center in Madison, Wisconsin and is discussed in detail in Jennifer Angelo's book, *Assistive Technology for Rehabilitation Therapists* [3].

Finally, remember to take into account the total demands of any task and not address too many goals at once. A more mature hand grasp requires greater concentration than the student is accustomed to during pointer tasks. This challenge may be just right when the student is performing a simple or familiar task such as a favorite computer game. If the presented task is perceptually or cognitively challenging, increasing the motoric demands may require too much from the student.

Alternatives to Hand-Held Pointers

Some students have no functional use of either hand, even for using a pointer. Fortunately, pointers can also be attached to other parts of the body that have better motor control. These alternative pointers include headpointers, mouthsticks, footpointers and thighpointers.

Headpointers and Mouthsticks

Headpointers and mouthsticks are the two most common types of alternative pointers, for two reasons: the head can perform movements on a wide variety of planes and the pointer is well within the visual field. The mouthstick is actually more versatile than a headpointer, because many mouthstick users are able to place the mouthstick in the mouth independently and remove it independently using a mouthstick stand, while most headpointers must be put on and taken off by another person. Some companies that sell both headpointers and mouthsticks include Sammons Preston, Maxi Aids, Inc., and Maddack, Inc. Unfortunately, commercially available headpointers have a somewhat robotic appearance which can frighten off many students. Sheryl Zelten, OTR/L, designed a very effective and much more attractive baseball cap headpointer which is fully described on page 140.

Mouthstick users cannot be mouth breathers and must have sufficient oral-motor skills to handle the mouthstick. Remember that over time, the design of a mouthstick will affect the muscles and joint alignment of the mouth area. The straight-dowel design, which permits tongue movements as well as head movements to control the mouthstick, is currently being called into question for this reason. Some dentists and therapists believe that the mouthpiece of a mouthstick should be carefully molded to the teeth in order to prevent oral-motor problems such as misalignment of the teeth and temporal-mandibular joint problems. This design stabilizes the mouthstick in one position, placing unfortunate limitations on the types of tasks that can be performed with the device.

One mouthstick user prefers to use just a simple straight dowel fitted with a piece of clear plumbing tubing, because he is very adept at using his tongue to maneuver the pointer in various positions and planes. He uses a variety of mouthsticks for different purposes. For example, he uses a mouthstick with an upside down embroidery needle fitted on the end to make intricate string-art projects for craft shows, and another mouthstick with a little cup at the end which he uses to "roll the dice". Using his tongue, he bounces the cup to shake the dice and toss them out of the cup. He would be unable to perform the latter task and would have less agility when doing his string-art projects if he were limited to using a molded mouthpiece.

The best solution to the controversy may be to use a mouthstick with a molded mouthpiece for all tasks that are performed frequently, repetitively, and don't require tongue manipulation (such as pushing computer keys). Perhaps tasks that require greater flexibility or finer control can be performed using a straight dowel with clear plastic tubing or other special padding.

SOME ATTACHMENTS THAT HAVE BEEN SUCCESSFULLY USED WITH MOUTHSTICKS:

1. Dice Cup - This is a small plastic cup with a straight handle (possibly a laundry detergent cup) taped to the end of the mouthstick; used to "roll the dice".

2. Brush - This is a regular toothbrush taped to the end of the pointer; used to clean the sawdust off of wood projects.

3. Steel Wool - This is a piece of steel wool taped to the end of the pointer; used for the final sanding of wood projects.

4. Bungy Cord Hook for Cutting - This is a bungy cord hook without the bungy cord, attached to the end of the dowel pointer; used to hook the loop handle of stabilized kitchen scissors to lift and lower it. Bungy cord hooks are available at Therapro (see Resource Guide) and some building supply and hardware stores. Cordless electric scissors can also be operated with a mouthstick.

5. Embroidery Needle for String Art - This is a regular embroidery needle taped upside down to end of mouthstick; colored string is threaded through the needle; user maneuvers the string around the pins of the string art project to form a picture or design. An assistant holds the spool to help control the tension of the thread.

6. Flexible Plastic Pointer Tip - Plastisol is a plastic dip material which can be found at building and electrical supply stores; the end of the pointer is dipped into the liquid plastic and then dries, forming a molded plastic tip for the pointer; provides a somewhat resistive surface to reduce the tendency of the pointer to slip off of buttons, etc.

7. Glue Tack - This gum-like substance is commonly used to stick posters and other papers onto walls without marring the walls; a small piece is placed on the end of the pointer to enable the user to pick up small items.

SOME ATTACHMENTS THAT HAVE BEEN SUCCESSFULLY USED WITH HEADPOINTERS:

1. A pencil eraser top or other rubber tip for keyboarding and other push-button tasks provides a resistive surface so the pointer does not slip off the keys.

2. A paintbrush or marker for artwork can be taped onto the pointer with masking tape.

3. A bent spoon for table-top gardening (planting potting soil and seeds in peat pots)can be taped onto the pointer; the bowl of the spoon is angled to allow both scooping the dirt and holding the dirt without letting it spill out of the spoon. Seeds are very sparsely sprinkled onto a separate pile of potting soil for easier spooning of seeds.

4. A roller-tipped pen for smoother drawing - this type of pen glides on the paper and eliminates the resistance that can sometimes occur when attempting to draw with headpointers.

5. Clay tools for carving or outlining the desired shape of clay.

☞ Any of the attachments recommended for mouthsticks can be used for headpointers and vice versa, except for the mouthstick attachments that require tongue manipulation (e.g. dice cup).

Thighpointers and Footpointers

These pointers are used only when the student has poor control of both head and upper extremity movements. They can enable such students to more fully participate in special subject classes such as Art, Music, and Industrial Arts. Due to their limitations these pointers should really be used as a last resort.

Although foot pointers can perform movements in a wide variety of planes it is difficult to monitor movements of the foot without using a complex mirror system. A single mirror produces a reverse image which can be perceptually confusing. Melissa Litton, OTR/L, set up a double-mirror system for one student that corrected this problem to the student's satisfaction. The student viewed his work through the second mirror which reflected the image of the first mirror.

Thigh pointers are pointers that are attached to the top of the thigh (see page 142). Using a thigh pointer is less visually straining than using a foot pointer, but has its own limitations. Thigh pointers can only move in one plane, which makes them most useful for tasks such as painting or drawing or strumming an autoharp (while another student presses the chord keys). Thigh pointers cannot perform a forward pushing movement, which makes pressing buttons nearly impossible, unless the object is positioned rather awkwardly and the pointer is bent up or down. The author has not yet seen this performed truly satisfactorily.

One student who uses a thigh pointer has no motor control whatsoever except in his right leg and foot. Until recent years, all efforts were directed to his foot. In fact he operates his power wheelchair and a computer with a foot-controlled scanning system. However, even following many years of practice, he continued to have great difficulty grading the force and direction of his foot. Placing a pointer on his thigh made a significant difference, allowing him to produce much finer gradations of movement. He can use the device to point on a miniature communication board, paint in Art Class, or play a rhythm instrument. Another student recently learned to use a thigh pointer to strum a vertically angled autoharp in Music Class, and showed off his new skill at an end of the year musical performance at school.

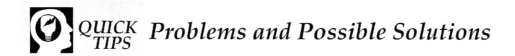

QUICK TIPS *Problems and Possible Solutions*

Following are some solutions which have successfully solved the identified problem for one or more students. Keep in mind that each student has a unique set of abilities and needs and may therefore require an original solution for the problem at hand. If a suggested solution is appropriate for a student, please adapt the design as necessary to best meet his or her needs.

Remember: fit the device to the student, not the student to the device!

1. Student needs a horizontal dowel handle to hold a pointer.

Use a plastic bicycle handle grip. Poke a hole all the way through to the opposite side and push a dowel or pencil through the hole.

(Paulette E. Binder, Home Economics Teacher, Cotting School)

Make one out of thermoplastic material (see page 136).

2. Student has involuntary movements of the arms and needs a weighted pointer to improve pointing accuracy.

Try an old golf club. Use a hack saw to cut off the head and shorten the shaft to the desired length. Dip the end of the new pointer in Plastisol (a plastic dip) to form a plastic tip. Plastisol can be found at an electrical or building supply store.

(Staff and Therapists at the United Cerebral Palsy Association in Watertown, Ma.)

3. The Y shaped mouthpiece of the Sammons Preston mouthstick is too large for the student.

Heat the mouthpiece using a heat gun and cut it to the proper size for the student's mouth.

(Contributed by Suzi Collins, M.S., OTR/L, Clinical Supervisor, Franciscan Children's School, Brighton, Ma. Designer unknown.)

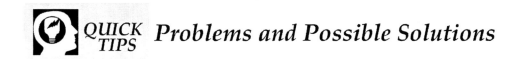

4. Student needs a special mouthstick to hold a marker and a good writing surface.

Refer to page 220 for instructions on how to make a mouthstick that holds a marker. This is used successfully with a vinyl-framed dry-erase memo board attached to the student's wheelchair using a universal mount.

(Barbara Steva, OTR/L, Director of Occupational Therapy and Therapeutic Recreation; Frances Maggiore, COTA/L, Certified Occupational Therapy Assistant, both at Franciscan Children's Hospital, Brighton, Ma.)

5. Student needs to use tongue movements to assist with manipulation of a mouthstick and will therefore need a simple dowel design, not a "Y" shaped mouthpiece.

One idea is to slide a short piece of non-toxic plastic or rubber tubing (such as a round pencil grip) over the end of a simple wooden dowel. This provides a more sanitary and cushioned contact surface for the teeth.

(Karen Conrad, ScD, OTR/L, Occupational Therapist, Founder and President, Therapro, Inc.)

☞ If possible, discuss the design of the mouthstick with the student's dentist before using it.

6. Student needs a slip-resistant tip for the end of his or her pointer.

Use a pencil head eraser.

Good tips for headpointers can often be found at a children's recycling center, such as the Children's Resource Center in Belmont, Ma., or the Children's Museum Recycling Center, Boston, Ma.

(Paulette E. Binder, Home Economics Teacher, Cotting School)

Dip the end of the pointer in Plastisol, a plastic dip which can be found at an electrical or building supply store.

(Staff and Therapists at the United Cerebral Palsy Association, Watertown, Ma.)

INSTRUCTIONS
FOR FABRICATING
SELECTED DEVICES

**SPRING-GRIP CYLINDRICAL HANDLE
FOR POINTERS & DRAWING IMPLEMENTS**

**HAND-GRIPPING THERMOPLASTIC
T-SHAPED POINTER**

BASEBALL CAP HEADPOINTER

THIGH POINTER

SPRING-GRIP CYLINDRICAL HANDLE
FOR POINTERS & DRAWING IMPLEMENTS

DESCRIPTION: A molded thermoplastic adaptive handle with a spring operated "gripper" which allows easy "click -in" and "click-out" mounting of dowel pointers, colored pencils, paintbrushes and other narrow ended tools.

PURPOSES:
1. To enable those with severe motor impairments to hold a pointer. Reinforces radial palmar grasp, making it especially beneficial for many students who exhibit a strong flexor pattern of the upper extremities, that is, those who attempt to grasp objects with a severely flexed wrist and adducted thumb.

2. To enable those with severe motor impairments to draw and paint by mounting a thin marker, paintbrush, or colored pencil in the handle instead of a pointer.

☞ The handle of this device is horizontal to compensate for the inability to adequately supinate the forearm (turn palm upward). If a student can supinate his arm sufficiently, it may be preferable to simply build up the handle of a pointer by fitting a piece of cylindrical foam over it to require and reinforce supination. The Spring-Grip Cylindrical Handle can also be held using a palmar-supinate grasp if used in conjunction with a vertical working surface.

MATERIALS:
1. Low temperature thermoplastic material, about 6" square piece
2. Spring-operated door latch (located next to the bins of drawer handles at building supply stores)

☞ Some types of low temperature thermoplastic materials require special solvent or light abrasion before bonding can occur. Please follow manufacturer's directions.

TOOLS:
Splinting pan or electric frying pan and water; heavy duty scissors; a dowel slightly smaller than the desired diameter of the device

MEASUREMENTS:

A 3 1/2" (allowing for 1/2" overlap) by 5" rectangle of thermoplastic material makes an appropriate-sized handle for many primary school students. The most precise method is to first experiment with different sized dowels to discover which diameter is best for the student. Then use a measuring tape to determine the circumference of the dowel and add an additional 1/2". The length of the dowel should be approximately 1 1/2" longer than the distance from the outside of the index M.P. joint to the outside of the little finger M.P. joint.

ASSEMBLY:

1. Draw the appropriate size rectangle on the low temperature thermoplastic material. Soften the material in the splinting pan and water, following manufacturer's instructions, and cut it out using heavy duty scissors.

2. While still soft, wrap one of the short ends of the rectangle around the spring-operated door latch, pressing it tightly around the metal extensions of the door latch without obstructing the operation of the latch.

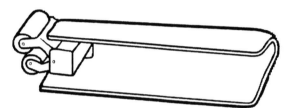

3. Bond the long edges of the thermoplastic material together by overlapping the edges and pinching them together.

MODIFICATION 1:

If preferred, the door latch can be attached to the side of the thermoplastic dowel using a small scrap of extra material.

MODIFICATION 2:

If heavy pressure will be placed on the pointer or drawing implement, it may be desirable to substitute an autoclamp for the spring-operated door latch. Autoclamps come in various sizes and have adjustable widths (accommodating various widths of pointers or drawing implements, including large markers). The disadvantage of the autoclamp is that a screwdriver or dime is needed to change the implement (such as when switching marker colors). If an autoclamp will be used, make a dowel shape out of the low temperature thermoplastic material first using same measurements as above. Then use a small thin scrap of thermoplastic material to attach the autoclamp to either the end or the side of the dowel.

(Designer Unknown - was discovered at Cotting School years ago.)

HAND-GRIPPING THERMOPLASTIC T-SHAPED POINTER

DESCRIPTION: A small T-shaped hand-held pointer formed around the palm, fabricated entirely of low temperature thermoplastic material. This design is reminiscent of the Typing Aid that is sold by Sammons Preston.

PURPOSES:

1. To enable a severely motorically challenged student to operate computers and other augmentative communication systems.

2. To enhance the motor control of certain students who have neurological impairments by enabling the fisted hand to remain on a keyguard while using the pointer.

MATERIALS:
1. Low temperature thermoplastic material - about 12" square piece
2. Pencil head eraser

☞ Some types of low temperature thermoplastic materials require special solvent or light abrasion before bonding can occur. Please follow manufacturer's directions.

TOOLS:
Splinting pan or electric frying pan and water; heavy duty scissors, measuring tape

MEASUREMENTS:
The top of the T needs to be long enough to curve around the palm to the back of the hand. If desired, use a measuring tape to measure the circumference of the hand just below the transverse arch, going through the web space. (The transverse arch is located at the large horizontal crease that forms when the fingers are bent.) Subtract about 1". Or do what most therapists do - "wing it"- cut the T too big and trim it later as it is fitted to the hand. The vertical piece needs to be whatever length produces the most effective pointing.

ASSEMBLY:

1. Draw a 1 3/4" thick T shape on the thermoplastic material using the measurement guidelines on the previous page. Soften the material in a splinting pan or electric frying pan and water until soft, and cut out the shape. Intermittently re-heat the material to maintain its flexibility while performing the following steps:

2. Roll the material (as if making a snake) so both sections of the T-shape are now thin cylindrical shapes. Make two slight cuts at the junctions of the "T" to facilitate rolling the vertical section.

3. Position the top of the T-shape against the palm, with the vertical section pointing away from the student's arm. Form the thermoplastic material across the palm and around to the back of the hand.

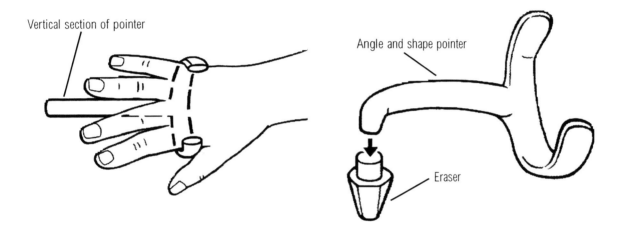

Vertical section of pointer

Angle and shape pointer

Eraser

4. The pointer should extend between the middle and ring fingers. Make sure the portion of the pointer that is in contact with these fingers is as thin as possible in order to maintain proper finger joint alignment.

5. Angle the pointer as desired, and trim off any excess.

6. Add a pencil head eraser to the end of the pointer.

Designed by
Amy Houghton, OTR/L, Occupational Therapy Team Leader, Cotting School

BASEBALL CAP HEADPOINTER

DESCRIPTION: An attractive, fun to wear headpointer made using a baseball cap. Two wide strips of thermoplastic material formed to the student's head provide stability and are hidden underneath the cap.

PURPOSE:
To provide a less intimidating alternative to commercially available headpointers, which tend to make the user look somewhat robotic. Some students who have rejected commercial designs are willing to use a baseball cap headpointer, especially since baseball caps are currently very much in vogue.

MATERIALS:
1. Low temperature thermoplastic material - 12" x 6" sheet
2. Baseball Cap - preferably chosen by the student. The cap should reflect the student's aesthetics, not the therapist's!
3. Two 7/8" long flat head screws
4. Small block of wood - 1 3/4" wide x 3/4" high x 7/8" deep
5. 3/16" diameter threaded metal rod - about 24" long (available at building supply stores)
6. Two 3/16" diameter nuts
7. 1/4" or wider elastic - 20" long strip for chin strap (available at fabric shops)

☞ Some types of low temperature thermoplastic materials require special solvent or light abrasion before bonding can occur. Please follow manufacturer's directions.

TOOLS:
Seam ripper or small pointed scissors; splinting pan or electric frying pan and water; heavy duty scissors; measuring tape; coping saw; sandpaper; power drill

MEASUREMENTS:
To determine the measurements for the thermoplastic stabilizing strips that form to the head, first have the student put on the baseball cap. Measure from the front edge of the cap (omitting the rim) up over the top of the head to the back edge of the cap. This should be the length of one of the strips. The length of the other strip should equal the distance from one side edge of the cap to the other side edge, at the location of the ears, going over the top of the head.

ASSEMBLY:
1. Use a seam ripper or small pointed scissors to split apart 1 3/4" of the front center seam of the baseball cap, just in front of the little button or junction point where all of the seams meet on top of the cap.
2. Make thermoplastic stabilizing cap:
    a. Soften the low temperature thermoplastic material in a splinting pan or electric frying pan filled with water, following the manufacturer's instructions. Then cut out two 2" wide thermoplastic strips following the length measurements determined above.

b. Re-soften the "front-to-back" strip in the pan, wait until it is cool to the touch, and form it to the student's head from forehead to back of head. Repeat with the "side-to-side" strip, forming it over the first piece and against the sides of the head. Remove from student's head and press the overlapping section hard so it bonds well. Resoften the junction of both pieces to improve the bond and smooth the edges, if desired. (The pieces will also be screwed together when the wood piece is mounted.)

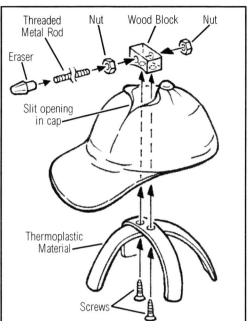

3. Shape and drill wooden block:
   a. With a coping saw, cut out a block of wood that is 1 3/4" x 3/4" x 7/8". Saw out a slight curve in one of the long sides of the block of wood so it matches the curve of the thermoplastic material where it will be positioned on top of the head.
   b. Drill a hole the same diameter as the threaded metal rod, through the center of the block of wood (hole should not go through curved side of block).

4. Attach metal rod to wooden block:
   a. Screw a nut a couple of inches onto the metal rod.
   b. Apply some epoxy glue or hot glue into the drilled hole in the wood and put the metal rod through the hole so it extends 3/4" through the back of the wood piece.
   c. Screw a nut onto the part of the rod sticking through the back of the wood piece. Add more glue on both sides of the wood piece and while glue is still wet tighten both nuts against the wood. Let dry.

5. Assemble the headpointer:
   a. Insert the thermoplastic cap inside the baseball cap.
   b. Spread the opened seam at top of the baseball cap apart and position the wooden block against the thermoplastic material, with the curved edge touching the cap. Clamp the block in place.
   c. On the inside of the cap, mark two spots on the thermoplastic about 1/2" from each edge of the block. Drill two pilot holes through the thermoplastic cap and into the wood block, using a drill bit slightly smaller than screw diameter. Screw in the two screws and remove clamp.
   d. Tuck the ends of the thermoplastic strips under the seam pocket of the cap.

6. Bend the metal rod to the desired angle. Place a pencil eraser head or other rubber tip on the end of the metal dowel furthest from the wood block. See page 131 and Quick Tip #6 for other ideas for pointer tips.

7. To add the elastic chin strap, poke a hole through the bottom, underside seam on each side of the cap, just in front of each ear. Then thread the elastic through the holes, adjust the tension, and knot the ends.

Originally designed by
Sheryl Zelten, OTR/L, Occupational Therapist
Modified by Val Greene, B.S. Ed., Industrial Arts Teacher at Cotting School.

THIGH POINTER

DESCRIPTION: A thermoplastic cuff formed to the thigh which has a pointer attached to it. This device allows an individual to point on a communication board, play certain musical instruments, paint, etc.

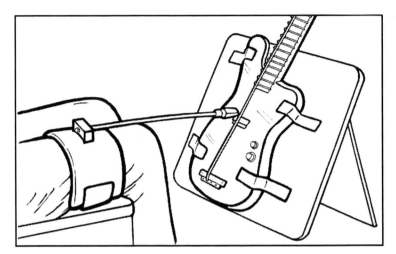

PURPOSE:
To offer students who have some control of hip movements (but very poor or absent head, arm, or hand control) a method for interacting with the objects in their environment.

MATERIALS:
1. Low temperature thermoplastic material, 14" x 3 1/2"
2. Piece of wood, 1 3/4" long x 7/8" high x 5/8" deep
3. 3/16" diameter threaded metal rod, 15" long (available at building supply stores)
4. Two 7/8" long flat head wood screws
5. Two 3/16" diameter nuts
6. Pressure-sensitive Velcro hook tape, two 3" long x 1" wide pieces
7. Velcro loop tape or Velfoam strip, enough for a short strap

☞ Some types of low temperature thermoplastic materials require special solvent or light abrasion before bonding can occur. Please follow manufacturer's directions.

TOOLS:
Splinting pan or electric frying pan and water; sharp heavy duty scissors; measuring tape; coping saw; sandpaper; power drill

MEASUREMENTS:
The thermoplastic cuff should be approximately 2/3 the circumference of the student's thigh and about 3 1/2" wide.

ASSEMBLY:

1. Make thermoplastic cuff:
   a. Soften the thermoplastic material in a splinting pan or electric frying pan filled with water, following the manufacturer's instructions. Then cut out a rectangle in the material following the measurements above.
   b. Re-soften the strip in the pan, wait until it is cool to the touch, and form it to the student's thigh in the correct position.

2. Shape and drill wooden block:
   a. With a coping saw, cut out a block of wood that is 1 3/4" x 3/4" x 7/8". Saw out a slight curve in one of the long sides of the block of wood so it matches the curve of the thermoplastic material where it will be positioned on top of the thigh.
   b. Drill a hole the same diameter as the threaded metal rod, through the center of the block of wood (hole should not go through curved side of block).

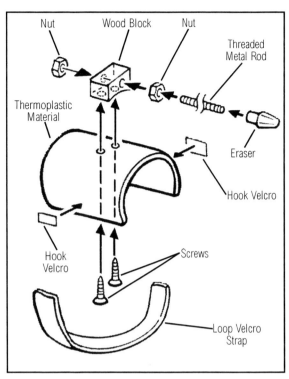

3. Attach metal rod to wooden block:
   a. Screw a nut a couple of inches onto the metal rod.
   b. Apply some epoxy glue or hot glue into the drilled hole in the wood and put the metal rod through the hole so it extends 3/4" through the back of the wood piece.
   c. Screw a nut onto the part of the rod sticking through the back of the wood piece. Add more glue on both sides of the wood piece and while glue is still wet tighten both nuts against the wood. Let dry.

5. Assemble the thigh pointer:
   a. Center the wooden block on top of the thermoplastic cuff, with the curved side resting on the thermoplastic. Clamp block in place.
   b. On the inside of the cuff, mark two spots on the thermoplastic about 1/2" from each edge of the block. Drill two pilot deep holes through the thermoplastic and into the wood block, using a drill bit slightly smaller than the screw diameter. Screw in the two screws and remove clamp.
   c. Attach a piece of pressure-sensitive Velcro hook tape to each side edge of the thermoplastic cuff. Add a Velcro loop tape or a Velfoam strap around the student's thigh to hold it securely.

6. Bend the wire to the desired angle. Place a rubber tip, such as a pencil eraser head, on the end of the metal dowel. See page 131 and Quick Tip #6 for other ideas for pointer tips.

Designed and built by
Robin Levy, OTR/L, Occupational Therapist,
and Val Greene, B.S. Ed., Industrial Arts Teacher, at Cotting School.

Chapter 10
Time Management

TIME MANAGEMENT AND ORGANIZATIONAL AIDS

In this often hectic, complex world, most people need to arm themselves with a variety of assistive devices just to keep pace and keep organized. The two categories of organizational aids that will be addressed in this chapter are time management aids and task sequencing aids. *Time management aids* have traditionally included such items as clocks, watches, calendars, daily schedules, simple "to do" lists, and daily planners. These devices have become more sophisticated with the advancement of high technology, and now also include such things as computerized organizers and miniature recorders that can fit in a pocket. *Task sequencing* aids include such things as instructional books, appliance manuals, recipe books, signs, or pieces of paper with step-by-step directions on how to record a show on the VCR or send a FAX on the computer.

Students who have perceptual and/or cognitive impairments often have an even greater need for organizational aids to compensate for decreased time awareness, motor planning ability, memory, and perceptual skills. However, they may not be able to effectively use the ones that work well for the general public. Typical lists or direction sheets are frequently too lengthy and complicated to understand, if they can be read at all, and watches and schedules likewise may be confusing. These students need their lists and schedules to be very simplified. For example, a student who is unable to follow a weekly school schedule may be able to use a daily schedule, because it eliminates the need to locate the correct day of the week (see Quick Tip #3 for more information). For students who have a very limited sense of time, the Schedule Book for Primary Level Students, described in detail later in this chapter, is an excellent aid for developing this sense. It also seems to help students feel more in control over their day (and lives).

Many of the high school students at Cotting School benefit from using a narrow 3-ring notebook containing the student's schedule, responsibility chart, separate homework pockets for different subjects, and sometimes other items such as communication boards. Important reminders for individual students can be taped (on the front cover if necessary) to these notebooks. Directions for assembling a notebook of this type, including sample schedules, charts, etc., are presented later in this chapter.

In addition to these time management aids and related "to do" lists, many special needs students benefit from simple visual aids such as signs and direction sheets (or, if necessary, auditory aids such as a cassette recorder) to assist with task organization and sequencing. These aids can be especially helpful for improving organizational skills during activity transitions, e.g. when students first arrive at the classroom or lunch, or when students finish their work. Direction sheets can be hung on the wall for all students to follow or can be taped to the notebooks, desks, or placemats of individual students. Direction sheets (or signs) have also been found to be extremely effective for helping some students to better organize their responses to frequently occurring stressful situations, such as when their bus is late or their work is too difficult. Detailed descriptions of to-do lists and direction sheets are supplied in the Quick Tips section of this chapter.

Also included in Quick Tips are some solutions for students who are physically unable to use standard time management and organizational aids due to severe motor impairments. For example, some are unable to see a watch that is placed on their wrists due to postural/motor impairments. Many of these students are also unable to write "to do" lists, homework lists, etc.

Remember that, when the potential exists, students need to learn not only how to follow lists and schedules but also how to make their own lists and schedules, in order to develop into independent, responsible adults in control of their own lives. Fortunately, today there are more devices available than ever before that can assist in this endeavor, such as computers, electronic organizers, and recorders.

$\bigodot$ QUICK TIPS *Problems and Possible Solutions*

Following are some solutions which have successfully solved the identified problem for one or more students. Keep in mind that each student has a unique set of abilities and needs and may therefore require an original solution for the problem at hand. If a suggested solution is appropriate for a student, please adapt the design as necessary to best meet his or her needs.

Remember: fit the device to the student, not the student to the device!

1. Student cannot read a watch placed on his or her wrist due to postural/motor impairments or perceptual impairments.

$\bigodot$ Attach a small, inexpensive digital clock with large numbers to the lap tray. One method for doing this: heat and bend a strip of thermoplastic material into an upright L-shape, mount the clock to the vertical part of L-shaped strip using pressure-sensitive Velcro, and mount the bottom, horizontal part of the L-shaped strip onto the wheelchair lap tray using a clamp or pressure-sensitive Velcro.

(Amy A. Houghton, OTR/L, Occupational Therapy Team Leader, Cotting School)

2. Student is unable to write and needs a method for recording homework assignments and other important information.

$\bigodot$ Some students may benefit from using a cassette tape recorder. If necessary, adapt it for switch use by making or purchasing a battery adapter (see page 95) and a simple switch.

(Sue Shannon, OTR/L, Occupational Therapist, Perkins School for the Blind)

$\bigodot$ Use a word processor and store the information onto a hard disk to bring back and forth from school.

3. Student is unable to follow a weekly school schedule due to visual perceptual impairments.

$\bigodot$ Make a large daily schedule for each day of the week, and laminate it so it doesn't get torn. If the student is a non-reader, color-code the schedule according to type of activity and/or include pictures depicting the various classes and activities. For students who have a very limited sense of time, the Schedule Book for Primary Level Students, described separately after Quick Tips, may be more appropriate.

4. Student has difficulty sequencing steps to a task and is unable to read direction sheets.

To describe each step, use photos, picture symbols and/or other visual communication symbols in place of or in addition to simple words. Simplify the visual information as much as possible, for example by providing one picture per step. Experiment to determine whether the steps are best presented in a single horizontal row, single vertical row, or as described in the next solution.

List each step on separate index cards to compensate for figure ground problems or the inability to follow directions in a left to right, top to bottom format. Attach the index cards together using two metal rings (obtainable at stationary stores). Attach the two metal rings to the top of a triangular stand made out of cardboard.

Record the steps of the task on a cassette recorder.

Record the steps on an augmentative communication device such as the MACAW by Zygo (using a separate key for each step) and place an appropriate picture over each key.

For manipulative tasks such as assembly, packaging, collating, or other prevocational tasks, set up work materials left to right (or top to bottom), following the order in which they need to be handled, to facilitate proper sequencing of steps. Tape a small card in front of each bin of materials identifying the step number.

5. Students appear disorganized when they first arrive in the morning and rely on the teacher to remind them to hang up their coats, sharpen their pencils, get their work out, etc.

Hang up a large, brightly colored sign on the wall that lists what is expected of the students first thing each morning, e.g.:
1. Hang up coat.
2. Put bag in cubby.
3. Sharpen pencil.
4. Start work in Unfinished Folder.

For non-readers, the list can consist of simple pictures: coat, bag, pencil, folder.

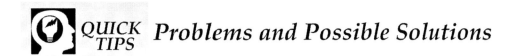

6. Student does not take responsibility for organizing himself or herself when arriving to the cafeteria.

Make a special placemat that lists (using words, pictures, or other symbols) what the student should do to prepare for eating, e.g.:
1. Remove helmet;
2. Put schedule book under chair;
3. Put napkin on lap; etc.

Also see Adapted Placemat, page 296 for other uses of the placemat.

7. Students have organizational difficulties (perhaps compounded by language impairments) and become extremely anxious and overwhelmed when:

- they do not know what to do next.
- things do not go according to plan.
- when their work becomes too difficult.
- when they do not understand what the teacher is saying.

These students may resort to inappropriate behaviors to relieve their stress.

Several students in Patricia Harlow's Upper School Class at Cotting School made very positive behavioral changes when she hung bright yellow signs on the walls with these instructions:

1. If your bus is late. . .Don't worry! Just come to homeroom, pick up your chart, check in and then go to class.

2. If you feel nervous or anxious. . . Take time to get yourself together.
Use the quiet desk if you want. (Note: Quiet Desk has fidget toys and stress busters on it.)

3. If you get an "X" on your chart. . . don't be upset! Just try harder next time.

4. If you don't understand a direction. . .Say, "I didn't understand what you said" or "Would you please repeat that direction?"

5. If your work is too hard. . .Don't pinch your hands or use inappropriate talk.
Just say, "This is too hard!" or "I am frustrated!"

Instructions should be specific to the needs of the particular students in the class. If only one or two students are having this difficulty, the list can be taped to the individual's notebook instead of hung on the wall.

INSTRUCTIONS
FOR FABRICATING
SELECTED DEVICES

SCHEDULE BOOK
FOR NON-READERSAT
THE PRIMARY SCHOOL LEVEL

ORGANIZATIONAL NOTEBOOK FOR
MIDDLE & HIGH SCHOOL STUDENTS

SCHEDULE BOOK FOR NON-READERS
AT THE PRIMARY SCHOOL LEVEL

DESCRIPTION: A cloth binder within which is attached (by two horizontal rows of self-stick Velcro) 2" square symbol cards depicting each of the student's various classes and activities for that particular school day, such as gym, music, lunch, recess, etc.

The pictures are stored in a zippered nylon pouch (velcroed to the inside of the binder) when not in use. At the beginning of each school day, the teacher helps each student position the appropriate symbol cards, in the sequence in which the activities will occur, on the horizontal Velcro strips. After each activity, the student removes the appropriate symbol card and places it back in the plastic pouch.

PURPOSE:
To help students begin to develop a sense of time awareness/sequence.
This schedule book is a "must" for those students who ask over and over if it's time yet for their favorite activity.

MATERIALS:
1. Cloth binder approximately 12" tall by 9 1/2" wide
2. Zippered nylon pouch intended for 3 ring binders
3. Pressure-sensitive Velcro hook tape - 2 yards long x 3/4" wide
4. Pressure-sensitive Velcro loop tape - 1 yard long x 3/4" wide
5. Approximately twenty-five 2" x 2" pieces of paper with words, pictures, and/or other symbols depicting the days of the week as well as the various activities of the day, such as the following:

Morning Meeting	Snack	Bathroom
Reading Class	Language Arts	Gross Motor
Lunch	Journal	Occupational Therapy
Free Choice	Recess	Music Class
Art	Bus	Home
	Communication Therapy	

Also include these two symbol/word cards: "Today Is" and "Finished".
6. Clear contact paper

ASSEMBLY:

1. Cut seven 9" lengths of Velcro hook tape. Attach two of these lengths of Velcro tape horizontally on the left side of the cloth binder, approximately 1 1/2" and 4" from the top of the binder (respectively), and place two more of these lengths of Velcro hook tape on the right side of the cloth binder, same distances from the top.

2. Attach the nylon zippered pouch to the bottom half of the right side of the cloth binder using two 9" lengths of Velcro hook tape as well as two 9" lengths of Velcro loop tape.

3. Tear off the backing of a long length of contact paper, lay the communication symbols face down on top of the contact paper, and place an additional sheet of contact paper on top of the symbols. Cut out the symbols from the contact paper.

4. Attach the remaining 9˝ strip of Velcro hook tape, about 3˝ from the bottom on the left side of the binder. Attach the "Today Is" card to this strip using a small bit of Velcro loop tape. Attach the "Finished" card to the front of the zippered nylon pouch using another small bit of Velcro hook and loop tape.

5. Place all the symbol cards in the zippered nylon pouch. During Morning Meeting, help the student arrange the cards sequentially on the strips of Velcro hook tape.

MODIFICATION 1: Attach the Velcro strips to a simple plastic binder and store the cards for the whole class in a index file box which is divided by activity: e.g. Journal Time, Recess, PT, etc. First thing in the morning, pass out the appropriate cards to each student to place on the Velcro strips.

MODIFICATION 2: If all of the students in the classroom follow the same schedule, hang an enlarged version of this Velcro schedule board on the classroom wall instead of giving each student their own notebook. This has been seen in some preschool classrooms.

Designed by
Cathy Mayo, M.Ed., Primary School Teacher, Cotting School
and
Elizabeth Miller, M.S., CCC-SLP, Speech-Language Pathologist, Cotting School

Modification 1 by
Marissa Shindell, M.Ed., Primary School Teacher, Cotting School

Modification 2 by
Karen Conrad, ScD, OTR/L, Occupational Therapist, Founder and President, Therapro, Inc.

ORGANIZATIONAL NOTEBOOK
FOR MIDDLE & HIGH SCHOOL STUDENTS

DESCRIPTION: A 2" thick 3-ring binder which contains the student's schedules and assignments; shows responsibilities and progress; and holds supplies and homework.

PURPOSE:
To provide an easy-to-understand and easy-to-follow organizational system to help older students successfully meet their responsibilities at school, including: arriving to the correct classes on time; completing homework on time; preparing for upcoming activities (classes, field trips); and fulfilling personal behavioral goals (as listed on the Responsibility Chart). Please see provided sample pages for examples of the items listed in the Description.

MATERIALS & ASSEMBLY:
Into a 2" thick 3-ring binder, insert the following, in sequence:

1. A label on the pocket on inside front cover of the notebook which reads: "Notices for Home".

2. A pencil case

3. The student's weekly schedule and school year schedule inserted back to back into one clear page protector

4. A yellow manilla folder within which is stapled the Field Trip Schedule on the left side and the Homework Assignments sheet (Weekly Planner) on the right side

5. A colored pocket folder for every class that has homework assignments. Label the left pocket "To Do"and the right pocket "Completed". (All classes can be combined into one folder if desired)

6. A colored folder (no pockets) within which is stapled a calendar of the month (to document the total number of earned points for each day) on the left side and the student's Responsibility Chart on the right side

OPTIONAL: Students who use communication boards sometimes insert these in the front of their organizational notebooks, inside a clear plastic page protector.

Designed by
Patricia Harlow, B.S. Ed., Upper School Classroom Teacher, Cotting School

---

STUDENT: _____ DATE: _____

RESPONSIBILITY CHART
PLEASE GET THIS CHART CHECKED OFF BY YOUR TEACHER
<u>BEFORE YOU LEAVE CLASS.</u>

RESPONSILITY:	#1	#2	#3	#4	#5	MARK BOXES: V = POINT X = NO POINT
HOMEROOM 8:20 - 8:30						
PERIOD 1 8:30 - 9:30						# LEGEND #1 - Arrive to class <u>ON TIME.</u>
PERIOD 2 9:30 - 10:30						#2 - Come prepared for school, community, trip, or work.
PERIOD 3 10:30 - 11:30						#3 - Follows directions and classroom rules.
PERIOD 4 11:30 - 12:30						#4 - Request help or materials independently.
LUNCH 12:30 - 1:00						
PERIOD 5 1:00 - 1:40						#5 - Use best speech and supports: - letter cues (wrist band, signs, letter board)
PERIOD 6 1:40 - 2:20						- rephrasing (different words)
HOMEROOM 2:20 - 2:25						- spelling

REMINDER:
Use word endings (ing, ed, s)
Try to produce <u>all</u> syllables of multisyllabic words.

HYGIENE:
Will be monitered by homeroom teacher
during homeroom only, unless it occurs
in your class during the day.

2 pts. - Are you appropriately groomed?
(hair, showered, shaved, clean clothes,
nails clipped, etc.)
YES _____   NO_____

** 47 Possible points (M,T,Th, F)
37 Possible points (W)
225 Possible Total Points
** **need 220 points to receive "pay"**

IF FOUND PLEASE RETURN (A.S.A.P) TO:

NAME: _____ RM NO.: _____

THANK YOU !!!!

WEEKLY PLANNER

Name ——————— Week ——————— of Month ——————— 19 ———

MONDAY

Subject	Done

TUESDAY

Subject	Done

WEDNESDAY

Subject	Done

THURSDAY

Subject	Done

COMMENTS

Field Trip Schedule
and special Events

March

P. Harlow

SUNDAY	MONDAY	TUESDAY	WEDNESDAY	THURSDAY	FRIDAY	SATURDAY

Part III

DEVICES USED IN SPECIFIC CURRICULUM SUBJECT AREAS

This section of the book describes handmade or modified assistive devices which may help some students increase their level of performance in specific school subjects.

It includes chapters on reading, writing, math, arts and craft activities, music, home economics, industrial arts, and the lunchroom.

The information provided in this section supplements the material presented in Part II, which is also highly applicable to these individual subject areas.

Chapter 11
Reading

ASSISTIVE DEVICES FOR READING TASKS

The ability to read affects all facets of life, not only at school or on the job but also the myriad everyday tasks. Written communication is one of the most common "assistive devices" used in our society to help people function. For example, it is used to help people:

- find the correct grocery aisle and distinguish between similar food items at the grocery store

- use an ATM machine

- adjust knobs to the correct settings on a washing machine, dryer, or dishwasher

- follow directions for using a particular laundry detergent, hair conditioner, medicine, or cleaning fluid

- assemble toys, furniture, and appliances

- follow road signs while driving or riding a bicycle

- use public transportation

- find locations within buildings, such as a doctor's office in a medical building or a particular store in a mall.

- understand mortgages and other business agreements

- maintain personal connections to others through letter writing or e-mail

- acquire knowledge about any subject using books and other written resources

Some of the above examples are high-frequency tasks typically completed within a few short seconds by those who can read. For non-readers, performing even these "quick" tasks becomes a time-consuming and laborious process. Anyone who has watched a student struggle to locate a specific item at the grocery store can begin to understand the frustration that often permeates the lives of those of those who cannot read.

A person who has difficulty reading will also have trouble writing. Poor readers may (and often do) learn how to copy written material using pen and paper or a computer, but they lose their place much more easily than others, because they are simply copying a bunch of meaningless letters that have meaningless spaces between them every once in a while. When asked, they may not have any idea what word they are printing or typing, although they have a better chance of figuring it out if they are copying from their own dictation, and if the dictation was only a sentence or two.

One strategy that can be used instead of taking dictation in writing from the student is to take dictation using a word prediction software program such as Co-Writer in combination with an auditory feedback program such as Write: Outloud (both available through Don Johnston Inc.) First type in a sentence or two dictated by the student using Co-Writer so the program becomes even more primed to correctly predict the words later on when it is the student's turn to type the sentence. Then erase the sentence and have the student re-type the sentence, also using Co-Writer. Co-Writer will automatically produce 5 (or as many as desired) words on the screen that are most likely to follow the previous word. Some students who have trouble decoding words out of context can nevertheless discriminate between these five words when they are looking for a specific word. This can be very motivating and will also reinforce the student's reading skills.

One of the best strategies for older students who continue to struggle with reading is to teach them to use context clues to help figure out words. This is often best accomplished while completing functional tasks such as writing, doing laundry, or other daily living tasks. Functional tasks are usually rich in context clues and also often hold more meaning for the student than book-reading tasks. For example, a long word beginning with the letter M may be impossible for a student to decipher when presented on a blank sheet of paper. However, the student might accurately guess that it stands for "machine washable" when found on the underside of a shirt tag.

As suggested by the above example, reading instruction shouldn't be limited to time with the reading teacher, but should take place in a variety of settings, with caregivers, teachers, and other support staff all helping to reinforce these skills wherever they are needed in daily life. Help the student read signs, food containers, etc., instead of simply supplying the information. Supplement reading materials such as recipes, direction words, etc. with pictures or other symbols as needed to aid in comprehension.

SOME GENERAL GUIDELINES
FOR 1:1 READING INSTRUCTION IN THE CLASSROOM

*Following are some basic guidelines to keep in mind
when setting up classroom reading tasks for students,
provided by Nancy McClintock, Ed.M., Reading Specialist,
while working at Cotting School.*

1. Arrange the seating so that glare from windows and lights is not a factor when reading from books or the blackboard. Good overhead lighting is essential.

2. Set up the reading materials at an optimum height and angle for the particular student. The optimum reading angle for most individuals is 20 degrees, though this may vary. In particular, those who have postural impairments may need reading materials placed higher and on a more vertical plane. Please refer to Quick Tips and also detailed write-ups of reading devices for ideas on positioning reading materials.

3. Print often needs to be enlarged for students who are experiencing reading problems. Compare textbooks from different publishers, as books that are intended for the same reading level may vary in size, darkness, and thickness of print. Larger, darker, thicker lettering is often best. If print needs to be enlarged on a copying machine, don't discard the text with colored pictures. Instead, use the colored pictures in the book along with the enlarged text. Colored pictures are generally easier to interpret than black and white pictures.

4. It is fairly common for remedial readers to have certain degrees of color-blindness. Since color cues are frequently used as a visual aid for poor readers, it is very important to test for this. If present, do not use colored markers or worksheets and text pages with confusing colors. Take color-blindness into consideration when choosing the letter colors and background colors for the student's computer monitor as well. Whether the lettering is in a book or on a computer monitor, make sure that it contrasts strongly with the background color.

5. Increasing the ratio of white space to print will reduce figure-ground problems. One way to do this is to leave an extra space between lines.

6. Before having the student read a paragraph, preview the color illustrations and introduce the key vocabulary words. Then have the student skim the paragraph to locate these key words (using a finger or highlighter). This provides the student with knowledge of the main subject matter prior to reading the lesson, giving the student important context clues.

In addition to the previous suggestions, McClintock has found that many students also benefit from using "experience writing" techniques to improve reading skills. With this approach, the student dictates and is instructed to watch as the teacher prints, making each sentence begin at the left and end at the right, to reinforce left to right reading progression. (Avoid ending the line of print in the middle of a phrase.) The student then rereads each line as the teacher's moving finger keeps pace with the student's spoken word. This is followed up with a grammar lesson, perhaps highlighting all nouns with a marker or highlighting tape. Since phrasing usually ends with nouns, the student will pause appropriately when reading the sentence following this instruction. Following sufficient time spent with pre-reading exercises and review, the student is now bound to recognize every word. At this point, the speed and phrasing of the student's reading can be directed by the teacher moving a finger at a consistent speed and stopping only at each pause.

Remember, this is just one approach to reading that is effective for some students. There are in fact a number of different reading approaches that have been successful for students who meet the criteria of the particular reading program. The trick is to match the right program with the right student.

Following are some solutions to common reading problems that have been very successful for certain students. This is not an exhaustive list by any means. Some of the Reading Specialists at Cotting School, who provided most of these Quick Tips, also stress that no two students are alike in terms of their learning needs. Therefore, what works for one student may not work for the next. It is very important to take into account the student's medical background to help determine the underlying causes for poor reading skills, and to choose strategies based on this knowledge as well as the knowledge gained from working with the student. By using this information, new strategies will often suggest themselves. Experiment with them!

QUICK TIPS *Problems and Possible Solutions*

Following are some solutions that have successfully solved the identified problem for one or more students. Keep in mind that each student has a unique set of abilities and needs and may therefore require an original solution for the problem at hand. If a solution below is appropriate for a student, please adapt the design as necessary to best meet his or her needs.

Remember: fit the device to the student, not the student to the device!

1. Student is unable to turn the pages of a book due to a motor impairment.

Try using a "rubber thumb" sold at office supply stores.

A pencil eraser head placed on the end of the student's pointer can often provide the necessary traction for turning pages. This simple solution can be used with a mouthstick, headpointer, or hand-held pointer.

If the student uses a headpointer, improve traction with an eraser head pointer tip described above and use in conjunction with a book holder that is designed to keep the pages open, such as the Magnetic Book Stand with Adjustable Ledge. A full description of this device follows Quick Tips.

(Sheryl Zelten, OTR/L, while working at Cotting School.)

Try Sammons Preston's Vacuum Wand, which is a suction mouthstick for turning pages. Also see the book holder suggestions for headpointer users, above.

Electric page turners are commercially available through various companies, such as Zygo Industries. Since electric page-turners can cost several thousand dollars and are also expensive to rent, obtain recommendations from a couple of different users before signing a rent-to-purchase agreement.

Using a reading scanner eliminates the need for page turning. Reading scanners scan any type of printed reading material, including documents, books or magazines. Most transfer the print and graphics to the monitor screen of a PC using special scanning software that comes with the scanner. In order to edit or format the scanned text, additional specialized software is required, called an Optical Character Recognition Program (OCR). There are several scanners and OCR programs to choose from. Some reading scanners (such as the Rainbow, available through Maxi-Aids) can stand alone or be connected to a PC. When used alone, the reading material is scanned and spoken - there is no visual output. Scanners can be purchased at large computer stores or through catalog companies such as MacConnection or Maxi-Aids. OCR programs (such as OmniPage Pro) can often be purchased at large office or computer supply stores.

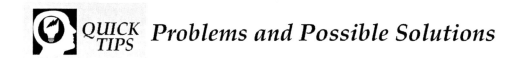 *Problems and Possible Solutions*

2. Student needs an angled surface to support reading materials.

Cookbook holders work well for some students. A clip can be added to the top to hold papers in position.

(Paulette Binder, Home Economics Teacher, Cotting School)

A 4" wide 3-ring notebook positioned as an inclined surface provides a 20 degree angle which is generally believed to be the best reading angle for most people. Another inclined surface is the Magnetic Notebook, described in the next chapter.

Students who require a more vertical book support may find the Magnetic Book Stand with Adjustable Ledge very effective (directions provided later in this chapter). The Triwall Easel is also effectively used as a vertical book support (page 47).

A vertical reading stand can be made to fit onto a lap tray, which is easily removable. Directions for fabrication are included at the end of this chapter.

(Beth Jackson, M.S, OTR/L, Occupational Therapist, Cotting School)

Angled book stands are also available through commercial suppliers such as Maxi-Aids and Sammons Preston (see Resource Directory).

3. Student has impaired reading skills and benefits from having additional visual input and/or auditory and visual input provided together to aid in comprehension.

Provide the student with book/storytape sets.

(Micki Rosenberg, M.Ed., Reading Specialist, Cotting School)

Use CD ROM tapes that are at the student's developmental level and which are full of sound and graphics.

Use books that include color pictures. Color pictures provide important color cues and are easier to interpret than black and white pictures. If reading materials need to be enlarged on a copying machine, still use the colored pictures that came with the original text.

(Nancy McClintock, Ed. M, Reading Specialist, while working at Cotting School)

The Ultimate Reader, from Universal Learning Technology, Peabody, Ma., is an "Advanced Literacy Development System" that adds a spoken voice and visual highlights to any electronic text. It has many additional features as well. Any text can be scanned into the program using a reading scanner (which must be purchased separately) as long as there is OCR in the scanner or computer. The text can also be down-loaded from any on-line service or moved in from a word processing program or CD-ROM. It is particularly beneficial for students who read below grade level, have difficulty decoding, and/or have impaired vision. There are versions for both Macintosh and PC.

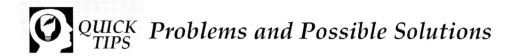 **QUICK TIPS** *Problems and Possible Solutions*

4. Student has visual or perceptual impairments which affect his or her ability to read standard print in books.

🔆 Enlarge the print on the copying machine. Some students also benefit from having very dark copies made on the copying machine.

🔆 Thicken print using thick markers.

🔆 Provide twice as much white space as print, to reduce the clutter on the page.

🔆 Provide good overhead lighting.

🔆 If a computer is involved, experiment with spacing, size/boldness/style of print, and whether the student reads best when all capitals are used or when mixed case letters are used.

🔆 Use strongly contrasting colors for letter and background colors. Test for color-blindness and avoid using colors that are confusing.

> *(All of the above tips were contributed by Nancy McClintock, Ed. M.,*
> *Reading Specialist, while working at Cotting School.)*

🔆 Maxi-Aids offers a very large selection of magnifiers as well as reading machines for those students who have very low vision.

🔆 Some computerized reading programs (such as the Ultimate Reader, from Universal Learning Technology, described earlier in this section) are excellent tools for accommodating vision problems.

5. Student has a poor sense of directionality and often reads words or numbers backwards, e.g. pot instead of top, 42 instead of 24.

🔆 If the student is not color blind, try the street-light color-coding system to compensate for directional confusion, using the colors green and red for stop and go:

- For reading words: Underline the first letter with green and the last letter with red.
- For reading multiple-digit numbers: Underline the first number with green and the last number with red.

☞ It is best if the same color-coding system is used for all areas in which the student is having trouble with directionality to provide a consistent approach. See Quick Tip #6.

Remember that this is a purely compensatory strategy; other remedial strategies may also be necessary.

> *(Reading and Math Tutorial Department, Cotting School)*

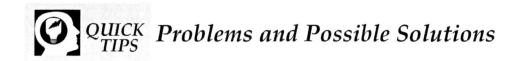

6. Student tends to read part-way across a line of print and then skip to the next line.

Use the street-light color-coded system (see Quick Tip #5): Draw a green line down the left margin of the page and a red line down the right margin of the page. The student is taught to start reading at the green line and not to skip to the next line until the red margin is reached. *Remember* to rule out color blindness before using this approach.

Note that students with this problem often have midline integration difficulties and/or a visual field deficit. Other remedial strategies may be needed to treat these problems.

7. Student is a beginning reader and has difficulty decoding words.

If the student will be choosing among single word answers on a reading sheet, print the first letter of each word in a different color from the rest of the letters in the word to assist in sounding out the word. If two of the words start with the same letter and are similar to one another (e.g. cold and cool) then also use another color to print a "key" letter which is different in both words (d and l in the above example).

(Marissa Shindell, M.Ed., Primary School Teacher, Cotting School)

8. Student's reading speed is too slow or too fast or student has difficulty phrasing sentences with pauses in the correct spots.

The teacher can use a moving finger, positioned under each word that should be read, to improve the student's reading pace or phrasing. Have the student try to pace his or her reading to the pace of the finger, not vice versa.

A homemade paper window cut-out can also be used to help the student modulate his or her reading speed. Make a paper window (described in Quick Tip #10) and place it over the print. The teacher controls the window card to improve reading speed.

☞ Reading speed and phrasing are often best addressed at the end of a thorough reading lesson, after the student has become familiar with all of the reading words. For more detailed information, please see General Guidelines for 1:1 Reading Instruction in the Classroom, earlier in this chapter.

(The above ideas were contributed by current and former members of the Reading and Math Tutorial Department at Cotting School.)

9. Student has a low reading vocabulary but is eager to read a "whole book".

Choose a book with lots of repetitive words and colored pictures.

(Nancy McClintock, Ed. M. Psychology of Reading, Reading Consultant.)

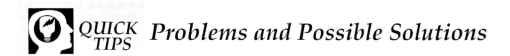

10. Student frequently loses his or her place when reading.

🔦 Enlarging the print and reducing the amount of lines on a page can help to reduce this problem.

🔦 Have the student use a marker to help keep his or her place. The best marker? The student's finger, positioned under each word as the student is reading it.
(Nancy McClintock, Ed. M., Reading Specialist, while working at Cotting School)

🔦 Other effective reading markers:
- a small plastic ruler placed under the row that the student is reading.

- a paper window cut-out, made by cutting the top left corner off of an index card, forming a rectangular window that only has two sides (right and bottom). This 2-sided window is easier to use than a 4-sided rectangular window, because the student can still view what was just read, making it easier to line it up correctly.
(Amy B. Milne, B.S. Sp.Ed., Learning Disabilities Specialist in Hudson, Ma.)

- Highlighter Tape, available through Therapro, is designed to be used as a reading marker, and is both removable and reusable.
(Karen Conrad, ScD, OTR/L, Occupational Therapist, Founder and President, Therapro, Inc.)

🔦 If the student does not have the fine motor skill to use any of the above approaches, try underlining each row of print with a different colored thin marker. Then the student only has to remember what color row they are currently reading or copying from.

🔦 Some students will need to have the teacher point to the next word to be read or hold a reading marker for them.

🔦 Some electronic reading systems provide a variety of highlighting options to improve tracking ability while reading. For example, the Ultimate Reader by Universal Learning Technology can highlight text by word, line, chunk, sentence or paragraph.

11. Student has difficulty with reading comprehension.

🔦 On the left margin of the page, draw a "key" with each of the protrusions of the key sticking out at the indentation that starts a new paragraph. Each indentation tells the reader that there is a new idea being presented. From Project Read [1].
(Idea contributed by Micki Rosenberg, M.Ed., Reading Specialist, Cotting School)

🔦 Before having the student read the paragraph, preview the colored illustrations and point out (and explain) the critical words in the text, using a finger or highlighter tape (available from Therapro, Inc.), so the student can start with the knowledge of the main subject matter.
(Nancy F. McClintock, Ed. M., Reading Specialist, while working at Cotting School)

🔦 Use color as a mode to focus attention to words. For example, highlight all of the names in yellow.
(Nancy F. McClintock, Ed. M., Reading Specialist, while working at Cotting School)

12. Student is a poor reader and needs compensatory strategies for performing functional tasks that entail reading, such as doing laundry, using an ATM machine, following cooking recipes, or following direction sheets for other functional tasks.

DOING LAUNDRY:

For sorting machine-washable from hand-washable clothes, teach the student to look at the first word on the underside of the clothing tag. If it's a long word that starts with M, it's machine washable, and if it's a four letter word that starts with an H, better hand wash it. This works for most clothing labels. Polaroids can also be taken of certain clothes, such as those that need dry cleaning and those that need to be hand-washed. Then tape the pictures to the top of the dryer or to the wall for easy identification of clothing.

Forget trying to distinguish between all of that hot/warm/cold wash gibberish - choose one setting that will be safe for all clothes, such as warm wash, cold rinse. Place a very thin strip of colored tape on the correct settings for both the washer and dryer. Now the student needs to simply turn the knobs of the washer and dryer so the indicators point to the tape.

USING THE ATM MACHINE:

Have the student carry a small pictorial chart in their wallet, showing each screen of the ATM machine in succession, with the correct button colored in for each screen. This tells the student (for example) to press the second button of the first screen, third button of the second screen, etc. Have the student learn to look for a particular word on each screen, to confirm that the student is on the correct screen.

FOLLOWING COOKING RECIPES:

Re-write cooking recipes and direction sheets, relying heavily on pictures, Picture Communication Symbols, Bliss Symbols, or whatever symbols the student can easily understand.

Some students who have visual or perceptual impairments need to have each step depicted on a separate sheet of paper, with all of the steps collated together to form a "book".

There are now some excellent recipe books on the market that are geared for non-readers. These are described in the Home Economics chapter.

FOLLOWING DIRECTION SHEETS:

Some students benefit from using an auditory approach, such as recording the directions on a cassette tape player (a large selection is available through Maxi Aids) or else recording them on a digital recording communication aid such as the MACAW (available through Zygo Industries, Inc.). With the MACAW, each step of the task can be recorded on a different key. On the key overlays, write the step number plus draw a picture that depicts the step. The student can then easily "replay" a step if necessary.

INSTRUCTIONS
FOR FABRICATING
SELECTED DEVICES

MAGNETIC BOOKSTAND
WITH ADJUSTABLE LEDGE

VERTICAL READING STAND
ATTACHED TO LAP TRAY

MAGNETIC BOOKSTAND WITH ADJUSTABLE LEDGE

DESCRIPTION: A vertically-angled, wooden book stand with an adjustable height support ledge. Mounted magnets and clips attached to the top of the stand allow two methods of holding pages in place. To use magnets, paper clips are attached in a staggered manner to the tops of several pages of the book. The paper clips stick to the magnets, keeping the book open to the desired page. The clips can be used to hold the pages of the book open when the magnet system is not appropriate (although the student will then be dependent on the teacher to turn the pages).

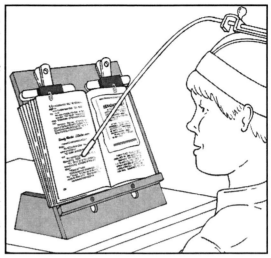

PURPOSES:

1. To enable positioning of the book at the proper height and angle to support the visual, motor, or positioning needs of the student.

2. To keep the book opened to the proper page. Often when books are placed on vertical book stands, the pages don't stay open the way they do on a flat horizontal surface. Many students who benefit from using vertical book stands are unable to use their hands to keep the pages open, due to motor impairments.

3. To enable independent page-turning for students who use headpointers or other types of pointers. A pencil head eraser placed at the tip of the pointer provides sufficient traction to turn the pages, and the pages stay open due to the magnets.

MATERIALS:
1. Plywood approximately 20" x 20"
2. Four 1/4" diameter flathead wood screws approximately 1 1/4" long
3. Two 3" long x 3/16" diameter bolts, each with a washer and wing nut
4. Two large potato chip bag clips; several heavy magnets; a box of paper clips

TOOLS:
Bandsaw (or other saw) to cut plywood; electric sander or sandpaper; drill; coping saw, scroll saw or router bit to cut holes in middle of plywood; heavy-duty glue such as hot glue

MEASUREMENTS:
The final measurements
of this book holder are:
    18″ high by 14″ wide.

One front supporting surface:
    14″ wide by 18″ high
Two trapezoid easel supports:
    TOP: 4 1/2″,
    BACK: 3 1/2″,
    BOTTOM: 6″
    (right angles between these three sides)
    FRONT 3 3/4″.

One book ledge: 14 1/2″ long by 2″ deep

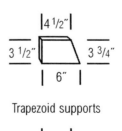

Trapezoid supports

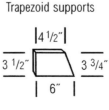

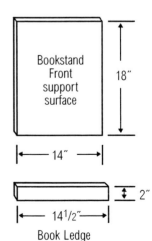

Book Ledge

ASSEMBLY:

1. Cut out the four pieces of wood described on the previous page using a bandsaw or other suitable saw.

2. Draw the two slots on the front surface of the book-stand for the bolts to slide through. Each should be approximately 6 1/2" long x 3/8" wide. Position these slots approximately 3 1/2" from the 18" sides, and 3" from the 14" bottom of the front supporting surface. Drill a hole at the top and bottom of each slot location and use a coping saw or scroll saw to connect the two holes, creating the slots. OR: Drill one hole and use a router to make the slot.

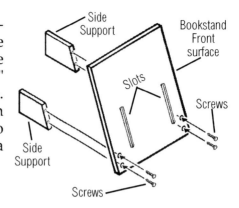

3. Sand all of the pieces of wood.

4. Drill holes in the supporting surface to attach the supports: Use a 1/4" bit to drill two pairs of holes one inch from each 18" edge, and 1 1/2" and 3" from the bottom (14") edge. Use a countersink bit to inset the screws, drilling again over your 1/4" hole just deep enough for the screw head to fit into.

5. Attach the two trapezoid-shaped supports to each side of the bookstand using two flathead wood screws for each support. Screw the screws from the front of the bookstand into the supports.

6. Drill two holes all the way through the adjustable ledge piece using a 1/4" bit, 3 3/4" from each end of this piece. Attach the ledge to the book easel by pushing a 3" bolt through each hole and positioning it in place on the easel with the bolts through the slots. Slide a washer onto each bolt from the back of the bookstand, add a wing nut to each bolt, and tighten ledge at desired height.

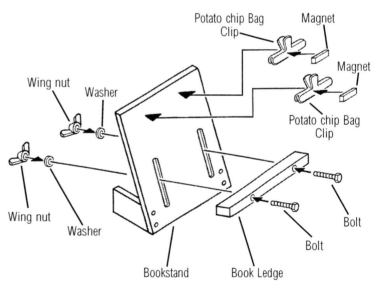

7. Glue the 2 large potato chip bag clips to the top of the stand, one on each side. Then glue one or more large heavy-duty magnets across the top of the clips.

8. To prepare a book to use on this magnetic stand, place the paper clips in a staggered manner at the top of several pages on either side of the page that the reader is on.

Idea conceived by
Sheryl Zelten, OTR/L, while working at Cotting School.
Designed and built by
Sheryl Zelten and Val Greene, B.S.Ed., Industrial Arts Teacher at Cotting School.

VERTICAL READING STAND ATTACHED TO LAP TRAY

DESCRIPTION: A 90 degree vertical triwall reading stand which easily attaches to a lap tray by slipping two wooden pegs at the bottom into corresponding holes in the lap tray. Two large metal rings attached at the top of the stand hold 2 hole punched reading materials.

☞ This stand is designed to support 2 or 3 hole punched sheets of paper, not books or other bound materials. Other reading stands are presented in this chapter that can be useful for supporting books.

This reading stand is currently used with a beginner reader for class activities such as Morning Meeting Time, Cooking, etc. For example, the reading sheets that are used for Morning Meeting time include the following headings and responses, which the student points to as well as verbalizes: How Do You Feel? (Happy, Sad, Mad, Proud, Tired); Who's Here Today? (Names of teachers and students in class); Our Specials Today Are . . . (Art, Music, Library, Gym, Assembly); The Weather is _____ (Sunny, Cloudy, Rainy, Snowy) And _____ (Cold, Hot, Cool, Warm).

PURPOSES:
1. To provide a means for supporting reading papers for those students who can benefit from vertical placement of reading materials and who are positioned in wheelchairs with lap trays.
2. To provide consistency of positioning for reading materials as well as ease of set-up and removal.
3. This stand can be particularly useful for the following students:
    a. beginning readers who can benefit from using individually-designed reading sheets geared to particular classroom activities to reinforce reading skills.
    b. students who benefit from using written instructions to assist with functional motor performance (e.g. Cooking Class).

MATERIALS:
1. Triwall material, approximately 13" wide by 10" high
2. Contact paper, enough to cover the Triwall material (13" by 21" sheet needed for a 13" x 10" stand)
3. Two 3" long pieces of 5/16" wide wooden dowel
4. Two large metal rings or four 1 1/4" metal rings - obtainable at a stationary store
5. Woodworker's glue

Tools:
Razor knife, saw for cutting dowel pieces, power drill for drilling holes in lap tray and top of reading stand, hammer or wooden mallet, sandpaper

Measurements:
Surface area of the Triwall stand should be large enough to support the reading materials, and it should be high enough to allow for optimal visual placement of materials.

Assembly:
1. Cut the Triwall to the desired size using a razor knife.

2. Cut two 3" long pieces from a 5/16" wide dowel using a wood saw. Sand the ends of the dowel pieces.

3. Insert the two dowel pieces into the bottom edge of the Triwall stand:
   a. Determine location for dowels (approximately 2" from each end).
   b. Pour wood glue into the holes (in the flutes of the Triwall) that the dowels will fit into.
   c. Hammer the dowel pieces into the Triwall until only 1" protrudes from the bottom. Let dry.

4. Drill two holes near the very top of the Triwall stand (one on each side) big enough to place a metal ring through each of them. Drill the holes to correspond to positions available on your 2 or 3 hole paper punch, so it will be easy to punch out holes in the reading materials to match the holes on the stand.

5. Attach the contact paper to the Triwall so it covers the front, top, and back surfaces.

6. Punch holes through the contact paper where it covers the drilled holes, and attach the metal rings through the holes. If 1 1/4" rings are used, attach one through each hole in the Triwall, and attach a second ring to the first one. Reading materials should be attached to the second metal ring.

7. Position the stand in the desired spot on the lap tray, trace around the wooden dowels where they contact the tray, and use a power drill with a slightly larger bit than the width of the dowels to drill holes all the way through the lap tray at the marked spots. Sand the holes.

8. To use Reading Stand: Punch holes in the desired reading materials and attach to the metal rings.

Designed and built by
Beth Jackson, M.S., OTR/L, Occupational Therapist,
and Val Green, B.S.Ed., Industrial Arts Teacher, both at Cotting School.

Chapter 12
Writing

ASSISTIVE DEVICES FOR WRITING TASKS

Students spend a great amount of their classroom time engaging in writing tasks. Those who are seriously challenged by handwriting skills often also experience difficulty in mastering those subject areas that employ handwriting. For example, number calculations will be incorrect if numbers are illegible. Important lecture information may be forgotten if the student cannot write fast enough to take down all of the notes, or if the notes are illegible. Compounding these problems is the tendency of teachers to bias test grades when papers are illegible. [1]

Having access to a word processor - as well as the skills to use one - can alleviate many of these problems in the classroom. However, despite the invention of lap top computers, there are still many everyday tasks that require handwriting, such as filling out applications and credit slips, and signing checks. Some quick and unpredictably occurring writing tasks, such as writing down car directions and taking phone messages, could theoretically be performed on a lap top computer, although the person providing the information might grow impatient waiting for the computer to be set up. Therefore, it continues to be crucial for teachers to help students maximize their handwriting skills whenever the student has any potential for handwriting at all.

When handwriting is impaired, consideration should be given to whether or not the student should also be taught word processing skills. A careful evaluation will determine if and when word processing skills should be taught as well as when it is appropriate to use them. Comparing the student's writing speed with his or her word processing speed can aid decision-making in this area.

Above all, it is crucial that the student's cognitive development not be hindered by the lack of adequate handwriting skills (or word processing skills, for that matter). Some students who have physical challenges possess a storehouse of knowledge, wit, and creativity that is eloquently expressed verbally, but struggle to write (or type) a couple of sentences in a 30 minute period. These students should be allowed to verbally dictate their written classroom reports to another person while they work to master a computer access method (such as a voice recognition program) which can keep up with (instead of disrupt) their flow of thoughts. Other students are equally intelligent but have no functional speech. Dictating their thoughts using their most functional augmentative communication method may be the best way for these students to complete their written work.

Assessing Handwriting Skills

When addressing a student's handwriting difficulties, it is important to evaluate the performance components that influence handwriting, including sensory/perceptual, motor, cognitive and psychosocial components. Occupational therapists are uniquely qualified to evaluate all of these components due to their extensive training in these areas, and should therefore be consulted whenever a student is experiencing significant handwriting difficulties. The therapist can target the specific causes of handwriting dysfunction and suggest appropriate remedial and/or compensatory strategies for the teacher to carry out.

It is best for therapist to become familiar with a variety of handwriting assessment tools as there is no single tool available that is optimal for every student. The student's age/grade level, reading ability, and attention span will affect the decision as to which tool to use. Resources that contain excellent information on handwriting assessment tools are noted in the Reference Section for this chapter, located at the end of this book.

Positioning the Student for Handwriting Activities

Writing tasks do not always need to be performed in a sitting position. In fact it can be beneficial for many students to perform writing tasks in alternative positions, such as prone-on-elbows or in a standing position. In the latter position, both arms should be positioned forward with slight elbow flexion, and with the base of the palms resting on a vertical writing surface. Both of the above positions increase proximal stability as well as dissociation of the hand from the forearm [2]. The student's level of alertness may also affect the choice of position. If a student tends to operate at an inappropriately low or high level of alertness, try experimenting with different positions to see if any of them makes a difference in the student's attention level.

When performing writing tasks in a sitting position, the student should be provided with a well-fitting chair with appropriate back support. The student should exhibit an upright posture with hips and knees at 90 degrees (as a general rule) and feet flat on the floor or other support surface. Also as a general rule, the table surface for writing tasks should be approximately 2" higher than the student's elbow to allow for at least 30 degrees of shoulder flexion.

Many students benefit from using angled working surfaces for writing tasks. A 4" or 3" wide 3-ring notebook positioned with the spine facing away from the student may provide an optimal inclined writing surface. The 4" wide notebook is often preferable as it provides the 20 degree angle often recommended by vision specialists. It also facilitates even more wrist extension/thumb opposition due to the more vertically-inclined surface. A possible solution for students who are unable to stabilize their papers independently is to magnetize the notebook, as is done to make the Magnetic Notebook with Ruler. Directions for making this device are provided later in this chapter. Commercially made angled working surfaces can be found in Therapro's catalog (EZ Writer, Study Buddy, Table Top Easel).

There are always exceptions to general rules, especially for students who have motor impairments, so be sure to consult with the student's physical or occupational therapist if there is any doubt as to how a particular student should be positioned.

Preparing the Student's State of Alertness for Writing Tasks

Writing is a task that requires a high level of integration of sensory, motor, perceptual, and cognitive skills. Many special needs students not only lack this level of integration but also have innate attentional deficits which further compound their difficulties with handwriting. Some students seem to always be operating in "low gear": they may appear sleepy, bored, lethargic, or even sad or depressed. In contrast, other students seem to operate in "high gear" much of the time: they may appear overactive or fidgety, and may find it difficult to settle their nervous systems down enough to fully concentrate on a writing task. Sometimes it is difficult to tell whether a fidgety student is in high or low gear, since some students who are in "low gear" may move around in order to try to wake themselves up. Very strong emotions - either positive (such as excitement) or negative (such as anger) can also put a student into "high gear".

Various sensorimotor-based treatment strategies can significantly help students adjust their levels of alertness so they are focused and able to attend to the task at hand [3]. These strategies may include putting something in the mouth, touch input (such as fiddling with objects or wearing a heavy shawl around the shoulders), changing the auditory and/or visual input that is present in the environment, changing body position, and/or engaging in movement activities (particularly resistive movements). The chart on the next page provides some activities that may be particularly helpful for students engaging in writing tasks. Those students who have potential to identify their own states of alertness and choose their own sensorimotor strategies may benefit from the *Alert Program for Self Regulation*, developed by Mary Sue Williams, OTR/L, and Sherry Shellenberger, OTR/L [3]. Remember that individuals may have different responses to the same sensory input: a strategy that works well for one student may make the situation worse for another. Observe the student's responses carefully to ensure that the strategies chosen are truly beneficial for the particular individual.

Some Strategies Which May Improve a Student's Attention to Writing Tasks

ORAL INPUT:
- Suck water through a sports bottle with a straw.
- Chew or suck on gum, candy or food (such as crunchy pretzels), making sure first that the student can safely handle the particular food item in his or her mouth.
- Have the students all blow whistles or other blow toys and/or sing a favorite class song very loudly prior to working on writing tasks. This improves respiratory function and facilitates better trunk control for sitting endurance [4].

TACTILE INPUT:
- Provide the student with an appropriate pencil grip if holding the pencil is uncomfortable.
- Place a pencil topper on the pencil that has interesting tactile qualities (such as troll's hair) for the student to fiddle with while gathering thoughts together for the next sentence.
- Provide the student with a stress buster to keep in his or her desk to play with when a short break from writing is needed. This might also be good for relieving cramped muscles when writing.

ALTERNATIVE POSITIONS:
- Allow the student the opportunity to perform some writing tasks at the chalkboard, such as copying spelling words.
- Allow the student to perform a short (5 minute) writing task while lying prone on a carpeted floor or mat.
- Give the student a Movin' Sit Cushion (Ball Dynamics, Inc.) or other special air-filled cushion that is designed to provide movement input to the student while seated in a regular chair. The Movin' Sit cushion has significantly improved the attention span of several students.
- A student who has excellent trunk control and balance may benefit from sitting in a straddling position on an air-filled peanut-shaped therapy ball, such as a Physio-Roll from Sammons Preston. This device provides vertical and side-to-side movement input while seated. The Physio-Roll provides more control and security than a typical therapy ball, and also provides increased touch pressure input which can be calming for some students.

MOVEMENT ACTIVITIES:
- Precede classroom writing tasks with basic stretching and movement activities, such as jumping in place, jumping jacks, wall push-ups or chair push-ups, arm swings, animal walks around the room, etc.
- Give student an errand to do prior to engaging in writing tasks, preferably one that involves going up and down a flight of stairs.
- Schedule writing tasks after activities that involve physical movement, such as recess, gym, or music.

AUDITORY INPUT:
- Eliminate avoidable auditory distractions. Some options: place tennis balls on the bottom of each leg of furniture; place the student's desk away from doorways, windows, and the teacher's desk, but keep it close to where the teacher lectures.
- In severe cases, try muffling remaining noises by introducing "white noise" in the room, such as an electric fan, or allow the student to listen to either "white noise" or music on a headset. As a last resort, some extremely auditorially distracted students may benefit from using an FM listening system to better attend to teacher instructions during writing tasks. Please see page 69 for further information on this device, which is available from Phonic Ear as well as other companies.

VISUAL INPUT:
- Position the student's desk away from visual distractions such as windows, doorways, and exciting bulletin boards.
- Make sure the student has a good storage system for books and school supplies so the desk can remain uncluttered while working.
- Have the student sit at a cubby desk, or make a cubby top (see page 50) for an existing desk, to block out visual distractions.

Developed by Lynn Ciampa Stoller, M.S., OTR/L, BCP

Choosing Writing Tools and Materials

Choosing the Appropriate Writing Paper

Sometimes the only adaptation a student needs to dramatically improve their writing performance is to change the type of writing paper they are using. Traditionally, beginning writers are given wide-ruled writing paper and do not progress to narrow-ruled paper until they have mastered printing. However, many students with special needs actually have better pencil control writing on a smaller scale using narrower ruled paper. Mary Benbow, MS, OTR/L recommends an excellent method for determining the appropriate vertical ruling for a particular child: Take a blank sheet of paper, use a ruler to draw a single straight line in the middle of it, and ask the student to write his or her name using their very best handwriting. Then measure the height of the student's writing. This measurement should match the height of the vertical ruling of the student's writing paper [5]. This technique has made all the difference for many students at Cotting School.

Paper with the appropriate ruling can usually be found at teacher supply stores. If the size you need isn't available, simply take a sheet of paper that has the closest ruling and use a copy machine to enlarge or reduce it.

Other students do in fact benefit from using wide ruled paper. This includes students who have impaired eye-hand coordination which makes it difficult to start and stop the pencil on the writing lines. Right Line Paper (sold by Therapro) has raised green lines which provide a proprioceptive cue whenever the pencil touches the line, and is available in both wide and narrow rule. Raised writing lines can also be made using Hi Marks, a 3-D fluorescent marker made by Kentucky Industries for the Blind. Colored glue may also be used to make raised lines on wide ruled paper, although the raised line will not be as thin and precise as that made by the Hi Marks marker.

Positioning the Paper

As a general rule, right-handed students should position the writing paper slanted to the left, between 20 and 35 degrees from parallel to the desk edge. Left-handed students should slant the paper to the right, often closer to 35 degrees for better visibility of their writing [2,3]. There are several methods to help students position their papers correctly. A strip of masking tape can be taped to the desk at the correct angle so all the student has to do is line the left edge of the paper up to the tape to ensure correct positioning. Or, the student can be asked to clasp hands in the air to form a "triangle", then put the "triangle" down on the desk and place the paper against the right forearm if right-handed, or left forearm if left-handed [6].

Solutions for Lack of Mature Pencil Grasp

Solutions will vary considerably depending upon the cause. An occupational therapist can diagnose the underlying problem, such as joint instability and/or decreased muscle strength, tactile hypersensitivity, poor initial instruction, etc. Some variations in pencil grasp are common in students who do not have any fine motor impairments. Generally speaking, if the web space is open and the student demonstrates good distal control of the pencil when using the grasp, then it should not be changed [2]. If in doubt, a therapist can determine whether or not a particular grasp pattern warrants intervention. Therapeutic activities designed to improve hand development and/or hand strength may also be necessary.

Devices to Improve Pencil Grasp

For students who need to modify their pencil grasps, there are a variety of solutions available. Simply placing a pencil grip over the pencil provides a solution for many students who have relatively minor difficulties with pencil grasp. Grips come in many variations and are available at Therapro, teacher supply stores, and increasingly at pharmacies and stationary stores. Following are some tips for choosing among various pencil grips:

FOAM GRIPS AND ROUND GRIPS: These are particularly helpful for those students who find the tactile sensation of the pencil against their fingers uncomfortable. These students sometimes demonstrate a maladaptive grasp in an effort to avoid these uncomfortable sensations.

STETRO GRIP: An advantage of the Stetro Grip is that it positions the thumb and fingers precisely; however, a student needs to demonstrate good stability and opposition of the thumb in order to use this grasp. Students who have perceptual and/or cognitive impairments sometimes find it difficult to figure out how to use this grip correctly.

TRIANGULAR GRIP: The shape of this grip naturally encourages use of a tripod grasp; however, the grasp may be only approximate as opposed to the more precise positioning required by the Stetro Grip. This grip has no up or down position, nor a specific spot for the thumb, and is therefore easier for some students who have perceptual and/or cognitive deficits to use. As an added benefit, this grip also prevents a pencil from rolling off an inclined surface!

THE PENCIL GRIP: This grip combines a triangular shape with a mushroom shape, which guides the thumb and fingers into a more precise tripod position than the triangular grip does, but not as precisely as the Stetro grip does. This grip does not require training in its use, a benefit for those who have perceptual and/or cognitive deficits. It is thicker than the Stetro Grip, so the grasp is more open. It is also very cushioned. This grip can reduce muscle cramping as well as the tendency to hold the pencil with a closed web space.

Ultimately, it is the student who makes the final decision as to which type of grip to use, and this decision is often appropriate to the student's needs. Simply put, if the student can't understand how to use a grip or if it is uncomfortable, the student will reject it.

If no available pencil grips is found which meets a student's needs, it is also possible to make a custom grip using a molding material such as Dyna-Form-It (available from Therapro, Inc. and Sammons Preston). A variety of writing aids are also available that attach to the hands, for those who are unable to support a pen or pencil using only their fingers.

Solutions for Impaired Thumb Stability

Students who have very low muscle tone or weakness of the hand muscles often demonstrate insufficient thumb stability to use a tripod grasp even with a pencil grip attached. For some students who have this problem, use of the D'Nealian handwriting grip may be helpful: Place the shaft of the pencil into the web space between the middle and index fingers and have the student support it with the pads of the thumb, index finger, and middle finger (in the typical tripod). This grasp was described by Don Thurber, MA, EdSp, many years ago [8,9] and is recommended by noted handwriting experts Mary Benbow, M.S., OTR/L [5,10] and Susan Amundson, M.S., OTR/L [2,6]. Placing the pencil shaft against the web space between the middle and index fingers significantly increases stability of the pencil, thus freeing the thumb from assuming this chore and enabling the thumb to move into better opposition with the index and middle fingers.

For certain students who have extremely low muscle tone, poor strength, or increased muscle tone and spasticity, Kristine Lopes, COTA, recommends the following modification of the D'Nealian grip, which was taught to her by David Gilbert, COTA: A pencil is pushed through the center of a hollow practice golf ball and the student holds the pencil using the adapted grasp over the golf ball [11]. Please see Quick Tip #3 for more specific information on how to make and use this device.

Other solutions for impaired thumb stability include providing the student with a neoprene thumb splint or taping the thumb using Coban [5] or transparent tape [12]. These solutions should only be tried under the supervision of an occupational therapist.

Solutions for Impaired Separation of Both Sides of the Hand

Some students have difficulty keeping their ring and little fingers bent into the palm while grasping a pencil with their thumb, index, and middle fingers. One solution is to give the student a small object such as a piece of sponge or a Koosh ball to hold in the palm (using the ring and little fingers) during writing tasks. Another is to clip a spring-loaded clothespin onto a pencil about 2 inches from the pencil tip, depending on hand size. The student bends the ring and little fingers around the clothespin while writing with the pencil. This adaptation also gives stability to the metacarpal heads [2].

Solutions for Impaired Pencil Pressure

Some students who have a weak grasp demonstrate very light pencil pressure when writing, often accompanied by wavy lines. Other students who have hand weakness overcompensate for this problem and exhibit very heavy pencil pressure, which may even result in tearing the paper. Students who have difficulty finely controlling the movements of their arms and/or hands due to poor proprioception will also often demonstrate difficulties with grading pencil pressure. Therapists all seem to have their own favorite techniques for improving pencil pressure. Several of these are described in Quick Tips.

Students who use insufficient or excessive pencil pressure are often compensating for joint instability, muscle weakness, and/or poor proprioception. This should be evaluated and treated by an occupational therapist. Pencil grasp may also need to be adapted.

Compensations for Visual-Perceptual
and Motor Planning Impairments

There are a number of handwriting methods in current use in this country, and this creates the potential for confusion if a student is taught different approaches by different teachers and specialists. This confusion will be magnified if the student has visual-perceptual or motor-planning deficits. It is therefore critical that all of the student's TEAM members decide together which handwriting system to use for a particular student, based upon the student's individual needs. The TEAM also needs to decide whether manuscript or cursive handwriting should be taught. The author has found that in general, students who have perceptual or motor-planning deficits find learning easiest when letters are taught in groups of similarly-formed shapes (such as a, c, d, g, q, which all begin with the same movement). This seems to be true whether the student is learning manuscript or cursive handwriting. This approach also adds a kinesthetic component to learning through reinforcement of particular movement patterns [5].

In addition to consistency of handwriting method, some students who have perceptual or motor-planning impairments also benefit from visual cues to aid in letter formation, alignment, and sometimes even spacing. Some of the most popular and effective visual aids are presented below.

Aids for Letter Formation

The author has found that the *Box and Dot Method for Letter Formation*, described by Charles H. Boardman, Capt. USAF, OTR, can be very successful with students who have a history of poor printing skills [13]. The sample on the left shows the box and dot

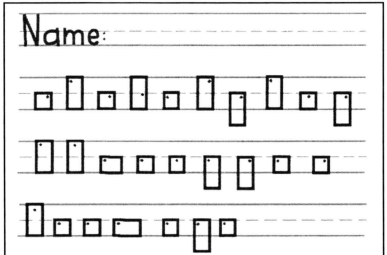

format for the lower case alphabet. The dots tell the student where to start printing the letter. The box provides a

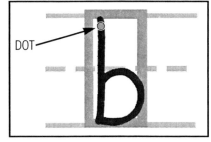

reference point for the dots, and also defines the writing space in which to form the letter. Combined, these visual cues provide the structure needed to facilitate correct motor planning for letter formation. After the proper writing patterns become habit, it usually is not a problem to remove the visual aids. The author uses the Box and Dot Method in combination with color-coding to help the student learn where to position the letters on the writing lines. This method is described next.

Aids for Letter Alignment

The following approach provides a very effective concrete system to enable students to learn where to position letters on the writing lines. First start with paper that has the appropriate vertical ruling for the student (discussed in "Choosing the Appropriate Writing Paper" earlier in this chapter). The paper should be double-lined and have a space between the bottom line and the top line of the next row.

Color-code the spaces between the writing lines to represent the sky (blue), grass (green), and dirt (brown).

The letters of the alphabet are organized into three different groups according to their location on the writing lines:

Sky Reachers (b,d,f,h,k,l,t),
Grass Grazers (a,c,e,i,m,n,o,r,s,u,v,w,x,z) and **Dirt Diggers** (g,j,p,q,y).

It is very important to use these name labels as they make the visual information more meaningful for the student, and therefore easier to remember. This approach has been used successfully at Cotting School for many years, and has also been attributed to Patty Oetter [6], though without the name labels.

If poor vertical alignment of letters is due to an eye-hand coordination impairment rather than impaired visual memory, consider providing the student with raised line paper during writing tasks, as discussed earlier in this chapter.

Aids for Word Spacing

Some students fail to leave spaces between words or leave inappropriate spaces between letters of the same word when writing. Many of these students have poor reading skills and do not recognize when a word has ended, or conversely, when it hasn't. These students are at a special disadvantage because all of their printing is merely an exercise in copying a long string of meaningless symbols with occasional spaces between them. Improving the reading skills of these students is undoubtedly the best strategy for improving their word spacing skills. Other common strategies which can be helpful include the following:

- Have the student use the index finger of the non-dominant hand to "keep a space" after each printed word while positioning the pencil just to the right of the finger to start the next word.

- Give the student a tiny strip of sticky note paper to use as a spacer between each word. [10]

- Have the student write sentences on graph paper upon which writing lines have been drawn; the student writes one letter in each box and leaves an empty box between words. [11]

QUICK TIPS *Problems and Possible Solutions*

Following are some solutions which have successfully solved the identified problem for one or more students. Keep in mind that each student has a unique set of abilities and needs and may therefore require an original solution for the problem at hand. If a suggested solution is appropriate for a student, please adapt the design as necessary to best meet his or her needs.

Remember: fit the device to the student, not the student to the device!

1. Student has poor hand grasp and needs an adapted handle for a marker, paintbrush, or pencil.

Many solutions are presented in the chapter titled Assistive Devices for Art and Craft Activities, in the Quick Tips Section. Typically, students use these devices to perform simpler writing tasks (e.g. marking multiple choice answers) or art activities (e.g. drawing, painting, gluing).

Also see solutions to Quick Tip #3.

2. Student does not use a mature pencil grasp due to uncomfortable tactile sensation.

A Foam Grip or a Round Grip (both available at Therapro) can often eliminate this problem.

3. Student does not use a mature pencil grasp due to thumb instability.

Try the D'Nealian pencil grasp, discussed earlier in this chapter.

Adapt a pencil with an inexpensive hollow practice golf ball (obtainable at sporting goods stores) and have the student hold the pencil using the D'Nealian grip over the golf ball. Find two holes that are exactly opposite each other on the golf ball and stick the pencil all the way through so the pencil tip protrudes through the opposite side. Widen the holes if necessary by twisting a scissors blade inside the holes. This device improves positioning and stability of the hand during handwriting tasks, and has been extremely effective for certain individuals who have extremely low tone, poor strength, or increased muscle tone and spasticity. It should be tried after commercially available pencil grips have been unsuccessful. The device is used most often on a slanted writing surface.

(Contributed by Kristine Lopes, COTA who learned of this adaptation from David Gilbert, COTA.
Both work in the New Bedford , Ma., Public Schools.)

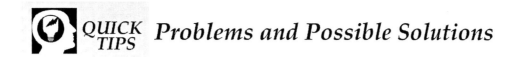 QUICK TIPS *Problems and Possible Solutions*

4. Student does not use a mature pencil grasp due to the continued use of a compensatory grasp which developed as a result of a fine motor delay.

❶ Pencil grips are very helpful for reinforcing the use of a mature pencil grasp for those students who are now developmentally ready to use one. Various types are available, each useful for different needs. Please see full discussion earlier in this chapter.

❶ Try giving the student small bits of crayons or chalk to use during writing activities. These small bits prevent the student from using compensatory grasps and help to develop a mature tripod grasp.

5. Student is unable to stabilize the paper with the non-dominant hand during writing tasks.

❶ If the student can operate a clip on a clipboard, simply add self-stick rubber feet or Dycem to the bottom of the clipboard (with double-sided scotch tape) and have the student position writing papers in the clipboard during writing tasks.

❶ If the student cannot operate a clipboard, and can also benefit from using an angled writing surface, then make a Magnetic Notebook and Ruler for Stabilizing Papers, described in detail on page 190.

❶ If the student cannot operate a clipboard and needs a flat (not angled) surface for writing, make a flat magnetic writing surface with magnetic ruler as described in the Magnetic Notebook Modification. The student stabilizes the paper between the writing board and the magnetic ruler.

6. Student uses a mouthstick for performing writing and drawing tasks and needs a good writing surface.

❶ A vinyl memo board, purchased at any department store, can be attached to the student's wheelchair (at a height appropriate to accommodate use of a mouthstick) using a universal mount, such as that sold by Sammons Preston. Make sure only a waterbased or dry-erase marker is used with this board! This board set-up works well in conjunction with the Mouthstick Marker Holder (page 220) for a student who has a C2-C3 spinal cord injury.

(Frances Maggiore, COTA/L, Certified Occupational Therapy Assistant,
Franciscan Children's Hospital, Brighton, Ma.)

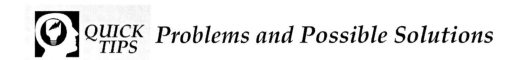

7. Student has difficulty drawing freehand and cannot stabilize stencils or other drawing aids using the non-dominant hand.

Attach magnets or magnetic tape to the bottom of stencils, rulers, and other drawing aids and use in conjunction with a Flat Magnetic Surface or the Magnetic Notebook (both described on page 190).

Attach Dycem to the bottom of rulers, stencils, etc. using double-sided scotch tape.

8. Student's pencil pressure is too heavy.

Put a putty substance around the pencil shaft to help reduce the tendency to grip the pencil too tightly.

Have the student use the Yellow Pages as a writing surface. This surface is spongy, giving the student instant feedback regarding pencil pressure.
(Karen Conrad, Sc.D, OTR/L, Occupational Therapist, Founder and President, Therapro, Inc.)

Sandwich a sheet of carbon paper between two plain sheets of white paper, and place these under the student's writing paper. If the writing goes through to the bottom sheet of paper, the student is pressing down too strongly. This provides good feedback to the student and facilitates self-monitoring.

9. Student's pencil pressure is too light.

Try the carbon-paper trick in reverse. Put the carbon paper directly under the writing paper, and tell the student to press hard enough so it goes through the carbon paper onto the plain paper underneath.

Try a weighted pencil - see page 192 for instructions for making one.
*(Beth Jackson, M.S., OTR/L, Occupational Therapist,
and Cindy Furbish, PT, Physical Therapist, both at Cotting School)*

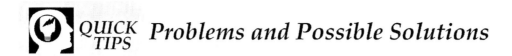

QUICK TIPS *Problems and Possible Solutions*

10. Student continues to exhibit poor printing skills using primary-ruled paper.

Make sure the paper isn't the problem. See the introduction to this chapter on how to determine the appropriate size ruling for writing paper. Many students actually print better using narrow ruled paper (often with a broken middle divider). Paper that has a 5/8" vertical ruling works well for many students. The Grade 5, 3/8" vertical ruling, blue baseline, broken midline paper (#140145) from Zaner-Bloser, made a tremendous difference for some students at Cotting School who have midline integration difficulties and who needed very narrow-ruled paper.

Raised line paper may be helpful for students who have impaired eye-hand coordination and need that extra proprioceptive cue to help them stay on the writing line. One type of raised line paper is called Right Line Paper and is offered through Therapro.

Raised writing lines can also be made using Hi Marks, a 3-D fluorescent marker made by Kentucky Industries for the Blind, Louisville, Kentucky 40206. Alternatively, colored glue may be used to make raised line paper.

11. Student needs increased tactile-kinesthetic feedback to improve performance with writing tasks.

Have the student write on a vertical surface, especially a resistive one such as a chalkboard.

The student's tactile-kinesthetic feedback may be improved by:
- Wearing wrist weights just above the wrist when writing on the chalkboard.

- Writing with a Squiggle-Wiggle pen.

- Drawing letters in clay or wet sand.

- Writing with chalk on rough pavement.

Make a screen writing surface: buy a screen mesh (used in screen doors) at a building supply store, cut it to the desired size using wire cutters. Cover the edges with duct tape, or "frame" it by nailing a long strip of wood over each of the four edges to attach it to a wooden easel or flat wooden base. Place the student's paper on the screen surface during writing and drawing activities. The feedback provided by the screen surface is especially beneficial for students who have visual impairments.

Writing 187

12. Student dislikes working on writing skills due to a long history of failure and frustration.

Have the student make signs around the school using Calligraphy pens. This worked like a charm for one student, who no longer found writing to be a chore and took great pride in his ability to perform a useful service to the school.

(Diane Long, M.S., OTR, President/Occupational Therapist,
New Directions Therapeutics, Inc., Auburn, N.Y. [11])

There are many additional ways to remotivate students to work on writing skills, including writing on Magnadoodles; using Squiggle-Wiggle pens; writing in messy media such as Funny Foam, shaving creme, finger paint, rice, clay, or sand; writing on the chalkboard or a dry-erase board using colored chalks or markers; "writing" or "tracing" with a flashlight, penlight, or laser light on a wall; writing in a sandbox or in the sand at the beach; writing with colored glue or fabric paint; printing the number words when making a hopscotch outside using chalk; or playing games that involve writing, such as playing Clue and writing down the clues on the appropriate writing paper instead of the checklist pad. Better yet, have the student practice writing by inventing his or her own board game!

13. Student is visually impaired and often writes outside the allotted space when filling out or signing checks, credit card slips, and other documents.

For signatures: Make a simple signature guide using a 3 1/4" x 2 1/2" rectangular piece of thin plastic material. Cut out a 1/4" x 2 3/8" long opening in this plastic rectangle. The opening of the plastic rectangle is positioned over the signature line to provide tactile cues to assist in staying on the line.

(Sue Shannon, OTR/L, Occupational Therapist, Perkins School for the Blind, Watertown, Ma.)

A variety of writing guides are available commercially through Maxi-Aids, including envelope writing guides, check writing guides, letter writing guides, signature guides, etc.

14. Student grasps the pencil too high on the pencil shaft.

Place a piece of colored or masking tape around the pencil in the location in which the student should grasp the pencil.

Wrap a rubber band around the barrel of the pencil in correct grasping spot.

INSTRUCTIONS
FOR FABRICATING
SELECTED DEVICES

MAGNETIC NOTEBOOK & RULER
FOR STABILIZING PAPERS

WEIGHTED PENCIL

WORD BOX TO ASSIST WITH WRITING TASKS

MAGNETIC NOTEBOOK & RULER FOR STABILIZING PAPERS

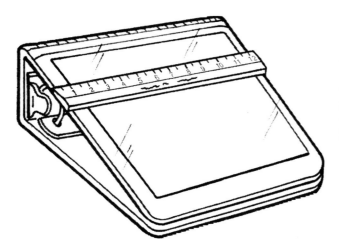

DESCRIPTION:
A 4" wide three-ring notebook with a sheet of metal (covered with contact paper) attached to the cover, paired with a magnetized ruler.

PURPOSES:
1. To provide the student with an angled writing surface to facilitate active wrist extension, open up the thumb web space and develop the hand arches. Also, vision specialists often recommend that reading materials be positioned at a 20 degree angle, which a 4" wide notebook provides.

2. To enable the student to stabilize their papers independently. Many students who can benefit from an angled writing surface also have difficulty stabilizing papers or rulers with their non-dominant hands.

MATERIALS:
1. 4" wide 3-ring binder (3" can be substituted, if necessary). A binder that has a clear cover sleeve is convenient but not essential
2. 11" x 11" square sheet of galvanized steel, obtainable in the plumbing department of a building supply store (Ask for steel sheets used for duct work or "joist panning".)
3. Attractive but visually non-distracting contact paper - enough to cover the metal sheet
4. 12" ruler
5. 12" long piece of magnetic tape
6. Duct tape to cover the rough edges of the metal
7. Optional: Dycem, for Flat Magnetic Surface Modification

TOOLS:
Metal cutters
Metal file

MEASUREMENTS:
The magnetic notebook provides a writing surface that is at least 11" x 11", which is sufficient to hold a standard sheet of paper.

ASSEMBLY:

1. Use the metal cutters to cut out a 11" x 11" square from the sheet metal. Remove any rough metal splinters (burrs) from the edges with the file. Then cover all the edges of the metal sheet with duct tape.

2. If the 3-ring notebook has a clear plastic sleeve, simply cover the metal with attractive contact paper and slip it into the sleeve.

3. If the notebook does not have a plastic sleeve, position the metal on top of the cover and place the contact paper over the metal sheet and around the edges of the cover to secure the metal sheet in place.

4. Stick a long strip of magnetic tape on the back of a ruler to use for the dual purpose of stabilizing paper as well as stabilizing the ruler when one is needed.

☞ If the student has potential to learn to stabilize their paper, put just enough magnetic tape so that stabilization with the non-dominant hand is still necessary, but now assisted (and thus successful). As the student's control increases, more and more magnetic tape can be removed, decreasing the amount of assistance being provided.

5. Position the notebook with the spine facing away from the student so it forms an angled work surface. Place the student's writing paper on top of the notebook and place the ruler on the top margin to stabilize it.

MODIFICATION: FLAT MAGNETIC SURFACE WITH MAGNETIC RULER

For those who perform best when using a flat versus an angled surface but yet could benefit from using a magnetic ruler, follow the directions above but do not place the sheet of metal into a notebook. The size of the metal sheet can be increased, if desired. Attach Dycem (with double-sided tape) to the bottom of the steel sheet to prevent the magnetic surface from sliding.

Designed by the author who was inspired by Paulette Binder's Cookie Sheet Paper Stabilizer an upside down cookie sheet used with two wood strips with magnetic tape on them. Steel cookie sheets are now difficult to find, and the joist panning eliminates the ledge often found on cookie sheets.

Paulette E. Binder is a Home Economics Teacher at Cotting School.

WEIGHTED PENCIL

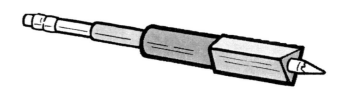

DESCRIPTION: A standard pencil with a weight placed over it, kept in place by a pencil grip on one end and tape at the other end.

PURPOSE:
To improve a student's line quality when writing, if the student tends to exhibit light and/or wavy lines due to tremoring or decreased pencil pressure.

MATERIALS:
1. Standard pencil

2. Pencil grip - whichever type works best for the student

3. Spacer (part # 1276-31-S), which can be obtained from Electronic Fasteners, Winter St., Waltham, Ma. 02154. (617) 890-7780. Mention the part number listed above as there are different types of spacers.

4. Cloth or masking tape

5. Pencil eraser head

ASSEMBLY:
1. Place the pencil grip on the pencil in the usual position.

2. Place the spacer on next, behind the pencil grip.

3. Wrap tape around the pencil just after the spacer, to hold it in place.

4. **OPTIONAL:** Put an eraser head on the end of the pencil.

Designed by
Beth Jackson, M.S., OTR/L, Occupational Therapist,
and Cindy Furbish, PT, Physical Therapist, both at Cotting School

---

WORD BOX TO ASSIST WITH WRITING TASKS

DESCRIPTION: An index card box with an alphabetical divider system in which to store the student's sight words alphabetically. During Journal Time, the student decides what sentence to write, finds all of the words of the sentence in the Word Box, sequences the words in the correct order, and finally copies the sentence onto the paper.

PURPOSE:

1. To enable students who have poor spelling skills but sufficient sight word vocabulary to independently write sentences. Some students who otherwise would need to have a teacher take dictation are able to complete their daily Journal Entries independently using this system.

2. To help students learn proper sentence structure.

MATERIALS:
1. Index card box with an alphabetical divider system

2. Paper

3. Clear contact paper or laminating machine

TOOLS:
Scissors
Marker
Ruler

ASSEMBLY:
1. Cut the paper into 2" squares. Write each of the student's sight words on its own square.

2. Laminate the squares (or cover them with clear contact paper).

3. Organize the words in alphabetical order in the index box using the alphabetical divider system.

Contributed by
Marissa Shindell, M.Ed., Primary School Teacher, Cotting School

Chapter 13
Math

ASSISTIVE DEVICES FOR MATH TASKS

Success in mathematics requires a multitude of skills beyond simply possessing the cognitive skills necessary to perform mathematical equations. Many math tasks also require reading skills and writing ability, as well as the ability to use mathematical tools such as rulers, compasses, and calculators. Students who have perceptual and/or motor impairments frequently have difficulty in one or more of these areas, as shown in the accompanying chart. Solutions to some of these problems can be found in the chapters on Reading, Writing, and Computer adaptations. Some solutions that were not covered in those chapters are presented here.

Functional Skills needed for Math Tasks:	SKILL COMPONENTS	
	Impairment of PERCEPTUAL SKILLS can result in:	Impairment of MOTOR SKILLS can result in:

READING SKILLS	•Number reversals or inversions when reading math problems: 2 may be read as 5, 6 may be read as 9, < may be read as >, 3/4 may be read as 4/3, 23 may be read as 32.
	
	•Poor comprehension of math problems due to poor reading skills
	
	•Poor comprehension of math problems caused by limited perceptual ability to:
	    -mentally rotate objects for geometry problems
	    -judge size differences to estimate answers
	    -understand parts-to-whole concepts such as
	      fractions and decimals
	
	•Difficulty remembering the meaning of math function symbols:
	    (+, -, x, division sign, %, =, <, >, etc.)
		•Difficulty setting up math book and turning pages of math book
		
		•Postural and ocular deficits may affect ability to keep one's place when scanning math problems

WRITING SKILLS	•Number reversals or inversions may occur when writing problems: 2 may be written as 5, 6 may be written as 9, < may be written as >, 3/4 may be written as 4/3, 23 may be written as 32, etc. •Poor formation of numbers leading to errors in number calculations •Poor alignment of numbers in problems, again leading to errors in number calculations •Errors in sequencing numbers: 235 may be written 532	•Impaired fine motor control of pencil
USE OF MATH TOOLS	•Difficulty figuring out how to use math tools such as rulers, compasses, etc.	•Difficulty operating calculators •Impaired fine and/or bilateral motor control necessary for using ruler, compass, or other math tools •Inability to use standard math computer software •Limited ability to use manipulatives for counting or other math tasks

Developed by Lynn Ciampa Stoller, M.S., OTR/L, BCP

Manipulatives: Still the Ideal Assistive Devices for Math Class

Despite the recent invention of math software, manipulatives continue to be the most popular assistive devices used in math class. Children must learn basic math concepts on a concrete level before they can understand more abstract mathematical information. For this reason, teachers usually encourage a high level of interaction with manipulatives to learn and reinforce math concepts.

Some students have severe motor impairments and are unable to manipulate the Unifix cubes, bread bag closure tabs, or other manipulatives that the rest of the class is using. This may lead the teacher to consult with the student's occupational therapist, providing the therapist with the golden opportunity to incorporate therapeutic motor goals into the student's academics.

The therapist will take into account any inappropriate movement patterns and/or gaps in motor development when choosing manipulatives for the student to use during math. The ideal manipulatives will discourage the use of inappropriate arm and hand patterns and will also help to develop the missing components of hand development [1,2]. This is accomplished by carefully choosing the shape, size, and consistency of the manipulatives and the size, angle, and distance of the work surface, and by carefully grading the difficulty in which the objects can be positioned and released onto a surface. Following are some examples of activity set-ups that may encourage the use of particular movement or grasp patterns.

SHOULDER FLEXION: Position manipulatives on a vertically-inclined surface, and gradually raise them to shoulder level, e.g. extra-large wooden pegboard on easel.

ELBOW EXTENSION: Increase distance between student and work surface.

WRIST EXTENSION: Use vertically-inclined surface.

PALMAR SUPINATE GRASP: Place very large cylindrical pegs in a pegboard positioned on a flat surface. Have student hold peg in fisted hand (i.e. peg against palm, with thumb opposed to fingers) with forearm in neutral or slightly supinated.

RADIAL PALMAR GRASP: Use large square blocks that fit against the radial side of palm, with thumb opposed to fingers. Gradually incline the work surface as the student develops the ability to extend the wrist using this grasp. Blocks can be adapted with magnets or Velcro for use on an inclined surface.

RADIAL DIGITAL GRASP: use smaller square, cylindrical, or mushroom-shaped pegs or blocks that encourage thumb opposition to index and middle fingers. Object is not held against the palm. Gradually decrease size of object until the student can manage 1/2" cubes well, using the finger pads.

PINCER GRASP: Start with small cubes (such as Unifix cubes) and progress to smaller items such as dried beans or sunflower seeds.

FINE PINCER GRASP: Use small bread bag closure tabs, toothpicks, pennies, or other thin small objects to encourage precise fingertip to fingertip grasp.

FACILITATING OBJECT RELEASE SKILLS: Adapt objects with magnets or Velcro, or use pegboards or other slotted boards. The student can also be encouraged to release the object by scraping it against the edge of a large, stabilized container. Occasionally, a student may need to release the object directly into the teacher's hand, so the teacher can assist with the release.

Designing Therapeutic Motor Activities to Help Meet Math Goals:
A Case Example

Math activities can be designed to reinforce therapeutic motor goals while enabling the student to perform math activities more easily. One former middle school student who has severe quadriplegia performed all of his math work on a computer. However, he was unable to regroup numbers on the computer to perform math equations (as math software tools such as Access to Math and MathPad had not yet been invented). His teacher consulted with the student's occupational therapist (the author), who had her own agenda as well: the student was getting progressively tighter and needed more frequent opportunities to perform active range of motion with emphasis on shoulder flexion, elbow extension, wrist extension, and thumb opposition.

The following solution simultaneously met the student's math and motor goals to the satisfaction of the teacher, therapist, and student. The teacher used chalk to draw a few math problems in the standard, vertical format onto a magnetic chalkboard easel (formerly available from Childcraft). Problems were chosen that required regrouping of numbers, such as 47 + 38. The student used 1 1/2" square magnetic wooden number blocks to "write" his answer, and also used blocks to "carry over" numbers from one column to another. This activity greatly assisted the student in learning the concept of regrouping while requiring all of the movements listed above that needed to be reinforced.

Although the magnetic chalkboard easel appears to be currently unavailable, Childcraft now offers a Magnetic Wipe-Off Board that can be mounted to a wall to serve the same purpose. Please see Quick Tip #6 for specific information on how to make the number blocks that go along with this adaptive solution. Using this same adaptive set-up without numbers printed on the blocks can reinforce simpler math concepts such as 1:1 correspondence skills, basic counting skills, and basic addition and subtraction, while simultaneously addressing motor goals.

Other Assistive Devices for Math

Students who have difficulty using manipulatives can also greatly benefit from using computer software programs designed to teach basic math skills. Many examples are presented in Quick Tips #1 and #6. There are also on-screen calculators for those who cannot operate a standard or adapted calculator (see Quick Tip #7). Please refer to the chapter on Computer adaptations for suggestions on how to set up computer activities for those who have motor, perceptual, or cognitive impairments.

Using Functional Tasks to Reinforce Math Skills

As with reading, there are innumerable opportunities to reinforce math skills during the every day activities of life. Purchasing items in a store, restaurant, or school cafeteria, playing board games that use dice, or dividing up a plate of cookies at the lunch table are just a few examples. A school job center is an excellent arena for applying math skills, such as when packaging groups of 10 items, counting up total amounts, etc. At Cotting School, many additional fun situations are set up during the course of the school year which help to reinforce concepts learned in regular math classes. Following are a few examples.

"Jeans Day": On this day, which occurs several times per year, staff are allowed to wear jeans, sneakers, and sweatshirts, at a cost of 50 cents per item. High school students are responsible for collecting money from the staff and must figure out for themselves how much each particular staff member owes. The money collected goes toward the senior class trip.

School Auction: Before the auction begins, students are each provided with 50 tickets, which are given in strips of 10. The students use the tickets to bid on slightly used items donated by staff members, such as games, books, toys, and tape cassettes. Through this activity, the students learn the concept of monetary value, i.e. that they can buy a couple of big items or many small items with the same number of tickets. They also are responsible for counting out their tickets, and if they give 2 strips of 10 tickets for a 16 ticket item, they must verbalize how much "change" they expect.

The Cotting School Store and the Cotting Bagel Shop: These enterprises are organized and staffed by students, and provide real-life situations to reinforce money management skills. Real items are sold, and real money is handled.

Following are some additional tips to help students overcome many of the stumbling blocks that interfere with math achievement.

⏻ QUICK TIPS *Problems and Possible Solutions*

Following are some solutions which have successfully solved the identified problem for one or more students. Keep in mind that each student has a unique set of abilities and needs and may therefore require an original solution for the problem at hand. If a suggested solution is appropriate for a student, please adapt the design as necessary to best meet his or her needs.

Remember: fit the device to the student, not the student to the device!

1. Student is having difficulty learning basic counting skills.

⏻ Provide manipulatives to assist in learning counting skills. Some guidelines for choosing appropriate manipulatives are presented earlier in this chapter. Some favorite manipulatives of the primary level teachers at Cotting School include: plastic bread bag closure tabs, plastic milk container lids, Unifix cubes and abacuses. Funtastic Therapy sells a "Beginning Math with Unifix Kit" designed for students at a very beginning level of math.

⏻ Students who have difficulty using manipulatives as an aid for learning beginning math skills can use software programs that are designed to teach these skills. Some examples follow.
☞ IntelliTools offers overlays for the first four programs listed so they can also be used in conjunction with IntelliKeys.

> *Millie's Math House* (Edmark): Macintosh or Windows.
>
> *Exploring Patterns* (IntelliTools, Inc.):
> > Macintosh: Intellikeys recommended but not required.
>
> *Monkeys Jumping on the Bed* (SoftTouch/kidTECH Software): Macintosh or Windows.
>
> *Five Green and Speckled Frogs* (SoftTouch/kidTECH Software): Macintosh.
>
> *Eensy and Friends* (Don Johnston, Inc.): Macintosh or Windows.
>
> *Blocks in Motion* (Don Johnston, Inc.): Macintosh.

2. Student has difficulty learning 1:1 correspondence skills.

⏻ Provide simple craft projects that reinforce 1:1 correspondence skills. A few examples include copying simple bead designs, copying simple Maxi Perler bead designs, and copying simple ceramic tile designs. Cover all but the row the student is working on to avoid confusion.

3. Student is having great difficulty understanding the concepts of more and less, even when manipulatives are used.

⏻ Are the manipulatives being stacked horizontally? If so, try stacking them vertically. This has miraculously solved the problem for more than one student.

(Lucy Kulis, M.S. Ed., Remedial Specialist, Cotting School)

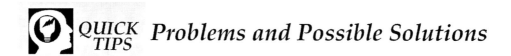

4. Student has difficulty with simple addition, subtraction, multiplication, or division.

The Number Line continues to be very popular and effective aid for this purpose. This is a long, horizontal strip of paper or masking tape with numbers written on it in sequential order, taped to a student's desk. The number line begins with the number 1 and ends with a number that is appropriate to the student's present level of skill. The numbers can be separated by vertical lines or alternately shaded, so they do not appear to run together. The student uses his or her finger to count along the line to add numbers or subtract numbers, or is taught to "skip count" along the line to perform multiplication. For example, when doing 4 + 5, the student places a finger on 4 and then counts out 5 more numbers, proceeding to the right, which lands the finger on 9, which is the answer. When doing 3 x 3, the student counts out 1, 2, **3**, 4, 5, **6**, 7, 8, **9**.

Standard number lines are also commercially available through teacher supply stores at local shopping centers. MathLine, by Howbrite Solutions (available through Don Johnston Inc.) is a combination number line and abacus. There are three different models available, any of which can be mounted on a desk top or blackboard.

5. Student has difficulty aligning math columns due to poor writing skills, resulting in calculation errors.

Have the student print math problems on a regular sheet of lined writing paper turned sideways, using the lines as guides to align the ones, tens, and hundreds columns.

6. Student is unable to write numbers and needs an alternative method for performing math work.

Use one of the math software programs on the market. Two examples:

Access to Math (Don Johnston, Inc.). Apple IIe/IIc/IIc+/IIGS.
MathPad (Intellitools). Macintosh.

A major purpose of both software programs is to enable students to do their own math problems when holding a pencil is not easy or possible. Both of these programs offer addition, subtraction, multiplication, and division problems. Math problems are presented in the correct vertical format and they also show regrouping of numbers as if written by a pencil.

Use a magnetic chalkboard or magnetic dry-erase board (such as the Magnetic Wipe-Off Board by Childcraft) in combination with 1 1/2" magnetic wooden number blocks. Mount the board on a wall or easel. Draw one or more number problems on the board and have the student place the magnetic number blocks in the correct locations on the board to answer the problems. To make the number blocks, buy a 2" x 2" piece of wood and saw it into 1 1/2" long pieces. Sand the blocks, and use a glue gun to glue heavy duty round magnets on the bottom of them (available through Childcraft, educational stores and craft supply stores). Number each block using black permanent marker or large number stickers.

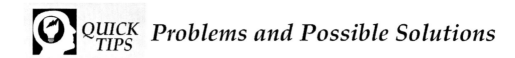 *Problems and Possible Solutions*

7. Student is unable to use a standard calculator due to motor impairments.

Use a calculator with enlarged keys.

Place a keyguard over the calculator. To make one, use the same method as described for making a computer keyguard (page 119).

Students who have involuntary movements (such as athetosis or severe tremoring) have successfully used a calculator with enlarged keys in combination with an angled calculator stand with attached angled wrist rest. This is identical to the Angled Keyboard Stand with Attached Wrist Rest, except the dimensions and angles of the stand and wrist rest sometimes need to be altered to accommodate the size of the calculator. Complete directions for the Keyboard Stand are presented on page 122.

Use an onscreen calculator, such as Big:Calc (Don Johnston, Inc.). Point the mouse to the desired keys and click, or, if necessary, access Big:Calc using an alternate access method such as a TouchWindow, Macintosh Switch Interface with switch, or Ke:nx with desired device.

8. Student lacks motivation for learning mathematics due to history of frustration and failure.

Provide the student with motivating games that reinforce math skills.
Some examples are:

Number Sense Dice (available through Therapro)

Math Bingo: Instead of calling out a number, call out a math problem.
If the answer is on the card, put a bingo chip on it.

Board games that use dice, and other types of dice games.

Card games such as black jack or war.

9. Student has difficulty stabilizing math tools such as a ruler or protractor using the non-dominant hand.

Add Dycem to the bottom of a ruler, protractor, or similar math tools using double-sided scotch tape.

Attach magnetic tape to the bottom of the ruler, protractor, or similar math tool and use in conjunction with the Magnetic Notebook or flat magnetic surface (both described on page ***).

☞ If the student can learn to use the non-dominant hand to stabilize a ruler, only apply as much Dycem or magnetic tape as necessary to ensure success. Remove when no longer needed.

INSTRUCTIONS
FOR FABRICATING
SELECTED DEVICES

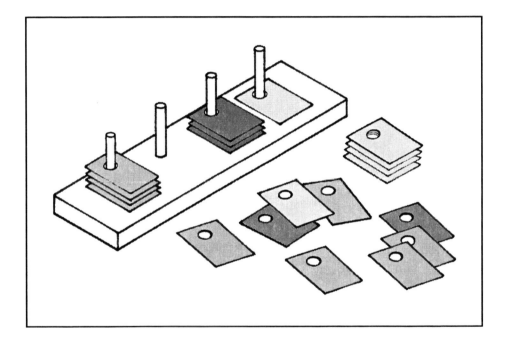

MATH PEGBOARD
FOR
NUMBER REGROUPING

MATH PEGBOARD FOR NUMBER REGROUPING

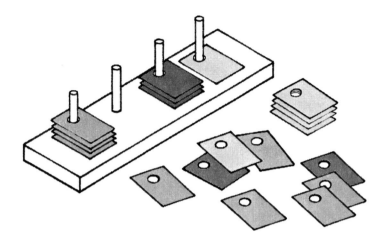

DESCRIPTION: A simple wooden pegboard consisting of three or four 3" high pegs aligned in one horizontal row. Each peg represents a number column, i.e. "ones", "tens", "hundreds" and perhaps "thousands". Cardboard counters (color-coded according to the numbers column in which they belong) are placed over the pegs. The student performs simple math problems that involve borrowing or carrying numbers using this device.

PURPOSE:
To help students to better understand the concept of regrouping numbers.

MATERIALS:
1. Rectangular piece of wood, 15" long x 4 1/2" wide x 3/4" thick
2. One 1/4" diameter wooden dowel
3. Four sheets of stiff posterboard, each a different color
4. Woodworker's glue

TOOLS:
Jigsaw or other appropriate wood saw
Hacksaw
Electric drill
Sandpaper, pencil and ruler
Wooden mallet or hammer
Heavy-duty scissors

ASSEMBLY:

1. Use the jigsaw to cut out the wooden base and sand all edges.

2. To make and attach the wooden pegs:
    a. Use a hacksaw to cut the dowel into 3 1/2" long pieces. Sand the rough edges.
    b. With a pencil and ruler, mark spots on the wooden base for the three or four pegs so they are approximately 3" apart in one horizontal row.
    c. Using a 1/4" diameter drill bit, drill a hole halfway through the base at each marked spot.
    d. Fill the holes halfway with woodworker's glue and hammer the dowel pieces into the holes.

3. To make the rectangular counters:
    a. On each sheet of posterboard, use the pencil and ruler to measure out at least ten rectangles 3" x 2 1/2".
    b. Cut out the rectangles using heavy-duty scissors. You may wish to make extra counters, in case any get bent or lost.
    c. Drill a hole in each rectangle, centered approximately 3/4" from one short edge, using a 3/8" drill bit.

4. Place the counters on the pegs, making sure each peg contains ten counters of a single color.

This version was designed by
Lucy Kulis, M.S. Ed., Remedial Specialist, Cotting School.

Chapter 14
Arts & Crafts

ASSISTIVE DEVICES FOR ARTS AND CRAFTS ACTIVITIES

Arts and crafts can offer an important outlet for creative self-expression for all students. Students who have an impaired ability (or are unable) to express their ideas in words can find it a freeing experience to use different art media to creatively express themselves. Exploring the various art and craft modalities provides opportunities for students to discover interests and talents which can develop into enjoyable hobbies. These hobbies can help promote a positive self-identity as well as provide purposeful, meaningful activity to fill leisure hours. Even a one-time experience with a particular art or craft activity can be very gratifying and provide students with insights into their own personalities.

Arts and crafts are also among the oldest treatment modalities used by occupational therapists, who carefully choose and set up the craft activities to help individuals meet therapeutic goals including improved strength, coordination, perceptual skills, motor planning ability, and psychosocial skills. Cognitive skills such as problem solving, sequential thinking, creative thinking, decision making, and learning about cause and effect are also strengthened through participation in art and craft activities.

Art class can provide an excellent arena for reinforcing information learned in the regular classroom setting. For example, students might be asked to make three-dimensional models of the solar system or the human body at the same time that these subjects are studied in class, allowing students to apply knowledge learned regarding sizes, proportions, forms, colors, distances, etc. This provides a truly multisensory learning experience. Learning situations can often be set up so the information is actually "discovered" by experimentation rather than "taught". For example, mixing paints will demonstrate the fact that combining blue and yellow produces green. These methods of learning greatly increase the chances that the information will be retained.

There are different teaching models that can be used to instruct a class of students who have special needs, when the focus is on the manipulation of materials, such as Art Class or a crafts group.

The Traditional Approach to Art Class

In the traditional approach used in most public schools, all of the students receive a demonstration showing how to produce a particular project and are then all expected to engage in that same art activity. Each student is also expected to complete their own project from beginning to end.

ADVANTAGES:

1. It is the most efficient teaching model for a group of students who have similar needs and abilities. When the group is homogeneous, the teacher can more easily choose a single project that matches the learning needs of all of the students, and only has to present the instructions once to the whole group.

2. The student gains a more complete understanding of the project when performing all steps from beginning to end.

DISADVANTAGES:

1. When this approach is used with a group of students who have widely divergent strengths and weaknesses, there is a risk that the project chosen is a poor match for some individuals.

2. If a poor student/activity match results in the need for intensive 1:1 assistance from an adult, the student may not feel as much ownership or sense of investment in the project.

STRATEGIES TO HELP OFFSET THESE DISADVANTAGES:

1. Allow the student to make all of the choices, even if another person needs to perform much of the manual work.

2. Employ the concept of cooperative learning by pairing students together who have complementary strengths and weaknesses. The two students can then assist each other in the completion of their projects.

3. Allow the student to use a different type of media to learn the same lesson, such as having a student draw a portrait using a computer while the rest of the class forms their portraits using clay. This allows the student to have an equivalent "hands on" experience while learning the same lessons regarding body proportions, body symmetry, etc.

The Production Line Approach

One alternative to the traditional approach is the production line approach, which is used very successfully in many vocational programs. In the production line approach, no one is expected to complete all steps of a project from beginning to end, but instead, individuals perform steps which are most suited to their abilities and interests. For example, one student can trace with a stencil, another can cut it out, and another can sew, glue, or whatever. In the school setting, the production line approach tends to be used more frequently for larger group (versus individual) projects, such as murals, making life-size statues out of boxes for the school lobby, etc.

ADVANTAGES:

1. Because tasks are chosen according to each individual's strengths, the student leaves the session feeling proud of what he or she can do, instead of feeling reminded about all of the things he or she can't do.

2. Students can participate in more complex (and often more prestigious) projects than they could complete on their own.

3. Peer interaction is increased since the students rely on each other to get the project completed, rather than on the staff. This can produce a sense of "team spirit" among the students.

DISADVANTAGES:

1. The student will be unable to claim full ownership of a finished product.

2. The student may not learn how to complete a whole project, in order to be able to perform the activity in the future.

The Activity Center Approach

Another approach that can be effectively used in an art or craft class is the use of activity centers. This is similar to the approach used in preschools and elementary classrooms, in which students have an opportunity to choose which center they want to work in at a particular time, such as the art center, science center, etc. To incorporate this concept in an art room, the teacher sets up a different art activity at each table, and allows the student to choose which activity to engage in. For example, one table might have modeling clay on it, another might have a collage or macrame project, and there may also be a computer art center in the room.

ADVANTAGES:

1. Theoretically, students will tend to choose activities that best match their needs, abilities, and interests.

2. The teacher no longer has to provide a single project that all students can participate in, allowing more intricate projects to be given to students who can benefit from them.

3. Students have more opportunities to develop their personal interests into real talents and hobbies, since the student has permission to repeat the same type of activity, session after session.

DISADVANTAGES:

1. This approach usually requires additional staff support as well as more time and effort on the part of the teacher to prepare activities and set up work stations.

2. If the student tends to choose the same station every session, he or she will forfeit the opportunity to experience other art and craft modalities.

It is important to consider the merits of each of the above approaches in relation to particular art projects and the needs of particular students. A combination of approaches may provide the most benefit to a classroom of students who have differing needs and abilities.

Devices that Promote Independence in Art Class

Many adaptive devices presented in earlier chapters can help to increase a student's level of independence during art class, especially those presented in the chapters on Positioning (which includes information on work surfaces), Pointers and Mouthsticks, and Assistive Devices for Writing Tasks. Many other suggestions are presented below.

A special thank you to Rosanne Trolan, B.F.A., Cotting School Art Teacher, who took the time to share some of her observations with the author, several of which have been incorporated into this chapter.

Following are some solutions which have successfully solved the identified problem for one or more students. Keep in mind that each student has a unique set of abilities and needs and may therefore require an original solution for the problem at hand. If a suggested solution is appropriate for a student, please adapt the design as necessary to best meet his or her needs.

Remember: fit the device to the student, not the student to the device!

1. Student has poor hand grasp and needs a cylindrical adapted handle for a paintbrush, marker, or other drawing implement to facilitate use of a radial-palmar grasp. (The cylindrical handle is held horizontally against the palm and protrudes through the web space with fingers on far side of the handle pressing it against opposed thumb and radial side of palm.)

Cut a hole all the way through a bicycle handle grip, approximately 1" from the thumb side of the grip, just big enough to stick the marker or other drawing implement through it.
(Paulette E. Binder, Home Economics Teacher, Cotting School)

Use the Spring Grip Cylindrical Handle for Pointers & Drawing Implements (page 136), replacing the pointer with a marker, pencil, or paintbrush.

For large markers that do not fit inside the spring-operated door latch that is used to make the above device, simply soften and roll a 3/4" wide by 6" long strip of thermoplastic material into a "snake" shape, form the center of the strip snugly around the marker and self-bond the extensions of the strip to the inside of the hollow cylindrical handle. Be sure to follow manufacturer's instructions for the particular thermoplastic material used.

2. Student has poor hand grasp and needs a spherical (ball-shaped) adapted handle for a paintbrush, marker, or other drawing implement to facilitate use of a spherical grasp. (Spherical handle is held against palm of hand with thumb and fingers abducted around the object.)

Work a hole all the way through a rubber racquetball (or other small, solid rubber ball),and stick a marker or paintbrush through it.
(Incorporates ideas by Amy A. Houghton, OTR/L, Occupational Therapy Team Leader, and Paulette E. Binder, Home Economics Teacher, both at Cotting School)

Make a custom grip: Take a long narrow strip of self-bonding low temperature thermoplastic material, melt it until it is very soft, following manufacturer's instructions, and wrap it around itself until it forms a spherical ball of the desired diameter. Mold this ball to the student's palm. Take another piece of thermoplastic material (perhaps 3" long by 1/2" wide) and roll it into a "snake" shape. Form the center of the strip around a pencil, and self-bond the extensions to the ball of material. Usually, the loop should be extended out from the ball far enough to protrude between the index and middle fingers, although it can be designed to protrude through other fingers instead. This extension should be very thin for comfort between the fingers. Make sure the material is pliable enough when forming the ball so the edges can be smoothed out well.
(Staff and therapists at the United Cerebral Palsy Association, Watertown, Ma.)

3. Student has poor directional control of a drawing implement and produces only scribbles.

☻ Provide the student with art activities that utilize scribbling movements yet produce an attractive product. Examples are:
- copper tooling projects
- making rubbings using metalsmith molds with paper and crayons
- other types of rubbings (e.g. leaves, stone plaques)
- scribbling on Multicolored Scratch Art Paper
  (available through art suppliers including S & S and Triarco Arts and Crafts Inc.)
- Rub-On Transfers (available through art suppliers including S & S)

☻ Provide the student with drawing aids such as stencils, rulers, protractors, or any of the more specialized drawing aids found at art or drafting supply stores.

☻ If the student has difficulty stabilizing stencils, etc., you can place magnetic tape on the bottom of them and use with the Magnetic Notebook (page 190).

☻ Have student create forms out of Wikki Stix or use colored glue to make raised outlines, and then color inside the created shape. The Wikki Stix form or glue line acts as a stencil to prevent the crayon or colored pencil from going outside the line. Wikki Stix are available at Therapro as well as toy and art supply stores.

☻ Although coloring books are presently considered to have no merit in the art room because they do not allow for creative self-expression, they can be a useful adaptive aid for students who are learning to start and stop their lines in specific spots and draw their coloring strokes in the same direction. Coloring books also help some students slow down, which improves their motor planning.

(Rosanne Trolan, B.F.A, Art Teacher, Cotting School)

☻ To help improve directional control of movements, provide art activities that increase awareness of joint and muscle movements, such as drawing on a wall-mounted chalkboard or using a wooden stick to draw in a tray of flattened modeling clay.

4. Student has no functional hand use and is unable to pick up and position materials for collages and other art projects that involve manipulatives.

☻ If the student is able to use a pointer, such as a headpointer, hand-held pointer, mouthstick, thighpointer, or footpointer, place glue tack on the tip of the pointer. This will enable the student to independently choose, pick up, and position materials as desired. Another person will need to hold the object in place so it can be released from the headpointer.

(Staff and therapists at the United Cerebral Palsy Association, Watertown, Ma.)

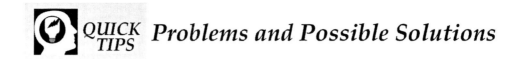

5. Student has difficulty performing scissor tasks because student pushes the fingers too far through the finger holes of the scissors.

🖐 Try wrapping Coban or other tape around the finger loops to narrow the holes.

🖐 For a younger student, try the Children's Scissors developed by Mary Benbow, MS, OTR/L, which have narrower finger holes than typical children's scissors. These are available from Therapro.

6. Student has difficulty performing scissor tasks because student does not keep the ring and little fingers bent into the palm when cutting with scissors but instead moves all fingers as one unit.

🖐 Have the student hold a small koosh ball, piece of sponge or foam, or other small object in the palm using the ring and little fingers during cutting tasks. This is recommended by many therapists.

7. Student has difficulty performing scissor tasks because student does not have sufficient finger isolation to use regular scissors.

🖐 Try loop scissors. These are available at teacher supply stores and from adaptive equipment or art supply companies such as Therapro, Sammons Preston, Childcraft, NASCO Arts & Crafts, and Sax Arts & Crafts.

🖐 Try hand held battery operated scissors. These are available from S & S and can also sometimes be found at discount stores such as Buck a Book.
Caution: These can be noisy and may be noxious to those who are hypersensitive to sounds.
(*Cathy Mayo, M.Ed., Primary School Teacher, Cotting School*)

8. Student is unable to control the size of the cut and instead makes each cut the length of the scissor blades, resulting in cuts that go through the lines when attempting curves or sharp turns.

🖐 Provide scissors with very short blades, such as the Children's Scissors, developed by Mary Benbow, MS, OTR/L. Or try Squizzers, which are child-size loop scissors. Both types of scissors are available through Therapro.

🖐 Bind the scissor blades with a rubber band so they cannot open up as wide. To do this, twist the rubber band several times around the scissor blade junction where the scissors screw is located.

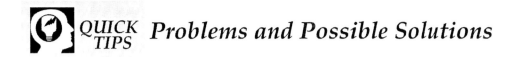

9. Student has difficulty performing scissor tasks because student can not grasp or squeeze loop scissors or battery operated scissors.

Stabilize loop scissors on a wooden base. For basic loop scissors that do not have finger holes, simply screw the scissors onto a flat piece of wood. Or, to angle the scissor tips slightly upward, use a chisel or router bit to carve an angled gully in the wooden base and screw the scissors into the gully. To stabilize household loop scissors (with finger holes) or to stabilize Table Top Spring Scissors (available through Sammons Preston), see separate directions included later in this chapter.

It is quick and easy to make a polyethylene foam base to stabilize battery operated scissors: take a 2" thick block of polyethylene (hard) foam, and use an electric carving knife (or steak knife) to carve out a gully just big enough for the scissors to squeeze into it snugly. Wrap 2" wide colored electrician's tape around the whole thing to make it look nice.
(Beth Jackson, M.S., OTR/L, and the author, both Occupational Therapists at Cotting School.)

10. Student has difficulty using the non-dominant hand to hold and turn the paper while cutting with scissors.

For some students who have difficulty with both finger isolation and bilateral motor coordination, allowing the student to use loop scissors eliminates the extra effort involved in using regular scissors and may allow the student to better focus on learning how to turn the paper correctly while cutting. Once paper holding and turning is mastered, the student can practice this skill using the regular scissors again.

Some students can learn to stabilize the paper on the desk using their non-dominant forearm while cutting with scissors. The Magnetic Notebook with Ruler can also be used to stabilize the paper during cutting tasks. See separate description of this device in the chapter on Assistive Devices for Writing Tasks.

The Crestalk Mount from Crestwood Company, which includes a flexible gooseneck arm with large clip at the top and a clamp to mount it onto a wheelchair or table, has been found to work very well for one student to stabilize the paper while he cuts with scissors.
(Cathy Mayo, M.Ed., Primary School Teacher, Cotting School)

Student may benefit from using an electrician's tool called "Helping Hands", available at electronic stores such as Radio Shack. The paper is clipped onto the "Helping Hands" tool which has a ball-bearing joint, enabling the student to easily turn the paper to the desired angle.
(Recommended by Schneck and Battaglia [1])

11. Student has involuntary movements due to athetosis or ataxia which affect object placement and release. This makes it difficult to place objects precisely when completing craft projects such as ceramic tile trivets or maxi perler bead designs.

💡 Cut off two adjoining sides from a lidless shoe box (or other box) and tape the box to the table with one open side facing the student and the other open side on the same side as the student's dominant hand. Place the project against the two remaining sides.

💡 Left-handed students who have involuntary movements or tremors often need to proceed right to left, instead of left to right, with certain craft projects in order to prevent displacement of already placed tiles, pegs, or other materials as they continue to add to their project.

12. Student has difficulty using glue due to impaired fine motor coordination.

💡 A glue stick can be secured in the Spring Grip Cylindrical Handle for Pointers & Drawing Implements if this device is made using an autoclamp as described in Modification 2 (see page 136). Also see Solution 3 of Quick Tip #1.

💡 Glue pens are thicker around and longer than glue sticks and can be more easily grasped using a palmar supinate grasp.

💡 White glue or similar liquid glue can be applied using a paintbrush or foam brush (in an adapted holder).

💡 A glue stick or paintbrush (for applying liquid glue) can be taped to the end of a headpointer, mouthstick, or other type of pointer.

💡 Eliminate the need for glue when making collages by using Prestax (brand) photo mount board, available from Sax Arts and Crafts. Remove the tacking paper from the back and have the student place the collage materials directly on the photo mount. A box filled with small cut-up paper pieces of various colors, shapes, and textures works wonderfully with this mount board.

(Rosanne Trolan, B.F.A., Art Teacher, Cotting School)

13. Student has impaired fine motor coordination and cannot keep the center strings taut when tightening knots of a macrame project.

💡 If the student has sufficient postural control, have him or her sit on a mobile stool while working on the macrame project. Tie the center strings to the base of the stool. When it is time to pull each knot tight, the student moves the stool away from the project while pulling the knot up, which keeps the center strings taut.

14. Student has no functional use of his or her hands and would like to participate in a clay project.

Clay tools can be taped to any type of pointer, such as a headpointer, mouthstick, hand-held pointer, foot-attached pointer, or thigh-pointer. If student lacks sufficient strength to actually carve the clay with the pointer, have him or her draw lines in the clay where he or she would like it cut away.

(Rosanne Trolan, B.F.A., Art Teacher, Cotting School)

15. Student is visually impaired and has difficulty seeing his or her finished product when drawing.

Use Hi Marks 3-D fluorescent marker made by Kentucky Industries for the Blind, and available from Therapro. This needs to be used with adult supervision, but when the product is dry, the student can feel their raised line drawings.

(Karen Conrad, ScD, OTR/L, Occupational Therapist, Founder and President, Therapro, Inc.)

Colored glue can also be used to make raised line drawings.

Have the student make forms using Wikki Stix and press on to the paper, so the student can feel the finished artwork. Student can also color inside the Wikki Stix forms.

16. Student has expressed an interest in doing needlepoint but has use of only one hand or has motor limitations in both upper extremities.

A very effective needlepoint project holder consists of two pieces of hard wire. The ends of one wire are soldered or welded together to form a circular base which allows a student to easily turn the project around on the wheelchair tray. The other wire is formed to look like three sides of a square. The ends of the wire are soldered perpendicularly to the base. The needlepoint project is attached to the device using clips. The needlepoint holder effectively stabilizes a needlepoint project at a good angle to allow those who have use of only one hand to enjoy this hobby. It has worked successfully even for some students who have severe motor impairments in both upper extremities.

(Thomas Capps, a welder and parent of a Cotting School Graduate)

17. Student is tactually defensive and avoids touching messy media in the art room.

When presenting messy media to the class, such as homemade play dough, putty, etc., be sure to offer a few varieties that have different consistencies, textures, and even temperatures, to offer students a choice. Never force a student to participate. There will often be at least one texture the student will try. In many cases, a student will tolerate the less sticky substances first (such as a bucket of dry kidney beans), and will gradually progress to the more sticky substances (such as play-do). Putty and dough recipes are provided in many craft books - check your local library

☞ This problem can often be effectively remediated by an occupational therapist trained in sensory integration theory and techniques.

(Rosanne Trolan, B.F.A., Art Teacher, Cotting School)

INSTRUCTIONS
FOR FABRICATING
SELECTED DEVICES

FOOT-ATTACHED
PAINTBRUSH/MARKER HOLDER

MOUTHSTICK MARKER HOLDER

STABILIZED TABLETOP SPRING SCISSORS

STABILIZED REGULAR OR
LOOP HOUSEHOLD SCISSORS

FOOT-ATTACHED PAINTBRUSH/MARKER HOLDER

DESCRIPTION:
An easily adjusted foot pointer, made with a threaded metal dowel attached to a thermoplastic "foot cuff". A paintbrush, marker, or other tool can be attached to the end of the pointer using masking tape. The metal dowel can be easily bent to position the drawing implement as desired.

PURPOSE:
To enable a student with no functional use of the arms and no potential to use a headpointer, mouthstick, or thigh pointer to participate in drawing and painting activities. Other approaches should be ruled out before choosing this device, since using a foot attached holder makes it very difficult for the student to see the project being created. Using a single mirror is often confusing because it reverses the image. A double-mirror system was successful with one student, and consists of one mirror reflecting the image of the foot/artwork which is reflected in another mirror, so the image is no longer reversed.

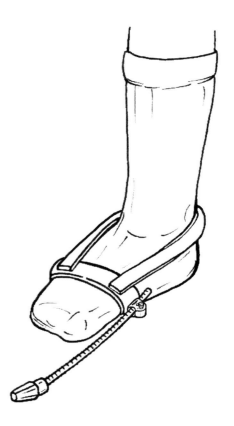

MATERIALS:
1. 6" x 12" sheet of low temperature thermoplastic material
2. 3/8" threaded metal dowel of desired length
3. Small autoclamp - one that can tighten securely around the 3/8" metal dowel
4. 1" wide non-adhesive Velcro loop tape - 12" long
5. 1" wide pressure-sensitive Velcro hook tape - 3" long, cut in half

☞ Some types of low temperature thermoplastic materials require special solvent or light abrasion before bonding can occur. Please follow manufacturer's directions.

TOOLS:
Splinting pan or electric frying pan and water
Sharp heavy-duty scissors
Measuring tape

ASSEMBLY:

1. Using the measuring tape, measure the circumference of the widest part of the student's foot and add a couple of inches. This should be the length of the thermoplastic strip. Also measure how wide the strip should be in order to fit comfortably against the foot.

2. Soften the thermoplastic material using the splinting pan and water, according to the manufacturer's directions, and cut to the desired size.

3. Allow the material to cool until comfortable to the touch, and then form to the widest part of the student's foot. Overlap the ends and bond them together.

4. Attach the autoclamp to the "big toe" side of the thermoplastic base using a tiny strip of thermoplastic material to bond it to the base. To do this, reheat the medial side of the base and soften the tiny strip, then sandwich the autoclamp between the two and press the 2 pieces of thermoplastic material together.

5. Position the dowel in the autoclamp as shown in the picture and use a screwdriver or a dime to tighten the autoclamp around the threaded dowel. Bend the dowel as desired.

6. Cover the rough tip of the metal dowel in one of the following ways:

   • place a pencil eraser head or other soft tip over it

   • dip it in Plastisol, a plastic dip which can be found at an electrical or building supply store

   • wrap it with tape

7. Position the device on the student's foot, and stick a 1 1/2" strip of pressure-sensitive Velcro hook onto the right and left sides of the thermoplastic base. Position the Velcro loop strap around the student's heel and press it against the two Velcro hook strips on the thermoplastic base. Trim off the excess loop tape.

8. Tape a marker or paintbrush to the end of the metal dowel.

This device was originally designed by the author.

Modified by
Jeanette Harney, OTR/L, BCP, and Robin Levy, OTR/L,
Occupational Therapists, Cotting School.

The double-mirror system was developed by
Melissa Litton, OTR/L, Occupational Therapist, Cotting School.

MOUTHSTICK MARKER HOLDER

DESCRIPTION: A mouthstick designed to holder a marker, made entirely of low temperature thermoplastic material.

PURPOSE:
To enable an individual to draw pictures or write using only head movements. This mouthstick marker holder is used successfully with a vinyl-framed dry-erase memo board mounted to the student's wheelchair using a universal mount.

MATERIALS:
1. 6" x 6" piece of 1/8" thick low temperature thermoplastic material. Two smaller pieces of different colors can be used, if desired: one for the mouthpiece and one for the marker sleeve.

☞ Some types of low temperature thermoplastic materials require special solvent or light abrasion before bonding can occur. Please follow manufacturer's directions.

TOOLS:
Splinting pan or electric frying pan and water, heavy-duty scissors

MEASUREMENTS:
The total length of this mouthstick holder is approximately 4", including the mouthpiece and a 2" section into which the marker is inserted.

ASSEMBLY:
1. Trace the shape of a commercial Y-shaped mouthpiece (such as a Sammons Preston mouthstick) onto the thermoplastic material. Include an inch or so of the pointer shaft when tracing the mouthpiece, so the second piece has something to bond to. If a commercial mouthstick is not available for tracing, have the student bite down on a plain piece of paper and draw a mouthpiece around the impression. Soften the material in the splinting pan and water, following manufacturer's directions. Cut out the "Y" shape.

2. Trace a 3" x 3" rectangle onto the second color of thermoplastic material (if two colors are used). Soften the material in the splinting pan or electric frying pan and water, following manufacturer's instructions. Wrap it snugly around a thick marker, leaving enough material extending off the end to bond to the bottom stem of the Y mouthpiece. Carefully remove the marker from the holder, trim the material as necessary, and allow to harden.

3. Resoften the material that extends from the end of the marker and self-bond it to the bottom stem of the Y mouthpiece. Trim and mold the material so it forms a smooth bond.

Designed by
Barbara Steva, OTR/L, Director of Occupational Therapy and Therapeutic Recreation, Franciscan Children's Hospital, Brighton, Ma.

Dry-erase board set up by
Frances Maggiore, COTA/L, Occupational Therapy Assistant
Franciscan Children's Hospital, Brighton, Ma.

STABILIZED TABLE TOP SPRING SCISSORS

DESCRIPTION: Tabletop Spring Scissors mounted to a two-piece angled wooden base.

PURPOSE: To enable students who have severe motor limitations to participate in cutting tasks. See following item for some of the ways in which students have used stabilized spring loaded scissors.

MATERIALS:
1. Tabletop Spring Scissors (available from Sammons Preston)
2. 5" or 6" square piece of 1/2" thick wood to form the base
3. 3 1/2" x 2" piece of 1 1/4" thick wood to form the angled support
4. Two 3/4" long round head screws

TOOLS:
Band saw or other wood saw, glue gun and hot glue, electric drill, screwdriver, electric sander or sandpaper, pencil

ASSEMBLY:
1. Using a band saw or other appropriate saw, cut out a 5" or 6" square piece of wood. Sand all edges.

2. Use a saw to cut the desired angle (perhaps 45 degrees) in the 3 1/2" x 2" x 1 1/4" thick piece of wood (see diagram). If using the band saw, tilt the table of the saw to the desired angle, as shown on the gauge under the table. Sand all rough edges.

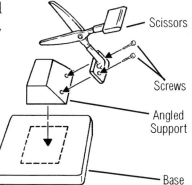

3. Using a drill bit equal in diameter to the screw shank, drill two holes all the way through the bottom scissors handle, approximately 1/2" in from each side edge.

4. Center the scissors on the angled portion of the wood as shown in the illustration, and use a pencil to mark the spots where the drilled holes contact the wood. Using a drill bit equal in diameter to the screw root, drill a pilot hole through each mark. If hard wood is used, drill the pilot hole to the same depth that the screw will enter the wood. If soft wood is used, drill the pilot hole to half the depth.

5. Using a screwdriver, screw the scissors to the angled support.

6. Position the scissors/angled support as desired on the wooden base and mark the location with a pencil. Use a glue gun and hot glue to attach the angled support to the base. Clamp until dry.

☞ If desired, the angled support can be screwed into the base instead of or in addition to being glued.

This device was designed and built by
Staff and therapists at the United Cerebral Palsy Association, Watertown, Ma.

STABILIZED REGULAR OR LOOP HOUSEHOLD SCISSORS

DESCRIPTION: Household loop scissors (that include finger holes in addition to the loop handle) or regular household scissors mounted onto a wooden base.

PURPOSE:
To enable students who have severe motor limitations to participate in cutting tasks. Following are some of the ways in which stabilized loop scissors have been used:
- the student presses the scissors with the dominant hand while an adult turns the paper.
- the student presses the scissors with a mouth stick and uses their functional hand to turn the paper.
- the student presses the scissors with their poorly coordinated hand and uses their coordinated hand to turn the paper.

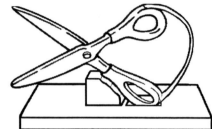

For those students who find it easier to pull a regular scissors handle rather than press down on spring loaded (loop) scissors, regular household scissors may be substituted for the household loop scissors.

If the cutting task does not involve intricate curves and twists, consider using stabilized battery-operated scissors (see Quick Tip #9). Cordless electric scissors perform cutting tasks more quickly and with less effort than the loop scissors, but are not practical for cutting intricate shapes due to their fast speed. Cordless battery-operated scissors can also be noisy, which may be distracting or irritating to those in the surrounding vicinity. Consider the student's particular needs and goals (as well as the needs of surrounding classmates) before choosing this option.

MATERIALS:
1. 11" long x 4 1/2" wide x 3/4" thick piece of wood for the base
2. 3" square by 1/2" thick piece of wood for the angled support
3. Household loop scissors or regular household scissors

☞ If the student finds it easier to pull rather than push a scissors handle, substitute a regular pair of kitchen scissors for the household loop scissors and follow remaining directions as written.

TOOLS:
Band saw or table saw to cut out rectangular base
Jigsaw or coping saw to cut out angled support
Drill and router bit or wood chisel to indent wooden base
Glue gun and hot glue
Pencil
Sandpaper
Wood clamp

ASSEMBLY:

1. Cut out a 11" long x 4 1/2" wide rectangular base from the 3/4" thick piece of wood. Sand all edges.

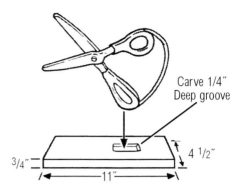

2. Position the scissors on top of the base with the scissor tips angled slightly upward and use a pencil to trace the contact area between the bottom finger loop and the base. Use a router bit or wood chisel to carve out the interior of the tracing to form a 1/4" deep groove. Sand the carved out area.

3. Make the angled support:

   a. With the scissors positioned at the desired angle on the base (and the bottom finger loop nestled in the 1/4" deep groove), place the 3" square by 1/2" thick piece of wood vertically against the scissors (see diagram).

   b. Trace the underside of the bottom scissors handle beginning approximately 1/4" from the junction screw of the scissor blades and ending where the scissors meets the top surface of the wooden base.

   c. Draw a line from the highest point of the tracing (near the junction of the scissor blades) straight down to the bottom of the piece of wood where it meets the base.

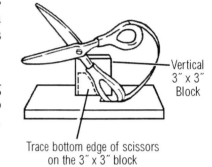

   d. Use a jigsaw or coping saw to cut along the lines.

   e. Sand the edges of the angled support.

4. Use hot glue to attach the angled support to the wooden base. Clamp until dry.

5. Position the scissors on the scissor stand and apply hot glue to secure the bottom finger loop into the groove in the base.

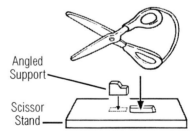

Optional: If desired, the angled support can be screwed into the base instead of or in addition to being glued.

☞ See Quick Tip #9 for directions on how to stabilize regular loop scissors.

Designed by
Amy Houghton, OTR/L, Occupational Therapy Team Leader,
Cotting School and Val Greene, B.S.Ed., Industrial Arts Teacher, Cotting School.

Chapter 15
Music

ASSISTIVE DEVICES FOR MUSIC CLASS

Welcome! You're just in time for the school-wide musical performance, directed by Noreen Murphy, Cotting School Music Teacher. The performers consist of forty or so actors, singers, and musicians who have a wide variety of special needs. The musicians are playing recorders, organs, handbells and a variety of other percussion instruments, and there is even an autoharpist and a guitar player or two. Some of the students have no functional use of their hands, others have extremely poor attention spans and low cognitive skills, and a large percentage have a poor sense of timing and rhythm. Everyone has their fingers crossed - the staff and parents in the audience, the students on stage, perhaps even Noreen Murphy.

The music begins, and lo and behold, most of the players are playing the correct notes, and are playing them on cue. It is not without error, but the song is recognizable and the instruments are being played in a reasonable synchrony with each other. No one is quite sure how Murphy accomplished this, but everyone relaxes into their seats and all greatly enjoy the show.

Conducting By Colors

Like a good magician, Murphy makes sure the audience is focused on the performers and not on the tricks up her sleeve. One trick that often goes unnoticed is her adapted system for conducting an orchestra. As she turns to point to a keyboard player, she simultaneously takes a step to stand on the *red* 5"- 7" paper square that has been strategically placed on the floor. This informs all of the handbell players and recorder players that have *red* pieces of electrician's tape on their instruments to play their notes. . .now! Now she points to the guitar player, and then steps on the *blue* paper square - and so on.

Red might stand for the F note. Recorder players that cannot keep their fingers properly pressed over the correct holes have white electrician's tape wrapped around their recorder so the F note will play no matter how their hand holds the recorder. White electrician's tape is used because it matches the color of the recorder and is therefore fairly unnoticeable. A small piece of red electrician's tape is also placed on the recorder to identify it as an F-note recorder. Recorders that are marked with a small piece of blue tape might be C-note recorders. They are wrapped in white electrician's tape so only the C note plays. There may also be G-note recorders, etc. Several recorders are not wrapped at all. Some students can use their fingers correctly to play various notes on a recorder, and either read music sheets or look at Murphy's feet to know which note to play.

The handbells work in a similar way. Each handbell plays a different note, and each is color-coded *not* to identify the particular note, but instead to identify the particular *chord* that the note belongs to. Since the "C" note is part of the C chord and the F chord, it is identified with both blue (C) and red (F) tape. Some students can play more than one handbell, and simply play the bell that matches the color Murphy is standing on. The perfect challenge for other students is to simply concentrate on playing one note, and watch Murphy's feet vigilantly to make sure they don't miss a note. All of the handbells are hung on bell stands in a very particular order according to the chord or chords they play. This color-coded handbell system is described in more precise detail near the end of this chapter.

Color-coding is also used on music sheets, organ keys, and other instruments for students who need it. Many of the color-coding adaptations are explained in Quick Tips or in the separate descriptions of devices. Color-coding is in fact the most frequently used adaptation in the Music Class at Cotting School, since many of the students are poor readers (of standard books as well as music sheets) but can discriminate between colors very easily. Of course, it is important to rule out color-blindness before using this approach.

Getting the Beat

The concept of rhythm is also very difficult for many students with special needs to comprehend. The inability to "feel the beat" is perhaps the most frustrating problem encountered by students in Music Class. There is at least one published account of an individual who developed this ability through sensory integration therapy [1]. Readers are referred to this article for detailed information on how this was accomplished.

Some students who can understand the concept of rhythm still may not be able to interpret the rhythm notes on a sheet of music. A simple adaptation such as printing little dash marks after each note - one dash for a quarter note, two for a half note, four for a whole note, etc., has worked well for some Cotting students. Other students need to rely on an external cue to indicate when to play each note - such as a metronome or the colored paper squares on the floor which were described earlier.

When playing chords, students can be taught to change the chord on a particular word, and when playing melody notes, students can learn to correspond each note to each syllable of the song.

Compensations for Motor Impairments

The lack of functional hand use is no excuse for bowing out of a school musical performance. Students have successfully used headpointers, thigh pointers, mouthsticks, and other aids to play instruments. Other instruments besides recorders and handbells have also been adapted for particular students - such as the one-string bass guitar. Occasionally, two students share the responsibility of playing a single instrument.

A few students use switches to play prerecorded music. One student may have only one switch to press; the goal for this student is to attend well to the external cues that tell the student when to press it. Another student may have three different switches that each contain prerecorded sections of a song. The goal for this student is to remember both the correct sequence as well as the correct timing for pressing the switches. Some organs have several memory banks for recording melodies and chords. These can be operated like the switches described above.

Some of the new, electronic musical or sound-effect toys can also be played alongside more traditional musical instruments in a music class or band. One example is the Body Wrap toy, available at any major toy store, which has eight buttons, each producing a different sound. The buttons are normally clipped to different body parts, but Suzi Collins, M.S., OTR/L, has successfully adapted this toy for a student by attaching each button with Velcro to a flat tray, to enable the buttons to be pressed by the student's hand.

More adaptations, as well as more specific details of the ones described above, are presented in the following pages. After finishing this chapter, you may be inspired to start your own band!

⊙ QUICK TIPS *Problems and Possible Solutions*

Following are some solutions which have successfully solved the identified problem for one or more students. Keep in mind that each student has a unique set of abilities and needs and may therefore require an original solution for the problem at hand. If a suggested solution is appropriate for a student, please adapt the design as necessary to best meet his or her needs.

Remember: fit the device to the student, not the student to the device!

A Special Thank You to
Noreen Murphy, M.Ed., Cotting School Music Teacher,
who contributed almost all of the following Quick Tips (identified as NM).

1. Student has impaired motor function of the upper extremities and would like to play the Recorder.

⊙ Recorder adaptations are discussed in detail earlier in this chapter.

2. Student has impaired motor function of the upper extremities and would like to play the Guitar, Autoharp or Other Stringed Instrument.

⊙ If the student cannot hold the guitar and play it at the same time, try lying the guitar flat on a table instead. Or choose an instrument that normally lies flat on the table, such as the autoharp or psaltery.

(NM)

⊙ If the student uses a thigh pointer, angle the autoharp or guitar on an easel slightly above the student's knee. If the student does not have sufficient range of motion in the thigh to strum all of the strings, try removing all but one string, such as to play a one-string bass guitar.

(NM and author)

⊙ If the student uses a headpointer, mouthstick, thigh pointer, or other type of pointer, consider pairing the student with another student to play the guitar or the autoharp. The first student uses the pointer to strum the strings while the second student pushes the chord buttons of the autoharp or, in the case of the guitar, performs the chord fingerings.

(NM)

⊙ If the student has functional use of only one hand and would like to play a stringed instrument, one solution is to have the student use a mouthstick to press the chord buttons of the autoharp and use the fingers of the dominant hand to strum the strings.

⊙ EZ Chord is an adaptive device for a guitar that allows the individual to play 4 basic chords in a variety of keys using only 1 finger. This is available from West Music.

(NM)

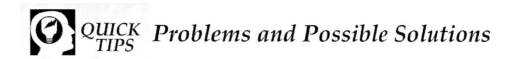
3. Student has impaired motor function of the upper extremities and would like to play the organ.

💡 Make an organ stand with keyguard and chord knobs to enable the student to press chord keys without hitting other keys. See directions following Quick Tips.

(Noreen Murphy, M.Ed., Music Teacher,
and Martha Carr, P.T., Physical Therapist, Cotting School)

💡 If the student is able to use computer keyguards, try making a similar keyguard for the organ (i.e. a clear cover made of plastic that fits over the keys with a hole drilled over each note).

💡 Pre-record sections of songs on the recording buttons of the organ and have the student be responsible for pressing these buttons to play the prerecorded music.

(NM)

💡 The organ can also be played using a headpointer, mouthstick, or hand-held pointer.

4. Student has impaired motor function of the upper extremities and would like to play the Drums, Tambourine, Handbells, or other Percussion Instrument.

💡 Mount a bass drum pedal on a piece of wood, and clamp it to the student's wheelchair foot rest or a low stool to enable the student to use his or her foot to play the drums, tambourine, handbells, or any other percussion instrument that can be played with a drum stick. Stabilize the rhythm instrument in front of the drumstick of the bass drum pedal so it will make a sound when the pedal is pressed.

(NM)

💡 The chimes is a good percussion instrument for a student who has gross arm movements. It can also be played by kicking it with a foot.

(NM)

💡 If the student does not have the wrist movement necessary to play the handbells, make a stand for the bells so the student can play it using a drum stick. Directions for making one follow Quick Tips.

(Noreen Murphy, M.Ed., Music Teacher,
and Bob Rudolph, Asst. Director of Buildings and Grounds, Cotting School)

💡 If the student cannot use a standard drumstick, perhaps a transverse mallet ("T" shaped drumstick) will work. These are available from West Music (see Resource Directory). Or, make one yourself by sawing a standard drumstick to 10″ and hammering it into a hole that has been drilled through the center of a 3/4″ thick by 4″ long dowel. The drilled hole should equal the diameter of the drumstick. Apply wood glue to both pieces before attaching them together.

5. Student does not have sufficient dexterity to perform the complex fingering required to play chords on an organ or guitar.

Have the student use an electronic keyboard that has single finger automated chords, such as the Yamaha PSR-310.

(NM)

Try the EZ Chord (West Music), an adaptive device for a guitar that allows an individual to play four basic chords in a variety of keys using only one finger.

(NM)

Consider having the student play an autoharp instead of a guitar. To play chords on an autoharp, the student simply pushes a button with the name of the chord printed on it.

(NM)

6. Student has the finger dexterity necessary to play chords on a piano, keyboard, or accordion but cannot remember which keys to press for which chords.

Pick a color to represent each chord (such as red to represent F, blue to represent C, etc.), and mark each key of the chord with that color. Then color code the music sheet to correspond with the colors designated for each cord. The student places his or her fingers on all of the keys marked with the color of the required chord.

(NM)

7. Student is unable to memorize the meanings of the different types of notes, i.e., that the quarter note means to play the note for one beat, the half note means to play the note for two beats, etc.

Use dashes to represent the number of beats each note represents. Place one dash next to each quarter note, two dashes next to each half note, etc.

(NM)

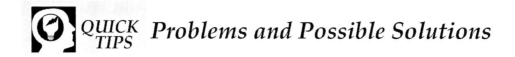

8. Student has poor potential for learning to read music and wants to play a musical instrument.

Use a color-coding system: Use markers to color the notes on the music sheet, using a different color to represent each note on the scale. If necessary, just make simple horizontal rows of colored dots instead of coloring notes on a scale. Also adapt the instrument as follows:

- For the piano, organ, accordion, or other type of keyboard instrument, place colored stickers or colored electrician's tape on the keyboard keys to correspond with the colors used on the music sheet.

(NM)

- If the student wants to play a stringed instrument, one good choice may be the psaltery, which comes with music sheets that look like dot-to-dot designs. These music sheets are placed under the strings. The student simply follows the line on the music sheet in a left to right progression and plays the string that the next dot is under.

(NM)

- Another option for students who cannot read notes on a scale is to play chords instead, such as on an autoharp, guitar, or organ. If the student can discriminate between letters, then he or she can identify the chords printed above the music scale. If the student does not have the dexterity to play chords or the ability to memorize chord fingerings, see Quick Tip #5 and Quick Tip #6.

(NM)

A very effective color-coding system for handbells is described in detail earlier in this chapter.

9. Student cannot sing in the key of the song.

Use an electronic keyboard that has a transposing function, such as the Yamaha PSR-310. The instrument will transpose the music to fit the student's voice range.

(NM)

INSTRUCTIONS
FOR FABRICATING
SELECTED DEVICES

TABLETOP ORGAN STAND
WITH KEYGUARD AND CHORD KNOBS

TABLETOP BELL STAND

TABLETOP ORGAN STAND WITH KEYGUARD
AND CHORD KNOBS

DESCRIPTION: A portable wooden organ stand with a removable keyguard that covers the organ keys. Before the song is played, the teacher slips two or three removable knobs into holes drilled to correspond with the organ's automated chord keys. The student presses the knobs to play the chords. This keyboard stand is effective for a small or medium sized organ, not a large organ such as the Yamaha PSR-310.

PURPOSES:

1. The keyguard with chord knobs allows students who have poor motor control to play specific chord keys without hitting other keys unintentionally.

2. Limiting the number of possible choices allows the student to work on switching from one chord to another in a timely manner.

3. Angling the stand promotes active wrist extension for students who need to work on this skill. The angled supports can be easily removed to accommodate students who work best on a flat surface.

MATERIALS:

1. 1/2″ thick hardwood - see Measurements to calculate amount needed
2. 2″ thick hardwood - see Measurements to calculate amount needed
3. 1/4″ thick wooden dowel
4. 1″ thick wooden dowel
5. Two hanger bolts, 1/4″ diameter by 2″ long.
   ☞ Hanger bolts have a machine screw thread on one end and a lag screw thread on the other end.

6. Two nuts to fit the machine screw threading of the hanger bolts
7. Two knobs or wing nuts to screw onto the hanger bolts.
8. Four 1 1/4″ wood screws
9. Four 1″ wood screws
10. Optional: 1/4″ rubber O-rings - one for each chord knob

TOOLS:
Table saw, band saw, or other wood saw; electric belt sander or sand paper, power drill, screwdriver, hammer, wrench, pencil, white wood glue

MEASUREMENTS:

1/2″ thick hardwood:

KEYGUARD:
Length = 2 1/2″ longer than the entire length of the organ;
Width = wide enough to cover organ keys but not organ settings (perhaps 5″)

BOTTOM BASE OF STAND:
Length = length of organ plus 6 1/2″
Width = wide enough to support the organ

FRONT SUPPORT OF ORGAN:
Length = length of keyguard
Height = height measurement of organ + 1/2″

2″ thick hardwood:

TWO SIDE PIECES:
Height = height measurement of organ + 1/2″
Width = width of keyguard.

TWO ANGLED SUPPORTS:
These are cut into identical right triangles. One of the sides adjoining
the 90 degree angle should be equal in measurement to the width of the base.
The other angle adjoining this side should be equal to the desired angle of incline.

1/4″ thick wooden dowel:

ORGAN STAND:
Eight 1″ pieces
CHORD KNOBS (PER KNOB):
One 1 1/4″ long piece

1″ thick wooden dowel:

CHORD KNOBS (PER KNOB):
One 1/2″ long piece

TABLETOP ORGAN STAND WITH KEYGUARD
AND CHORD KNOBS
(continued)

ASSEMBLY:

1. Cut out and sand all pieces of wood.

2. Attach the side pieces to base:

    a. Find and mark the locations for the screw holes: With a pencil, draw a line 2 1/2″ in from each short end of the organ base. Position the bottom edge of the side pieces next to the pencil lines, 1/2″ from the front edge of the base (to allow space for the front piece to be attached later). On the line drawn on the base, mark 1″ in from both the front and back edges of the side pieces.

    b. Drill holes through the base, using a drill bit the diameter of the screw shanks. Use a countersink to widen the top of the holes, just deep enough to recess the head of the wood screw.

    c. *Center* one side piece over one of the lines, 1/2″ from the front edge of the base, and clamp it to the base. Repeat this step with the other side piece.

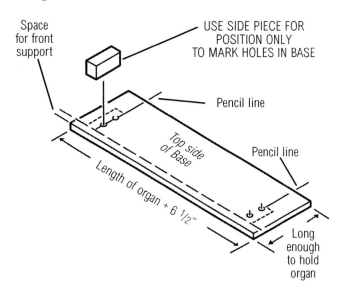

Space for front support

USE SIDE PIECE FOR POSITION ONLY TO MARK HOLES IN BASE

Pencil line

Top side of Base

Length of organ + 6 1/2″

Pencil line

Long enough to hold organ

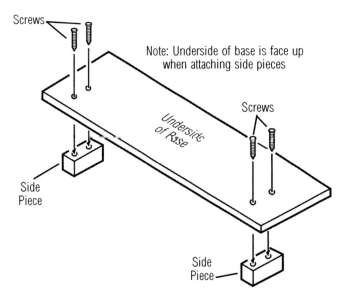

Screws

Note: Underside of base is face up when attaching side pieces

Underside of Base

Screws

Side Piece

Side Piece

    d. Turn the clamped organ stand upside down, and using the same drill bit used to drill the base, extend the holes very slightly into the side pieces to ″mark the spots″. Remove the clamps and separate the wood pieces. Now use a slightly smaller drill bit to drill a hole 3/4″ deep at each of the marked ″spots″ on the side pieces.

    e. Screw the side pieces onto the base, using the 1 1/4″ screws.

3. Make and attach the keyguard:

   a. Drill a hole, *slightly bigger* than the diameter of the 1/4″ thick wooden dowel pieces, at each of the four corners of the keyguard. Each hole should be 1/2″ from the side edge and 1″ from the front or back edge of the keyguard. The 1/4″ thick dowel "pegs" should be able to slide in and out of these holes.

   b. Place the keyguard in position on the organ stand. The front and side edges of the keyguard and organ stand should line up with each other. Mark the point where the holes contact the side pieces of the organ stand by placing a pencil in each hole of the keyguard.

   c. Drill a hole 1/2″ deep at each of the pencil marks on the side pieces, using a 1/4″ drill

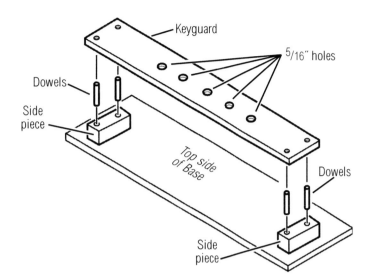

bit. The dowels must fit snugly into these holes. Fill the holes half way with white glue and tap the dowels into the holes with a hammer.

   d. Mark where the holes should go in the keyguard to correspond with desired organ keys and drill 5/16″ diameter holes.

4. Attach the front support to the side pieces:

   a. Use a pencil to mark the spots for four screws. Each screw should be 1/2″ from the top or bottom of the front piece and 1″ from the side edge (the screw should be centered in the side piece).

   b. Drill a hole the diameter of the screw shank all the way through the wood at each mark. Widen the top of each hole using a countersink, drilling just deep enough to recess the head of the screw.

   c. Place the front piece in position in front of the side pieces and on top of the base, and use a slightly smaller drill bit to extend the drilled holes to "mark the spots"

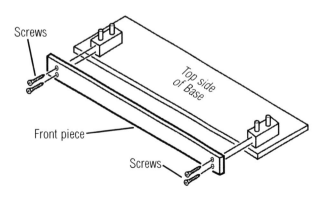

where the screws will go. Remove the front piece and drill a 1/2″ deep hole at each marked spot.

   d. Screw the front support to the side pieces, using the 1″ screws.

5. Attach the triangular supports to the underside of the base:

a. Place the triangular supports in the correct positions under the base of the organ stand, making sure the edges are flush together.

b. Mark 4 spots on the organ stand base, directly over the location of the triangular supports, which are centered on the supports and 1″ from each end. These are the locations where the pegs in the triangular support will fit into the organ stand base. Remove the organ stand base from the supports and drill a hole slightly larger than the 1/4″ thick dowel pieces through the base at each mark.

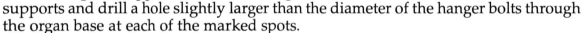
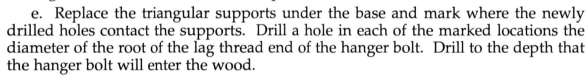

c. Replace the base on the triangular supports and mark where the holes contact the supports. Remove base and drill 1/2″ deep holes in the marked spots using a 1/4″ diameter drill bit. Fill the holes half way with white glue and tap the dowels into the holes with a hammer. Let dry.

d. Slide the base onto the pegs in the triangular supports and mark the spots where the hanger bolts will protrude through the base. The hanger bolts should be in the exact center of the triangular supports. Remove triangular supports and drill a hole slightly larger than the diameter of the hanger bolts through the organ base at each of the marked spots.

e. Replace the triangular supports under the base and mark where the newly drilled holes contact the supports. Drill a hole in each of the marked locations the diameter of the root of the lag thread end of the hanger bolt. Drill to the depth that the hanger bolt will enter the wood.

f. Screw two nuts on the machine screw end of each hanger bolt until they are locked together. Using a wrench placed around the locked nuts, screw each hanger bolt into a triangular support. Remove the nuts from the hanger bolts.

g. Slide the base onto the triangular supports and screw on a knob or wing nut to hold the supports in place.

6. To make each chord knob: Using a 1/4″ diameter drill bit, drill a hole 1/4″ deep in the center of the cut end of a 1″ thick dowel piece. Fill the hole half way with white glue and tap a 1/4″ thick dowel piece into the hole.

Chord knob

7. Slide organ into assembled keyboard stand. Place chord knobs.

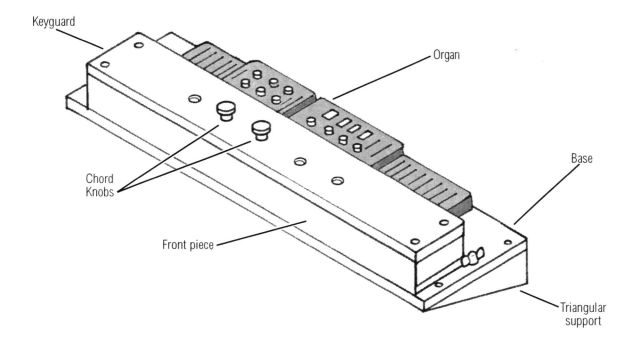

OPTIONAL: Before placing the organ in the keyboard stand, position chord knobs in the desired holes and place rubber O-rings on the bottom of each knob to prevent it from popping out of the keyguard. (This "popping-out" tendency may occur from rough handling by certain students.)

Designed and built by
Noreen Murphy, M.Ed., Music Teacher and Martha Carr, P.T., Physical Therapist,
and modified by Val Greene, B.S.Ed., Industrial Arts Teacher; all at Cotting School.

TABLETOP BELL STAND

DESCRIPTION: A free-standing frame with coat hooks attached at the top for hanging handbells. The bell stand is only 13″ high and is positioned on a table or other raised surface.

PURPOSE:
To enable students to play the handbells using a stick or simple touch. Many students do not have sufficient wrist control or technique to operate the handbells in the conventional manner.

MATERIALS:
1. 2″ x 2″ x 65″ piece of hardwood
2. 2″ x 6″ x 12″ piece of hardwood
4. Five brass coat hooks, each 1 1/4″ deep from front to back with screws
5. White woodworking glue
6. Two 5/16″-18 x 3 1/4″ joint connector bolts
7. Two 1/2″ long x 1/2″ diameter joint connectors with 5/16″-18″ hole.

TOOLS:
Table saw or other suitable saw, electric sander or sandpaper, electric drill, screwdriver, chisel, measuring tape, pencil

MEASUREMENTS:
The measurements provided make a bell stand that can hold up to five handbells. Any of the measurements can be altered to suit the requirements of the student and situation. For example, smaller stands have been made that hold only three handbells.

Top of frame: 2″ x 2″ x 45″
Side supports: Two pieces, each 2″ x 2″ x 10″
Base of frame: Two pieces, each 2″ x 6″ x 6″

ASSEMBLY:

1. Use a table saw or other suitable saw to cut all of the wood pieces. Sand all pieces using an electric sander or sand paper.

2. Drill a hole 1″ in from each end of the top of the frame, using a drill bit slightly larger than the shank of the bolt. Drill all the way through the wood.

3. Using the same drill bit, drill a hole down into the center of one end of each side support, 1 1/2″ deep (slightly deeper than the bolt will enter the wood).

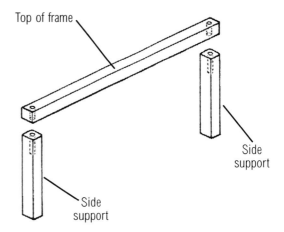

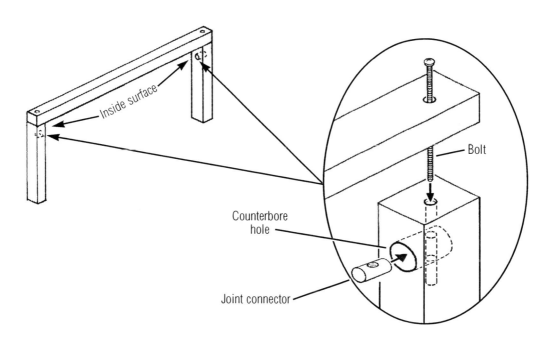

4. On the inside surface (i.e. the side that will face the hanging bells) of each side piece, mark and drill a hole (using a counterbore bit) that is less than 1″ from the top of the piece for the joint connector, which must fit on the bolt). This hole must go straight through the hole just drilled for the bolt. Hole should be slightly larger than the diameter of the joint connector, and should be just deep enough so the threaded hole in the joint connector can match up with the bolt.

5. Position the joint connector in the hole drilled in step #4, and use the screwdriver to screw a bolt through the top of the frame, down into the side support, and into the joint connector. Repeat with second bolt and side support.

TABLETOP BELL STAND
(continued)

6. Make a recessed hole (mortise) in the square base pieces:

    a. Carefully trace the bottom edge of one side support onto the center of a square base piece.

    b. Use a large drill bit to drill holes inside the tracing, each exactly 1/2″ deep (use the depth gauge on the drill), removing as much excess wood as possible. Use a wood chisel to finish carving out the square tracing to the 1/2″ depth. Carve it out carefully so the side support fits tightly into the hole.

    c. Repeat with second base piece and side support.

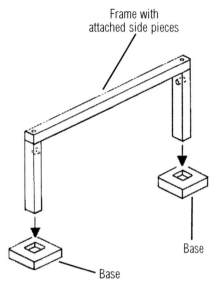

Frame with attached side pieces

Base

Base

7. Use woodworker's glue to glue the side pieces of the frame into the mortise joints in the bases.

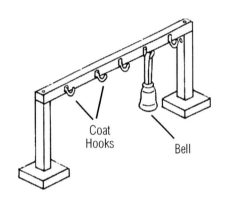

Coat Hooks

Bell

8. Determine the desired positions for the coat hooks, approximately 8″ apart. Mark the screw holes with a pencil. Drill holes at each marked spot and screw the coat hooks onto the frame.

9. Place one hand bell on each hook.

MURPHY'S RECOMMENDED METHOD FOR SETTING UP THE HANDBELLS:

Place two or three bell stands together so handbells representing all eight notes of an octave can be hung on the stands. Position the bells in this order: FACEGBD. The first three notes, FAC, belong to the F chord; the middle three notes, CEG, belong to the C chord, and the last three notes, GBD, belong to the G chord. Most of the students are responsible for one bell, though a few can handle two bells. The task is more complicated for those who are assigned the C or G bell, because these notes are each used in two chords. Notice that the C note is positioned between the F and C chord "teams", and the G note is positioned between the C and G chord "teams".

Designed by
Noreen Murphy, M.Ed., Music Teacher,
and Bob Rudolph, Asst. Director of Buildings and Grounds, at Cotting School.
Built by Bob Rudolph.

Chapter 16
Industrial Arts

ASSISTIVE DEVICES FOR INDUSTRIAL ARTS

Industrial Arts Class has always been popular with students, who derive great enjoyment from seeing their creative efforts immortalized in wood. The end product does not simply get placed on a refrigerator for a few days and then tossed into the trash barrel, like many paper creations! In fact, most wood creations are not purely decorative but also serve a functional purpose, such as stools, wind chimes, napkin holders, key holders, puzzles, jewelry boxes, and so on. Wood creations therefore have the power to continue to give the student pleasure and foster a sense of pride for years following the completion of the project.

All of the possible benefits that a student might derive from engaging in Arts and Crafts also apply for wood crafts. The Arts & Crafts chapter also provides a comparison of the various teaching models that may be used with students in a class that involves the manipulation of materials. Choosing a teaching model that is most appropriate for particular students and particular projects may enable students to gain the most benefit from their experiences in the Industrial Art room.

Benefits and Risks of Resistive Activities for Certain Student Populations

In addition to the benefits described earlier, many woodworking activities possess two special qualities that can be particularly beneficial for many children who have special needs: first, they provide a high degree of muscle resistance and second, they usually require repetitive movements. These qualities make woodworking activities an excellent treatment modality for those who need muscle strengthening. When used for this purpose, it is important to consult with a occupational therapist, who is trained to evaluate muscle strength as well as to analyze the muscle requirements of particular activities. Both of these are necessary to ensure that the activity chosen will be a good match to meet the student's specific strengthening goals.

The high degree of muscle resistance and repetition provided by woodworking activities also provides intensive feedback to the muscles and joints (proprioceptive input). Proprioceptive input is used extensively in sensory integration treatment to help those who are sensory defensive to better integrate other sensations (i.e. tactile, vestibular, and auditory). Strong proprioceptive input is also used therapeutically to improve a student's body awareness in space, which is necessary for optimal motor planning. These goals can be incorporated into the Industrial Arts class for certain students. In fact, woodworking activities can be included in a student's "sensory diet" to help provide the amount of proprioceptive input necessary to better integrate sensory input throughout the day. (Remember to have some *Hearing Protectors* available for those who are sensitive to sounds, since Industrial Arts can be pretty noisy with all of those power tools! These "ear muffs" can also be placed over FM listening devices, discussed in the Mobility chapter).

As beneficial as resistive activities are for certain students, they may actually do harm to other students. For example, some types of resistive exercise may exasperate certain medical conditions, including cerebral palsy and other neuromuscular conditions, muscular dystrophy, orthopedic conditions (including some forms of arthritis), as well as some cardiovascular and pulmonary diseases. *In many cases, whether or not a resistive and/or repetitive activity is harmful or beneficial depends upon the muscles used, as well as the intensity, frequency, and duration of the activity.*[1] Due to the risks involved, it is very important that each student's medical file be carefully reviewed before engaging the student in resistive or repetitive movement activities in the Industrial Arts room. The student's physician, physical therapist, and/or occupational therapist should be consulted whenever a medical condition exists, or whenever there is any doubt as to the appropriateness of a specific woodworking activity for a particular student.

Safety Concerns

Finally, it is very important to consider the issue of safety in the Industrial Arts room. Does the student have the sensory, motor, perceptual, and cognitive skills necessary to use the materials and tools in a safe manner? For example, do not jump to the conclusion that a student can use an electric belt sander safely simply because he or she does not have any apparent motor problems and appears to be cognitively bright. Many students who have learning disabilities lack the attention and judgment skills to use tools safely, and need close 1:1 supervision when doing so. Otherwise, the potential for sustaining a serious injury can be great. Therefore, it is important to be fully aware of the student's strengths and weaknesses (by reviewing the student's medical and educational file) before introducing woodworking activities.

Students also need to be repeatedly instructed in proper safety precautions when handling tools and materials - not just during the first class, *but during each class.* In addition, the Industrial Arts teacher will probably need the assistance of the classroom teacher, teacher's assistant, and perhaps other specialists as well, in order to ensure both the safety and the success of an Industrial Arts class that includes students who have special needs.

Problems and Possible Solutions

Following are some solutions which have successfully solved the identified problem for one or more students. Keep in mind that each student has a unique set of abilities and needs and may therefore require an original solution for the problem at hand. If a suggested solution is appropriate for a student, please adapt the design as necessary to best meet his or her needs.

Remember: fit the device to the student, not the student to the device!

1. Student has limited or no functional use of the upper extremities but would like to engage in sanding activities in Industrial Arts Class:

Electric sanders can be adapted for single switch use to enable operation by any part of the body. (See Solution 1 of Quick Tip #4)

If the student has adequate control of leg movements, make a "Sandal Sander": Use a heavy duty glue (such as super glue) to attach sandpaper to the sole of a sandal with Velcro straps. First flatten the treads on the sandal or else use a sandal with flat soles.
(Scott Whidden, Developmental Specialist, UCPA Community Experience Program, Watertown, Ma.)

If the student has gross control of arm movements, try using a sanding block. These are available commercially through hardware stores. If the commercial ones don't work, consider making a sanding block that is better designed to accommodate the student's hand skills. Two designs are presented later in this chapter. Also, wrapping sandpaper over a dowel can be an effective way to sand curves and the dowel handle can be easily held by most students. Students who demonstrate wrist flexion when holding dowels may benefit from wearing a wrist splint or brace such as a Futuro - please consult with the student's occupational therapist.
(Val Greene, B.S. Ed., Industrial Arts Teacher, Cotting School and
Scott Whidden, Developmental Specialist, UCPA Community Experience Program, Watertown, Ma.)

If student can use a mouthstick or headpointer, attach steel wool to the end of the pointer to sand between coats of paint. This involves light sanding; heavier sanding would put too much stress on the teeth and neck muscles.

Caution: Please make sure paint is non-toxic if using a mouthstick for sanding.

(Staff and therapists at the United Cerebral Palsy Association, Watertown, Ma.)

2. Student has limited or no functional use of the upper extremities but would like to paint wood in Industrial Arts Class.

Painting wood can be an extremely satisfying activity for some students who have poor directional control of arm movements. Unlike painting on paper, which usually requires eye-hand coordination, the goal of many wood projects is to paint the whole thing one single color - such as to make a foot stool green. It is impossible to make a mistake with a project like that!

Paintbrushes can be taped to any type of pointer: headpointer, mouthstick, thigh pointer, foot-attached pointer, or hand-held pointer.

Adapted handles for paintbrushes are described in the chapter on Adaptive Devices for Arts and Crafts Activities.

Stencils can be taped to the wood project if designs are desired.

3. Student has limited or no functional use of the upper extremities but would like to use hand saws in Industrial Arts Class:

If the student has good strength in the elbow flexors but weak elbow extensors, consider adapting a miter saw with bungy cords. (See directions on page 252) The student pulls the saw backwards and the bungy cords pull the saw forwards. A benefit of a using a miter saw is the student does not have to control the direction of the saw, as it is secured in a frame.
 (Scott Whidden, Developmental Specialist, UCPA Community Experience Program, Watertown, Ma.)

Caution: This device may be contraindicated for certain students who have a neurological condition, especially those that exhibit a flexor pattern in the upper extremities. Please consult with the student's occupational or physical therapist if there is any question of its appropriateness for a particular student.

Students who have gross arm control may be able to use a coping saw. This type of saw is operated using up and down arm movements, rather than forward and backward arm movements like most saws. The vertical handle can be easily adapted to compensate for impaired hand grasp or muscle weakness. For those who need a vertical handle, use as is or, if necessary, build up the handle with foam to improve the grip. For students who need a horizontal handle, stick a thick wooden dowel (that has a diameter suitable for student's hand size) through the hole in a wire-handled coping saw. First cut a notch in the middle of the wooden dowel for the wire handle of the coping saw to fit into, to stabilize the dowel. Then use duct tape to secure it in place. A teacher may need to help control the direction of the saw.

 (Val Greene, B.S. Ed., Industrial Arts Teacher, Cotting School)

Problems and Possible Solutions

4. Student has limited or no functional use of the upper extremities but would like to use power tools in Industrial Arts Class:

Most power tools can be adapted for single switch use with an environmental control unit (ECU). The ECU that is used to adapt power tools at both Cotting School and the United Cerebral Palsy Association's Community Experience Program is The AbleNet Power Unit. When switches are used, the teacher and student often work as a team with the teacher performing the actual sanding, drilling, sawing, etc., while the student controls when to turn the machine on and off. Please refer to the chapter on Switches and Switch Mounts for information on the different types of switches available.

(Val Greene, B.S. Ed., Industrial Arts Teacher, Cotting School and
Scott Whidden, Developmental Specialist, UCPA Community Experience Program, Watertown, Ma.)

Self-standing power drills have been adapted so they can be operated by a foot pedal or by pulling a handle suspended from the ceiling. These designs are based on the same mechanical concept (using rope and pulleys) which can be adapted in other ways as well, depending upon the student's needs. Directions for both modifications are provided later in this chapter.

(Scott Whidden, Developmental Specialist, UCPA Community Experience Program, Watertown, Ma.
and Val Greene, B.S. Ed., Industrial Arts Teacher, Cotting School)

Information on bicycle-type and treadle-type woodworking machines (e.g. jigsaws, sanders, lathes) which are designed for use by (or rehabilitation of) the lower extremities, can be obtained from the book *Craft Techniques in Occupational Therapy*, 1971, written and published by Department of the Army. (The book is available from the Superintendent of Documents at 202-512-1800, Order # 008-020-01018-9, and is also available for loan to occupational therapists through the AOTA library.)

5. Student needs to stabilize his or her arms when doing manipulative tasks, but the tables of self-standing power tools are too small to support the arms.

Make an arm support for the self-standing power tool. The arm support makes it much easier to stabilize the project and is less fatiguing and more comfortable for the arms. Directions for an Arm Support for Band Saw, Jig Saw or Scroll Saw are provided later in this chapter.

(Val Greene, B.S. Ed., Industrial Arts Teacher, Cotting School)

6. Self-standing power tools are inaccessible for students in wheelchairs due to their height.

Lower the height of the power tools. The heights of several power tools in the Industrial Arts Room at Cotting School were adjusted as follows:

> •Drill Press: Using a hacksaw, cut down the metal legs of the drill press and also the rack and vertical column to suit the new height. Rebevel the edge of the rack before reassembling it.
>
> *(Val Greene, B.S. Ed., Industrial Arts Teacher, Cotting School)*

> •Delta Scroll Saw: Unscrew the metal legs of the scroll saw from the table. Use a metal-cutting band saw to cut 7" off from the TOP of each leg (not the bottom) so it will still stand straight.
>
> *(Val Greene, B.S. Ed., Industrial Arts Teacher, Cotting School)*

INSTRUCTIONS
FOR FABRICATING
SELECTED DEVICES

ARM SUPPORT
FOR
BAND SAW,
JIG SAW,
OR
SCROLL SAW

ADAPTED MITER
SAW

ADAPTED DEVICE TO LOWER A DRILL PRESS

FOOT-OPERATED DRILL PRESS

SANDING BLOCK WITH HAND STRAP

SANDING BLOCK WITH DOWEL HANDLE

ARM SUPPORT FOR BAND SAW, JIG SAW, OR SCROLL SAW

DESCRIPTION: A wooden surface (consisting of 3/4" thick solid core plywood with laminate top) with two extensions to support the arms, attached underneath the metal table of a power saw.

 This arm support was made for a scroll saw, but the directions can be used with most other power tools.

PURPOSES:

1. To provide a solid surface to support the arms so they can better stabilize and control the wood project during cutting.

2. To improve comfort and reduce fatigue while using power tools.

MATERIALS:
1. 36" square piece of 3/4" thick solid core plywood with laminate top (total thickness, with laminate, is almost 1")
2. Four #8 flathead wood screws

TOOLS:
Band saw
Pistol drill or drill press
Screwdriver
Pencil
Ruler or measuring tape
Butcher paper, for drawing the pattern.

MEASUREMENTS:
Specific measurements are provided on the pattern shown here. This pattern produced an arm support that has worked well for most of the students and adults that use the scroll saw. Measurements for the rear portion that is cut out for the scroll saw may need to be adjusted to suit the dimensions of the power saw being adapted.

ASSEMBLY:

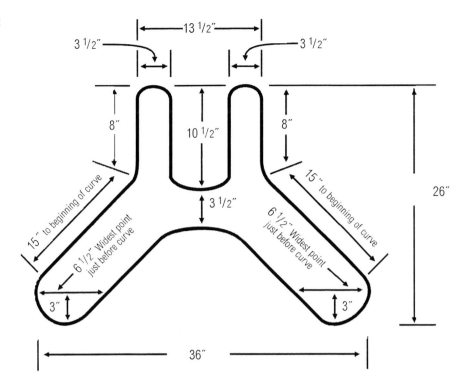

1. Copy the pattern onto the butcher paper, following the measurement guidelines shown. Cut out the pattern.

2. Trace the pattern onto the wood. Cut out the wood along the tracing lines using the band saw. Sand the wood.

3. Disassemble the metal table (that supports the wood) from the power saw. Using a pistol drill (or drill press), drill a hole using a drill bit the same size as the screw shank, near each of the four corners of the metal table. Each hole should be approximately 1/2" to 3/4" from each of the two edges that form each corner.

4. Place the arm support on top of the metal base that usually supports the metal table, and then position the metal table on top of the arm support. Make sure they are positioned properly and then clamp the metal table and arm support securely to the metal base. Using the same drill bit used in Step #3, extend the shank holes very slightly into the arm support - just enough to mark the spots for the pilot holes.

5. Disassemble the pieces from the clamp and drill a pilot hole at each of the marked spots on the arm support (drill bit = diameter of root of screw).

6. Use a countersink bit to widen the holes in the metal table, just deep enough so the head of the screw will be flush with the surface of the table.

7. Reclamp the arm support and metal table in position on the power machine and screw in the wood screws.

Designed and built by
Val Greene, B.S. Ed., Industrial Arts Teacher at Cotting School.

ADAPTED MITER SAW

DESCRIPTION: Miter saw (a back-saw in a miter box) adapted with two short bungie cords. The bungie cords pull the saw forward and all the student has to do to operate the saw is to flex the arm toward the body, pulling the saw backwards. The saw can be further adapted by adding a horizontal dowel handle or a nylon rope handle to accommodate various grasp and arm movement patterns. One individual placed the rope handle around his trunk and used trunk extension to operate the saw.

☞ The table will need to be bolted to the floor or be braced with a very heavy object (such as a heavy, old fashioned typewriter!) to prevent it from sliding forward when using the saw.

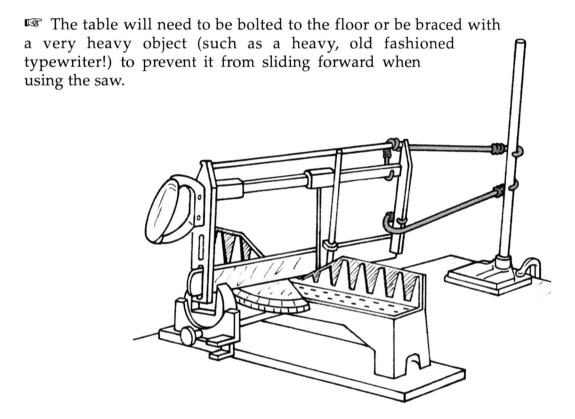

PURPOSE:
1. To enable students who have poor strength in elbow extension to independently use a miter saw.

2. For those who have no functional use of the upper extremities but who have good trunk control, further adapting the miter saw with a rope handle (Modification 2) may enable the student to operate the saw using trunk extension.

Caution: This device may be contraindicated for certain students who have a neurological condition, especially those that exhibit a flexor pattern in the upper extremities. Please consult with the student's occupational or physical therapist if there is any question of its appropriateness for a particular student.

MATERIALS:

1. Two short bungie cords (perhaps 6" long, though this may vary depending upon the distance between the clamped pole and the end of the miter saw)
2. 12" tall, thick metal or wooden pole attached to a flat base
3. Large C-clamp to clamp pole base to table
4. OPTIONAL: Thick dowel or 3' long, thick rope to adapt handle

TOOLS:

None, if pole is already attached to a base. To attach pole to base, a drill press and screwdriver will be needed. Please refer to Materials and Processes chapter for information on inserting dowels into wood.

ASSEMBLY:

1. Clamp the base of the pole to the far end of a very sturdy table, in line with the miter saw.

2. Attach one end of each bungy cord to the vertical edge of the forward end of the miter saw. Attach the other end of each bungy cord to the pole. One bungy cord should be positioned at the very top of the miter saw and the other bungy cord should be positioned at the very bottom of the saw. The ends that are placed on the pole should start out rather high up on the pole and will need to be adjusted downward as the project progresses. Experimentation will determine the proper positions of the bungy cords.

MODIFICATIONS:

1. To add a horizontal dowel handle, simply stick a dowel that is thick enough to stay wedged in place in the hole of the handle.

2. To make a rope handle, simply thread a thick rope through the handle of the miter saw and tie the ends together.

Designed and built
by Scott Whidden, Developmental Specialist,
UCPA Community Experience Program, Watertown, Ma.

ADAPTIVE DEVICE TO LOWER A DRILL PRESS

DESCRIPTION: A drill press adapted with a rope pulley system with handle. The student pulls the handle to lower the drill press. There are three pulleys used with this system. The first pulley consists of a 7" diameter homemade wooden pulley attached to the handle of the drill press. After the rope is threaded through this pulley, it is threaded through two additional pulleys which are attached to the ceiling.

PURPOSE:
To enable students to operate a drill press who are unable to pull (or get close enough to access) the drill press handle.

MATERIALS:
1. 3/4" thick pine board, about 8" x 12"
2. Two large metal pulleys, strong enough to take body weight
3. Approximately 12 feet of strong cable cord
4. Exercise pulley handle (or other suitable handle)
6. One eye screw, large enough to thread the cable through
7. Two ceiling pulleys with screws
8. Strong duct tape

TOOLS:
Band Saw
Drill Press
Belt Sander
Screwdriver
Drummel
Pistol Drill
Clamp

ASSEMBLY:

1. Cut out wooden parts. Using the band saw, cut out a 7" diameter circle and a strip 1" x 6".

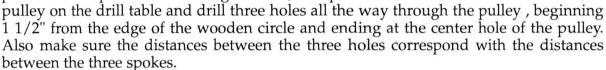

2. Make and install wooden pulley:

   a. Using the drill press, drill a huge hole halfway through the center of the 7" wooden circle. Hole should be just big enough to fit over the center hub of the handle of the drill press.

   b. Drill three diagonal holes in the wooden pulley to mirror the angles of the spokes of the drill handle, as follows: first, determine what degree (from vertical) the spokes are angled on the drill press handle, and tilt the table of the drill press to correspond with this angle. Next, clamp the wooden pulley on the drill table and drill three holes all the way through the pulley , beginning 1 1/2" from the edge of the wooden circle and ending at the center hole of the pulley. Also make sure the distances between the three holes correspond with the distances between the three spokes.

   c. Use a hand-held drummel to carve a groove into the circumference edge of the wooden pulley. Also carve a groove from the center hole to the outer edge of the pulley.

   d. Sand the wooden pulley, and then attach it to the handle of the drill press (unscrew the spokes off the drill press, place pulley into position, and rescrew the spokes back on).

3. Screw the two ceiling pulleys to the ceiling. One should be directly above the rear edge of the wooden pulley and the other should be directly over the spot from which the handle should hang.

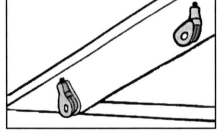

4. Drill a shallow hole with a drill bit slightly smaller than the screw, and then screw the eye screw into the rectangular piece of pine. Position the pine horizontally onto the side of the drill press so that the eye screw is located a few inches directly above the back edge of the wooden pulley. Attach the pine board to the drill press using two pieces of duct tape.

5. Thread the cable as follows:

   a. Tie the cable to the center hub of the drill press handle.

   b. Feed the cable into the groove leading from the center hub to the outer edge of the pulley.

   c. Feed the cable around the edge of the wooden pulley (in the groove), feeding the cable forward, then downward and under to the back.

   d. Next, feed the cable up through the eye screw, then through the rear ceiling pulley, then through ceiling pulley that is in the forward position.

6. Tie the handle to the end of the cable, adjusting it to hang at the desired height.

Designed and built by
Scott Whidden, Developmental Specialist,
UCPA Community Experience Program, Watertown, Ma.

FOOT-OPERATED DRILL PRESS

DESCRIPTION: A hinged wooden foot pedal which is attached to the feed lever that raises and lowers the drill with a length of insulated wire cable. Pressing on the foot pedal pulls the cable, which turns the feed lever of the drill press to lower the drill. A series of pulleys are used to guide the cable from the feed lever to the foot pedal.

PURPOSE:
To enable a student with the use of only one arm or with impaired use of both arms to operate a drill press independently.

☞ The power drill needs to be positioned on a table that can have a hole drilled through it to accommodate the cable, or else there should be enough space between the drill table and the wall to feed the cable between them.

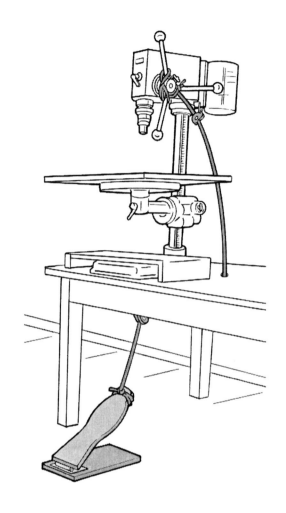

MATERIALS:
1. 5/8" thick plywood, approximately 26" x 5"
2. 3" long x 1 1/2" wide metal hinge with screws
3. Several yards of wire cable, enough to reach from the floor pedal to the handle of the drill press (including feeding through whatever pulleys are necessary to get from pedal to handle) plus an additional 12 inches or so for knotting.
4. Two small (1/2") pulleys with screws
5. One or more large (2") pulleys with screws - the exact number will depend on the cable "route". This will vary depending upon drill model and table type.

TOOLS:
Band saw, jig saw, or suitable hand saw
Drill
Screwdriver
Electric sander or sandpaper

ASSEMBLY:

1. Use a saw to cut the wood into 2 pieces, a 14" long piece for the foot pedal and a 12" long piece for the base. If desired, shape the 14" long foot pedal to resemble the shape of a shoe sole, as shown in the illustration. Sand both pieces.

2. Drill a hole just big enough to fit the insulated cable wire through, approximately 1" from the "toe" end of the foot pedal.

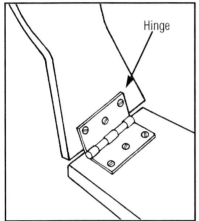

3. Join the base and the foot pedal, using the metal hinge:

    a. Position the hinge so it is centered at one of the short ends of the 12" long base, with the hinge joint approximately 1/2" in from the edge of the base. Use a pencil to mark where the screws should go, and then drill 1/4" deep pilot holes, using a drill bit that equals the diameter of the root of the screw. Screw in the screws to attach the hinge to the base.

    b. Position the "heel" end of the foot pedal (the end without the cable) under the unattached half of the hinge, approximately 1/8" from the hinge joint, with the hinge centered, and mark where the screws should go. Drill the pilot holes. Screw in the screws to attach the foot pedal to the hinge.

4. Attach a small pulley to the drill as follows:

☞ These directions may vary depending upon the model and type of drill.

    a. Using a pistol drill, carefully drill a small hole through the metal piece to which the drill motor drum is attached. Drill the hole 1/2" from the lower right corner of this metal piece. Do NOT drill a hole through the metal drum that protects the drill motor.

    b. Slip the metal pulley ring through the drilled hole.

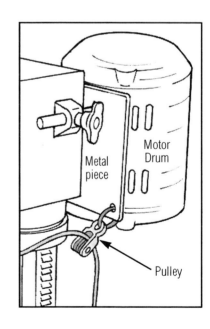

FOOT-OPERATED DRILL PRESS
(continued)

ASSEMBLY:

5. Attach remaining pulleys:

This step depends upon the individual set-up of the drill. At Cotting School, the drill is supported on a wooden table (with shortened table legs). A hole is drilled into the table directly below the pulley that is attached to the drill. A second small pulley is attached immediately in front of the drilled hole on the underside of the table. A large pulley is attached under the front edge of the table. If a hole cannot be drilled in the table, simply design the cable route to travel behind and under the table, and arrange the pulleys accordingly.

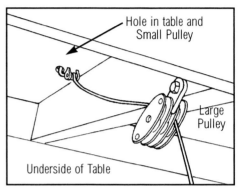

6. To run the cable wire:

    a. Tie a reinforced knot at the end of the cable wire and thread it through the hole in the wooden foot pedal.

    b. Thread the wire through each of the pulleys, in sequential order along the cable route, from the foot pedal to the drill.

    c. Wrap the cable clockwise around the hub of the feed lever, going first under and then around the front and over the top of the hub. Loop the end of the cable around the feed lever handle that is positioned forward when the drill is resting in the raised position, and tie a knot.

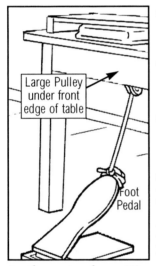

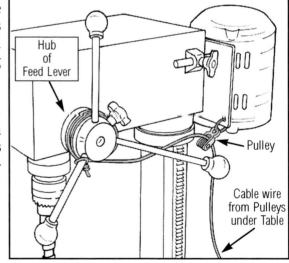

☞ Make sure the foot pedal is positioned correctly on the floor, and also adjust the length of the cable wire until the optimal tension has been found, before tying the cable to the handle of the drill press.

Designed and built by
Val Greene, B.S. Ed., Industrial Arts Teacher, Cotting School.

SANDING BLOCK WITH HAND STRAP

DESCRIPTION:
A sanding block made of polyethylene (hard) foam with two beta pile hand straps. The foam can be carved to support the hand in a desired position (like a splint).

PURPOSE:
To enable a student with impaired hand grasp to perform sanding tasks.

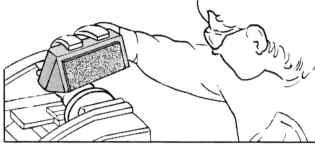

MATERIALS:
1. 7" x 5" block of 2" polyethylene (hard) foam
2. 20" length of 2" wide Velfoam loop or other suitable strapping material
3. 8" of 2" wide pressure-sensitive Velcro hook tape
4. Double-sided tape
5. Sandpaper

TOOLS:
Electric carving knife (preferred), steak knife, or saw; pencil, scissors

MEASUREMENTS:
This sanding block measures 7" long by 5" wide, but can be adjusted if necessary to better accommodate the size of the student's hand.

ASSEMBLY:
1. Use the electric carving knife (or steak knife, or saw) to cut out a block of 2" thick polyethylene (hard) foam that is 7" x 5". If desired, shape the top surface of the sanding block to support the hand in an optimal hand position.

2. Cut out a piece of sandpaper that is also 7" x 5".

3. Attach the sandpaper to the bottom of the foam using double-sided tape.

4. Position the student's hand on the sanding block and mark locations for two hand straps. Cut the Velcro hook tape into four 2" strips. Attach pieces of Velcro hook to the block, one on the left side and one on the right side, at each of the marked locations.

5. Cut the Velfoam or other strapping material in half and attach the ends of each strap to the Velcro hook to secure the student's hand on the sanding block. Trim any excess.

MODIFICATION FOR SANDING GROOVES: Cut the sanding surface of the foam block into a downward facing triangle before covering it with sandpaper.

Designed by Sharon Bridson, COTA, Certified Occupational Therapy Assistant
and Val Greene, B.S. Ed., Industrial Arts Teacher, at Cotting School.

SANDING BLOCK WITH DOWEL HANDLE

DESCRIPTION: A sanding block made of polyethylene (hard) foam with a horizontal dowel handle.

PURPOSE:
To enable a student with impaired hand grasp to perform sanding tasks. The dowel handle in this particular design can facilitate development of a radial palmar grasp. Important components of this normal hand grasp are commonly absent in students who, due to a neurological disorder, exhibit an abnormal pattern of flexed wrist and adducted thumb. For these students, grasping cylindrical shapes helps to develop the normal pattern components needed to fill in the sequential gaps in their fine motor development. [3]

MATERIALS:
1. 7" x 5" block of 2" polyethylene (hard) foam
2. 3/4" thick wooden dowel
3. Two 1 1/4" long flathead wood screws
4. White woodworking glue
5. Double-sided tape
6. Sandpaper

TOOLS:
Steak knife
Wood saw
Electric belt sander
Electric drill
Screwdriver
Optional: Electric carving knife

MEASUREMENTS:
This sanding block measures 7" long by 5" wide, but can be adjusted if necessary to better accommodate the size of the student's hand.

ASSEMBLY:
1. Use the electric carving knife, steak knife, or saw to cut out a block of 2" thick polyethylene (hard) foam that is 7" x 5".

2. Use a saw to cut the 3/4" thick dowel into three pieces: two should be 2 1/2" long to form the vertical uprights of the dowel handle, and one piece should be 5" long to form the horizontal crossbar of the handle.

3. Shape and drill crossbar:
     a. Use an electric belt sander or sandpaper to flatten one side of the crossbar. The flattened side will be attached to the vertical uprights and face the sanding block when handle is assembled.
     b. Clamp the crossbar with flattened side down, to stabilize it, and drill shank holes downward, 1" in from each end of the crossbar, into the flattened side of the crossbar, using a drill bit the same size as the screw shank. Make sure both holes are aligned so they are parallel, and drill all the way through the dowel. Use a countersink bit to widen the top of each shank hole (on rounded side) to recess the heads of the screws.

4. Attach the vertical uprights to the hard foam:
     a. Mark the spots where the uprights will be inserted into the foam. Each should be positioned 1" from a side edge and perhaps 2" from the far edge of the hard foam block.
     b. Use a steak knife to carve two 1" deep holes in the foam at the marked locations, to snugly fit each of the uprights.
     c. Fill each hole half way with white woodworker's glue and then press the two uprights into the holes. Clamp until dry.

5. To attach the crossbar to the two vertical uprights:
     a. Mark and drill a pilot hole through the center of one of the vertical uprights, with a drill bit slightly smaller than the screw.
     b. Place the crossbar in the correct position on top of the uprights and screw it onto the drilled upright.
     c. Next, position the drill inside the remaining hole in the crossbar and drill a hole into the remaining upright. Screw the crossbar to the second upright.

6. Cut out a 5" x 7" piece of sandpaper and attach it to the sanding block using the double-sided tape.

MODIFICATION FOR SANDING GROOVES:
Cut the sanding surface of the foam block into a down-ward facing triangle before covering it with sandpaper.

Designed by
Sharon Bridson, COTA, Certified Occupational Therapy Assistant,
and Val Greene, B.S. Ed., Industrial Arts Teacher, at Cotting School.

Chapter 17
Home Economics

ASSISTIVE DEVICES FOR HOME ECONOMICS CLASS

Cooking activities add a new twist to the concept of providing students who have special needs with a "multisensory approach to learning". Nothing quite motivates like the smell, taste, and texture of food! Engage a group of students who have learning impairments in a cooking project and you will likely notice a significant improvement in attention and organizational skills. In fact, Beth Jackson, M.S., OTR/L, has done just that and has recently published a series of recipe books based on her experiences with her cooking groups at Cotting School [1,2]. As Jackson notes in her books, cooking is an excellent modality for addressing a wide variety of skills, including fine motor and bilateral motor skills, visual-motor/perceptual skills, sequencing, problem solving and safety awareness, functional mobility, and social skills. Most important of all, cooking activities teach students an essential life skill that will help to prepare them for community living. And students gain these skills while engaged in a favorite activity- what could be better?

Orienting Students to the Kitchen

One of the first tasks that needs to take place when beginning a cooking group is to orient the students to the lay-out of the kitchen in which they will be working. Have you ever been at a social gathering at someone's house and offered to help the hostess cook or clean-up? Sounds easy, you do it all the time at your own house. The problem is, you don't know where the hostess stores the dishes, silverware, pots and pans, etc., or his or her unique procedure for loading the dishwasher (forks up or down? dishes sideways or facing forward?). So you ask a lot of questions, leaving the hostess wishing he or she were left alone to do it themselves!

Learning the lay-out of a kitchen is a more challenging task for students who have learning impairments, especially those that have visual memory problems. Paulette Binder, Home Economics Teacher at Cotting School, has made kitchen organization and orientation a high priority, realizing how much this one issue affects a student's level of independence with cooking tasks. She is lucky to have a plethora of drawers and cabinets to store equipment in, and each one has a picture and name label on it showing what is inside. To conserve time and energy, items should be stored as close to the location where they will be used as possible. Commonly used items should be located in lower cabinets to enable independent access by those who use wheelchairs. During the first session or two, after the students have been oriented to where the supplies are, Binder has students play games trying to locate certain items. This is both fun for the students and helps to avoid frustration later during actual cooking tasks.

Safety Issues

Safety is another important issue to address with students before beginning cooking activities. Many students who have special needs have impaired perceptual, memory, and judgment skills which may result in safety hazards. Students must remember to turn off a stove after use, wear an oven mitt before touching hot objects, avoid reaching over hot burners, stabilize foods correctly when cutting them with a knife, and hold the knife correctly with cutting edge down. These are only a few examples. Sufficient time must be spent instructing students on safety issues, and whenever possible, visual cues should be employed to reduce the chances of injury. Examples are placing brightly colored stickers on the stove knobs to denote the "off" position, hanging brightly colored oven mitts next to the stove as a reminder instead of placing them in a drawer, and visually highlighting the cutting surface of a knife (see Quick Tips for method).

Students who have physical disabilities often find themselves in safety-compromised positions because the kitchen is not sufficiently adapted to compensate for their impaired mobility skills. For example, one former student (a young adult) with athetoid cerebral palsy and spastic quadriplegia regularly performed cooking chores at home. He never used his wheelchair at home and instead crawled around the kitchen, sometimes getting into a kneeling position to use the microwave or sink. He performed cutting and mixing tasks on the floor because the counter was too high for him to perform these tasks while kneeling.

One day, he suffered a burn while transferring hot spaghetti from the microwave to the floor. After exploring various solutions with the author, it was determined that kneeling on a thick (folded) mat placed against the counter (under the microwave and sink) was the safest method for him to perform cooking tasks. This would allow him to perform all tasks at the counter instead of transferring foods back and forth between the counter and the floor. This was a low-budget solution, with one major pitfall: the mat might be inconvenient for his mother who used the same kitchen. A more aesthetic (and also more expensive) solution that would eliminate this inconvenience would be to install a sturdy kneeling bench similar to the ones seen in many churches which could fold up against the bottom of the counter when not in use.

For those who do use wheelchairs in the kitchen, using the stove can pose an increased safety hazard. Not only is it difficult to reach the pots on the stove, but due to the lowered body position the arms are much closer to the burners which increases the risk of burns. Fortunately, as Paulette Binder points out, most cooking activities can be performed without using a regular stove top. Alternative solutions are presented in Quick Tips.

Teaching Approaches for Cooking Tasks

There are two different approaches to teaching cooking activities to groups of students who have special needs:

1. The class prepares a group meal with each student performing only certain steps of the task (similar to the production line approach described in the Art chapter).

2. Each student in the class completes all steps of making a simple meal, such as a peanut butter and jelly sandwich.

The second approach provides the student with practice in sequencing a whole (though simpler) meal from start to finish, thus teaching the student an essential survival skill. Although the merits of this approach are self-evident, the production line approach has its own advantages as well. For instance, some students who are severely motorically involved may never be able to make a peanut butter and jelly sandwich, but they can control a switch to turn on a blender, and thus participate in an enjoyable group activity to make a special meal. The production line approach allows emphasis of each student's strengths instead of his or her weaknesses. Therefore, it is important to consider the goals of the group and its individual members when determining which approach to use. Very often, students benefit from a combination of these two approaches.

Sources of Assistive Equipment for the Kitchen

Assistive devices for kitchen tasks are readily available through several adaptive equipment companies, including Sammons Preston, Maxi-Aids, North Coast Medical, Inc., S & S adaptAbility, Concepts ADL, and Therapro, Inc.. Also check local retail stores, especially those that specialize in kitchen supplies, as they now often carry some gadgets that are designed for those who have impaired vision or motor skills. Due to the wide availability of assistive devices for cooking tasks, Quick Tips in this chapter is mostly limited to solutions that are not generally found in a catalog.

Recipe Books

A standard recipe book is in actuality a task sequencing aid which is designed for use by the general population. Many students who have special needs often do not have sufficient cognitive or reading skills to use these books, yet they may have an even greater need for aids that can help compensate for impaired memory and task organizational skills during cooking tasks. The following recipe books are designed to serve this purpose for those who have special needs:

The Stepwise Breakfast Cookbook [1] and *The Stepwise Lunch Cookbook* [2], both by Beth Jackson, M.S., OTR/L (published by Therapro, Inc.). These recipe books include directions for making several simple breakfast or lunch meals. They are geared for students who have poor reading skills as well as poor task organization and sequencing skills. The books, which come with a fold-out cardboard stand (for hands-free viewing), describe each step of making a simple meal on a separate page, with emphasis on pictures to describe the step. These books have worked very well with some Cotting students and are highly recommended.

Making It Easy: Crafts and Cooking Activities [3], by Elaine F. Marcus and Randy F. Granovetter. This book breaks over 100 tasks (including many cooking activities) into easy to follow steps. Available from Therapro, Inc.

A Special Picture Cookbook [4], by Frieda Reed Steed. This is a well-illustrated, step-by-step manual intended to help children who are poor readers learn a few basic recipes. Available from PRO-ED and Therapro, Inc.

Home Cooking Cookbook [5], *Home Cooking Cookbook Plus* (laminated) [6], and *Color-Your-Own Cookbook* (reproducible) [7], by Ellen Sudol, all published by the Attainment Company, Inc. These three picture-oriented cookbooks contain the same collection of easy-to-prepare recipes in different formats.

Look 'n Cook [8], also by Ellen Sudol, illustrates easier recipes than the *Home Cooking Cookbook*, ranging from main dishes to desserts. It is also published by the Attainment Company, Inc.

⚡ QUICK TIPS *Problems and Possible Solutions*

Following are some solutions which have successfully solved the identified problem for one or more students. Keep in mind that each student has a unique set of abilities and needs and may therefore require an original solution for the problem at hand. If a suggested solution is appropriate for a student, please adapt the design as necessary to best meet his or her needs.

Remember: fit the device to the student, not the student to the device!

A Special Thank You to
Paulette E. Binder, Home Economics Teacher at Cotting School,
who provided most of the following Quick Tips (identified as PB).

1. Student cannot reach the stove burners safely from his or her wheelchair.

💡 Use a portable burner, such as the ones students use in college dorms. These can be placed on a table appropriately sized for the wheelchair.

(PB)

💡 Many foods can be cooked in an electric frying pan, which can be placed on a suitable table.

(PB)

2. Student cannot safely use the stove burners due to impaired safety awareness.

💡 Many students have sufficient safety skills to use an instant water boiler, such as the Sunbeam Hot Shot. These are much safer than boiling water in a pot, though one still must be cautious. Many instant foods can be made using one of these, such as oatmeal, soups, stews, hot chocolate, etc.

(PB)

💡 Many students are able to use a microwave oven to cook certain foods. Enough recipes adapted for the microwave can be found that almost any kind of food can be prepared.

(PB)

☞ Pictorial or written instructions may be necessary for using either of the above appliances safely.

3. Student does not have functional use of the upper extremities except for switch use, and would like to actively participate in cooking class.

Adapt kitchen appliances such as a blender, toaster, frying pan, etc., with an environmental control unit such as the AbleNet Power Unit. This will allow the student to turn the appliance on or off. More information can be found in Chapter 7, Switches and Switch Mounts.

4. Student cannot tell which side of a knife is sharp due to visual perceptual deficits.

Paint nail polish on the cutting surface of any type of knife to identify it.

(PB)

5. Student has impaired grasp and has difficulty holding tomatoes, onions, or other vegetables for peeling.

Have student use an onion holder to hold the vegetables.

(PB)

6. Student has difficulty spooning and shaping cookie dough due to fine motor impairments.

Have the student use an ice cream scooper or meatball scooper to scoop and shape the dough.

(PB)

7. Student needs a built-up handle on a vegetable peeler due to impaired hand grasp.

Adapt the handle of the vegetable peeler with a crutch-grip handle. Crutch-grip handles can be bought at some creative recycling centers including the Children's Resource Center in Belmont, MA.

(PB)

The Good Grips vegetable peeler has a built-up handle and is available through Sammons Preston as well as large department stores and kitchen specialty stores.
(Karen Conrad, Sc.D., OTR/L, Occupational Therapist, Founder and President, Therapro, Inc.)

8. Student has difficulty using a spatula or other kitchen utensils due to impaired grasp or coordination.

Some ideas to accommodate hand grasp:

- adapt the handle with cylindrical foam, available from Therapro, Sammons Preston and other adaptive equipment suppliers.
  (Beth Jackson, M.S., OTR/L, Occupational Therapist, Cotting School)

- for those who find vertical handles easier to grasp or handle, try the Ergonomic Spatula and the Ergonomic (serving) Fork from Sammons Preston.

- to adapt short, wood-handled utensils with a ball handle, see directions for the Wooden Spoon with Ball Handle provided later in this chapter.
  (PB)

For some students, the angle of the spatula can make a critical difference in the ability to use one well. Experiment with different types of spatulas, or adjust the angle of a spatula by bending it (if it is metal) or using a heat gun (if it is plastic).

9. Student has difficulty stabilizing mixing bowls, etc. due to use of only one hand or poor ability to coordinate both hands together.

Buy 1/3" thick adhesive-backed rubber foam sheets, sometimes available at creative recycling centers (including the Children's Resource Center in Belmont, MA.). Cut out small pieces of it to stick on the bottom of bowls, cutting boards, etc. to stabilize them. If none is available at the local recycling store, check with local rubber companies.

(PB)

Another effective alternative to using Dycem matting is using the rubber foam padding which is designed to pad and stabilize carpets. This has a sticky consistency although it is not adhesive-backed. It can often be purchased very cheaply at discount stores that sell second quality merchandise or overstocks.

(Virginia Birmingham, P.T., Physical Therapist, Cotting School)

Adhesive-backed neoprene padding is available from Therapro, Inc.

Commercially available adaptive devices which address this problem are available through suppliers listed earlier in this chapter. Reminder: If this task would provide an appropriate challenge for improving the use of both hands together, do not use any adaptations.

10. Student has visual or perceptual impairments and cannot read a standard measuring cup.

Since it is easier to fill a measuring cup to the brim than to a specific line, use measuring cups that stack together instead of a standard measuring cup. Two brands which are designed to compensate for visual and/or perceptual skills:

- Color-Coded Measuring Cups by Maxi-Aids: Each measuring cup is a different color, and also has raised numbers on the side indicating the size.

- GOODCOOK Measuring Cups and Spoons: available at large department stores and kitchen specialty shops.

(Beth Jackson, M.S., OTR/L, Occupational Therapist, Cotting School)

Another option is to tape pictures of the particular food on the measuring cup that would be used with it (e.g. picture of hot cocoa and "cup of soup" on the 1/2 cup measuring cup).

INSTRUCTIONS
FOR FABRICATING
SELECTED DEVICES

ADAPTED CUTTING BOARD

WOODEN MIXING SPOON
WITH BALL HANDLE

ADAPTED CUTTING BOARD

DESCRIPTION: Any standard, commercially available cutting board with a handle, adapted by nailing two stainless steel nails in it. The food to be cut (vegetable, fruit, etc.) is pushed onto the nails to stabilize it during cutting. The nails are covered with small pieces of plastic aquarium tubing when not in use, to help prevent injuries. *BE CAREFUL WITH THIS CUTTING BOARD - THE NAILS ARE SHARP!*

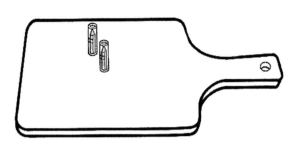

Caution:
Nails made from other materials should not be inserted into food as they may be toxic.

PURPOSE:
To enable those who are unable to stabilize objects with their non-dominant hand to slice food more safely.

MATERIALS:
1. Any standard, commercially available cutting board with a handle
2. Two stainless steel nails, 1/8" diameter by 1 3/4" long
3. Two 1 1/2" long pieces of plastic aquarium tubing sized to fit snugly over nail tips

TOOLS:
Hammer, drill, scissors

ASSEMBLY:
1. Using a drill bit that is slightly smaller than the diameter of the nail shaft, drill two holes in the cutting board approximately 1" apart from each other.

2. Hammer the two stainless steel nails through the holes so the sharp ends of the nails stick up through the cutting board.

3. Cover each nail with a small piece of plastic aquarium tubing when not in use.

☞ This type of cutting board is also commercially available through suppliers such as Therapro, Inc. and Sammons Preston.

Built by
Paulette E. Binder, Home Economics Teacher, Cotting School

WOODEN MIXING SPOON WITH BALL HANDLE

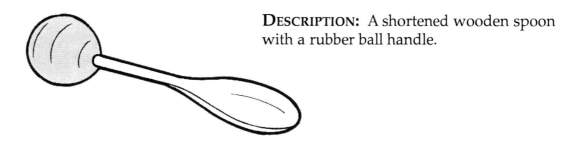

DESCRIPTION: A shortened wooden spoon with a rubber ball handle.

PURPOSE:
To enable some students who have impaired hand grasp to mix ingredients in a bowl. This adaptation can be therapeutic for some students who have a neurological disorder such as cerebral palsy, as it requires a spherical grasp which helps to open up the web space between the thumb and index finger.

MATERIALS:
1. Wooden mixing spoon
2. Solid rubber ball - about tennis ball size
3. Clear general purpose goop (it's waterproof!)

TOOLS:
Saw, knife

ASSEMBLY:
1. Use a saw to cut the wooden spoon to the desired length. Ball handles work best on shorter-length utensils.

2. Carefully work a hole in the rubber ball using the knife or other sharp object.

3. Put clear general purpose goop in the hole and on the end of the utensil handle and push the utensil handle in the ball.

Designed by
Paulette E. Binder, Home Economics Teacher, Cotting School

Chapter 18
Lunchroom

ASSISTIVE DEVICES FOR THE LUNCHROOM

Lunchtime for students should be a time to relax and enjoy good food and conversation with peers. However, for some students who have special needs, it can instead be a source of frustration. The crowd of students and noise level in a lunchroom can be noxious to those who are sensory defensive, and the list of expectations can be overwhelming: sit up straight, hold the fork better, look at your plate, keep chewing, wipe your mouth, don't put your napkin in your food, chew with your mouth closed, don't use your fingers, use your communication board-and use full sentences, clear the table, don't throw the fork in the trash...And this was suppose to be the most fun part of the day!

The truth is, it can be difficult to observe a behavior that is generally considered unacceptable without correcting it. However, as with any other activity, it is important to prioritize goals and let the low priority ones slide for a while to maximize learning of the higher priority goals as well to avoid eroding the student's self-esteem. Chewing food thoroughly before swallowing is a high priority; chewing with the mouth closed may not be. Learning to use a mature grasp to hold a fork can take much effort and concentration. If there are also major lunchtime behaviors to contend with, it may be best to deal with these behaviors first. Addressing both may be asking too much from the student. Remember that lunchtime goal expectations may be set by various members of the student's interdisciplinary team (e.g. occupational therapist, speech and language pathologist, classroom teacher). Therefore, it is not sufficient to simply prioritize goals within one's own discipline; ideally goals should be prioritized as a team.

In a school that serves students who have special needs, safety is the number one concern in the lunchroom. Feeding assistants should receive full training before working with children who have feeding difficulties, especially those who have oral motor impairments. They need training in proper positioning, food textures, food temperatures, and bite sizes; as well as proper feeding methods and training strategies. A short and simple introduction to the normal development of oral feeding skills, as well as the abnormal patterns that can evolve when normal development is blocked, is also very helpful, so the staff understand the "why" behind the "what". Some believe that this is not essential, as long as appropriate strategies are used. However, it is often the "why" that finally sparks real interest in the subject on the part of the feeding staff, because it enables them to see how some of the puzzle pieces fit together.

The reader is referred to the Additional Reading section at the end of the book for more specific information on the topics listed above. Positioning is also extremely applicable to eating tasks, since the position of the student strongly influences all muscles, including the muscles involved in chewing and swallowing food. In addition to looking at body positioning, also look at head positioning, making sure the student keeps the head forward with chin slightly tucked. When the head is extended, the tongue naturally retracts, which directly affects chewing and swallowing ability.

In addition to promoting good chewing and swallowing skills, another important lunchtime goal for many students who have special needs is to improve self-feeding skills. For those who have neurological disorders, this may require some preparatory activities to help normalize muscle tone, which can be taught by a physical or occupational therapist. Facilitating more normal muscle tone helps to improve the range and ease of arm and hand movements, enabling better control of the eating utensils and cup.

There are several standard pieces of adaptive equipment that help promote self-feeding skills, which can probably be found in most schools serving students who have impaired motor skills. The charts on pages 278 and 279 describe commercially available adaptive eating equipment. These items are obtainable through suppliers such as Sammons Preston, North Coast Medical, Maxi-Aids, S & S adaptAbility, Concepts ADL, and Therapro. Please consult their equipment catalogs for further information on these and other commercially available adapted equipment.

For some students, using this equipment is not sufficient for solving their difficulties with self-feeding. Possible solutions to some of these problems are presented in Quick Tips, and directions for making some adapted feeding devices are provided at the end of this chapter.

Meeting Social and Behavioral Goals in the Lunchroom

Lunchtime is one of the biggest social hours of the school day, and for many students, this can be perfect time to address certain communication goals and further develop relationships with peers. This can be a missed opportunity if the student is immersed in a one-to-one training session to learn how to feed himself independently. Feeding assistants who are sensitive to this issue can facilitate social interactions between peers during lunch. Unfortunately, for certain students with high-level feeding needs, most social interactions with peers need to be primarily reserved for the beginning of the meal (during set-up) and during the free time available at the end of the meal (if there is any). The assistant can also provide brief breaks during feeding training which coincide with particularly interesting topics being discussed at the table, to allow the student to participate in the conversation. Remember that talking or laughing while eating can increase the risk of choking, so if someone at the table is in the middle of telling a good joke, or if the student looks like he or she has something to say, have the student take a break from eating.

On the other hand, don't let the student get so absorbed by all of the social interaction that he or she doesn't have enough time to eat a full meal. Some students have particular caloric goals they have to meet, and this usually cannot be done during the last 15 minutes of lunch. Some students with motor impairments need to focus all of their attention on getting their food to their mouth. Other students (who have severe attention disorders) are so distracted by conversation that they would forget to eat altogether if someone was not there to prompt them! And students who are hypersensitive to noise and crowds can be so hypervigilant in the lunchroom that it disrupts their ability to focus on eating as well as demonstrate organized behaviors. In many of these cases, efforts need to be made to reduce the social stimulation during lunch (ideas are presented in Quick Tips), but extra "free time" (such as recess) might be scheduled following lunch to help make up for the time lost to socially interact with peers.

Many students who have special needs also have behavioral goals, and these should not be thrown out the door when they enter the lunchroom. If students use a responsibility chart which outlines specific behavioral goals during class (see chapter on Time Management and Organizational Aids), it should be checked off during lunch as well. Certain students may need a separate responsibility chart specific to the lunchroom which addresses behavioral issues which only occur in this setting and/or goals relating to general table manners (e.g. will use eating utensils rather than fingers, will wipe mouth, will place rather than throw trash into the trash barrel). These can even be incorporated into an adaptive placemat if the student uses one (complete description provided later in this chapter). It is recommended that responsibility charts be laminated as they can get pretty grungy-looking otherwise!

Solutions that have solved lunchtime problems for particular students are described in the Quick Tips section later in this chapter.

COMMERCIALLY AVAILABLE ADAPTIVE EQUIPMENT
FOR EATING TASKS

MATS

DYCEM: a rubber mat placed under a plate (or cup) to prevent it from sliding around when eating.

PLATES

SCOOP PLATE: plastic round dish molded with a high lip (like a bowl) on one side and a low lip on the other side. The individual scoops the food against the high lip to help position the food on the spoon. Also prevents food from falling off the plate. A nonskid, rubber bottom prevents the plate from sliding when scooping.

PLATE WITH INSIDE EDGE (INNER LIP PLATE): Serves similar purpose as scoop plate, except the plate has a lower lip that completely surrounds the circumference of the plate. Many students progress from using scoop plates (which have the higher lip) to using inner lip plates.

PLATE GUARD (OR FOOD GUARD): Plastic or metal ring that snaps onto a standard plate to prevent food from spilling off the plate. Not quite as effective for scooping as the scoop plate is, but does prevent food spillage.

DIVIDED PLATE: A plate with section dividers to keep food items separated. Especially useful for blind individuals to help identify the specific locations of food items.

SUCTION PLATE: A plate that has one large or several mini suction cups on the bottom of it to prevent it from sliding.

UTENSILS

BUILT-UP HANDLE UTENSILS: Forks, spoons, and knives with thickened handles to accommodate weak or impaired hand grasp. Several styles are available. Or, buy cylindrical foam padding (also available from many of the suppliers listed earlier in this chapter) and slip on to any standard utensil to build up the handle. Sammons Preston and Theraprosell a moldable material called Dyna-Form-It for those who require a custom design to improve hand grip.

ANGLED UTENSILS: Angled utensils are useful to accommodate individuals who demonstrate decreased range of motion during eating tasks, especially in the forearm and wrist (due to real range of motion deficits or abnormal movement patterns). Some models are designed at preset angles while other models can be easily bent to adjust the angle. The latter are generally more effective, as it seems no two students require the exact same angle.

PLASTIC-COATED OR NYLON-COATED SPOONS: Spoons which have a special coating over the bowl to protect the teeth and lips and reduce temperature sensitivity. If used with a heavy biter, check with the manufacturer to see if the particular model is designed to withstand that treatment.

UTENSIL HOLDERS: Strapping material or elastic cuffs that have a pocket for holding an eating utensil and are strapped onto the hand. Used especially for those who have very weak muscle grasp and who can not hold an eating utensil even if it has a built-up handle.

ROCKER KNIVES: Knives with curved blades which enable individuals who have functional use of only one hand to cut food. There are two basic models, one with a standard knife handle (for those who have intact arm strength and coordination) and one with a T-handle design that works better for those who have decreased strength and coordination. The latter model in particular is very sharp; therefore, its use needs to be closely supervised until the student demonstrates the ability to use one independently and safely. Keep away from other students.

Developed by Lynn Ciampa Stoller, M.S., OTR/L, BCP.

COMMERCIALLY AVAILABLE ADAPTIVE EQUIPMENT
FOR EATING TASKS

CUPS

☞ Many older students prefer to use standard travel mugs because they are popular with the general population and they serve the same purposes as the covered, wide-based, handled cups described below which are sold by adaptive equipment companies.

WIDE-BASED AND WEIGHTED CUPS: Designed to prevent tipping over by those who have poor coordination. Special weighted cups help those who have tremors to control movement while drinking.

CUP OR GLASS HOLDERS: These fasten onto the cup or glass to provide a handle for those who have impaired hand grasp or coordination. They come in one-handled and two-handled models. Some models are also heavy which helps prevent the cup from tipping over.

COVERED CUPS: Designed to prevent spillage by those who have poor coordination.

SPOUT CUPS: Cups that have a lid with a spout. These should only be used if recommended by a speech and language pathologist or occupational therapist, since many models are actually detrimental to the development of oral motor skills. A professional can recommend a model that meets therapeutic criteria.

NOSE CUTOUT CUPS: Plastic cups that have a cutout for the nose to allow proper head positioning during drinking.

STRAWS

EXTENDED STRAW: An extra-long, reusable straw. These are especially useful for those who cannot pick up a cup and who need a longer straw to maintain an upright posture when drinking.

ONE-WAY STRAW: Straw with a one-way valve which keeps the straw filled to the top with liquid even when the lips are removed. These are excellent for individuals who have not developed good enough sucking skills yet to bring liquid up to the top of the straw each time they want a sip.

SANDWICH AIDS

SANDWICH HOLDER: A plastic holder for a sandwich that has a handle which can either be covered with cylindrical foam padding or can be inserted into a utensil holder. The angle of the sandwich holder can be adjusted using a heat gun. Very useful for those who have difficulty holding a sandwich due to impaired hand grasp.

Developed by Lynn Ciampa Stoller, M.S., OTR/L, BCP.

QUICK TIPS *Problems and Possible Solutions*

Following are some solutions which have successfully solved the identified problem for one or more students. Keep in mind that each student has a unique set of abilities and needs and may therefore require an original solution for the problem at hand. If a suggested solution is appropriate for a student, please adapt the design as necessary to best meet his or her needs.

Remember: fit the device to the student, not the student to the device!

1. Student has difficulty controlling arm movements resulting in the fork jabbing the roof of the mouth during eating.

A "wave fork" has solved this problem for one student: A junior plastic handle fork (Sammons Preston #1192) was bent in such a manner so the prong tips would not hit the hard palate when entering the mouth. The metal part of the handle was curved downward; the base of the prongs was curved slightly upward, and the outer half (tip) portion of the prongs were bent downward.

(Kate Moore, M.S., CCC-SLP, Speech-Language Pathologist, Cotting School)

2. Student tends to put his or her whole hand in the plate when eating with a spoon, resulting in a very messy hand.

Try making a circular "shield" out of low temperature thermoplastic material to place over the spoon handle. The shield is made by simply cutting out a small round shape out of the thermoplastic material and sticking a spoon through the middle of it. This keeps the hand positioned higher on the handle of the spoon, thus preventing the student from sticking the whole hand (not just the bowl of the spoon) into the plate.

(JoAnn Kluzik, M.S., PT, PCS, Physical Therapist, while working at Cotting School)

SecurGrip Cutlery by Ableware (available from Therapro, Inc.) has a collar to prevent the hand from slipping off the front of the handle onto the plate.

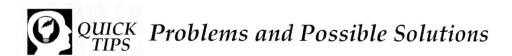

3. Student drinks out of a juice box or milk carton at school and tends to knock it over due to incoordination.

Make a juice box or milk carton stabilizer (complete directions provided later in this chapter).
(Suzi Collins, M.S., OTR/L, Clinical Supervisor, Franciscan Children's School, Brighton, Ma.)

4. Student has no room to place his or her communication book or augmentative communication device while eating a meal.

Incorporate a communication board onto an adapted placemat, and have the student store his or her regular communication book under the chair. Directions for the adapted placemat follow Quick Tips.
(Beth Jackson, M.S., OTR/L, Occupational Therapist,
and Deena Gulezian, M.S., CCC-SLP, Speech-Language Pathologist, Cotting School)

5. Student has no functional use of the arms and cannot feed him or herself.

If the student is able to maintain a bent elbow, see Quick Tip #6.

Make a sandwich stand to hold a sandwich. Directions follow Quick Tips.
(Sheryl Zelten, OTR/L, Occupational Therapist, while working at Cotting School)

Have the student try an electric self-feeder (such as the Winsford Self-Feeder). These enable the individual to feed themselves by simply touching a switch, which can be activated by a slight touch of the head (or by any other body part). Requires sufficient control of the neck and oral muscles to remove the food from the spoon. These are available from adaptive equipment supply companies including Sammons Preston and North Coast Medical, Inc.

6. Student cannot hold a sandwich and is also unable to use a commercially available sandwich holder due to wrist instability/poor grasp.

Sometimes pairing a foam-handled sandwich holder with a wrist brace is sufficient to solve the problem.

Make a sandwich holder splint. This allows for more customized adjustments. See directions following Quick Tips.
(Sheryl Zelten, OTR/L, Occupational Therapist, while working at Cotting School)

7. Student is positioned in a wheelchair with trunk supports, and cannot pick up a cup. Therefore, student needs an extended straw. However, student does not have sufficient sucking skills to suck the liquid all the way up that long straw each time he or she wants to take a sip.

Connect an extended straw to a one-way straw by cutting small slits at the end of the extended straw to fit it over the one-way straw.

8. Student has a gross grasp and can only maintain the forearm in neutral position which makes functional grasp of a spoon difficult.

See description of the Mother Care (or Maroon) Spoon with Vertical Handle which follows Quick Tips.
(Suzi Collins, M.S., OTR/L, Clinical Supervisor, Franciscan Children's Hospital, Brighton, Ma.)

9. Student does not remember to wipe his or her mouth following the meal.

Place a small mirror at the student's place setting as a reminder to check and wipe his or her face.

QUICK TIPS *Problems and Possible Solutions*

10. Student is so distracted by conversation, noises, and visual stimuli in the lunchroom that it is hard to focus on the task of eating.

If the student must sit in a crowded cafeteria, there are a few options:

Position the student at a table with only a few other students in a far corner away from the doors and other well-travelled areas and, if necessary, use a room divider (such as a ceiling-hung curtain) to further reduce distractions.

Try having the student wear an FM listening device (see page 69), which allows the feeding assistant to deliver training instructions to the student (such as for self-feeding) through a wireless microphone while significantly reducing extraneous environmental noises. (Please check with the student's communication specialist first).

Assign a small group of distracted students to the same table and have them begin lunch 15 minutes before the other students arrive - or schedule the time so it doesn't overlap at all with the other students.

The therapeutic application of certain types of sensory input (especially deep touch pressure or proprioceptive input) can significantly reduce anxiety, overactivity, disorganization, and hypervigilant behavior in some students in the lunchroom. Please consult with an occupational therapist who has training in the treatment of sensory processing disorders to determine which technique(s) might work well for a particular student.

Make sure the chair and table are not contributing to poor attention at lunch. The Positioning chapter earlier in this book can provide more information.

Reduce the acoustics in the lunchroom, if possible, such as by placing tennis balls or other sound-dampening material on the bottoms of furniture legs (see page 37, Quick Tip #5), using plastic plates and cups instead of china and glass, etc.

11. Student uses a wheelchair and has difficulty clearing dishes from the table.

Have the student place Dycem on his or her lap before placing the plate and utensils on it, to reduce the chances of the dishes/utensils falling on the floor.
(Virginia Birmingham, P.T., Physical Therapist, Cotting School)

Adapt a washbasin with neck strap for clearing dishes. Caution: Basin must rest on the lap, not hang from the neck strap! See detailed directions later in this chapter.
(Helen Denham, Program Aide, Perkins School for the Blind)

INSTRUCTIONS
FOR FABRICATING
SELECTED DEVICES

SANDWICH HOLDER STAND

SANDWICH HOLDER SPLINT

MOTHER CARE (OR MAROON) SPOON
WITH VERTICAL HANDLE

ANGLED SCOOP DISH STABILIZER

HARD FOAM CUP HOLDER

HOLDER FOR MILK OR ORANGE JUICE CARTON

ADAPTED PLACEMAT

TABLE CLEARING BUCKET

SANDWICH HOLDER STAND

DESCRIPTION: A Quad-Quip Sandwich Holder attached to a wooden base by a threaded metal rod. The base is clamped to a table.

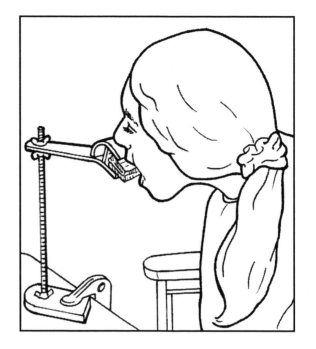

PURPOSE:
To enable a student who has no functional hand use to eat a sandwich independently following set-up.

MATERIALS:

1   Quad-Quip Sandwich Holder (available from Sammons Preston)

2. 3/16" thick threaded metal rod.   Determine length of rod by measuring the distance between the student's mouth and the surface of the table.

3. 3/4" x 4 1/2" x 2 1/2" piece of hard wood

4. 4 wing nuts to fit the threaded rod

TOOLS:
Band saw
Drill press
Belt sander

ASSEMBLY:

1. Use a band saw to cut the wood into a rectangle. (Note: It is possible that this device would not need to be clamped if the base was larger.) Sand the wood, and round the back two corners to form a semi-circular shape if desired.

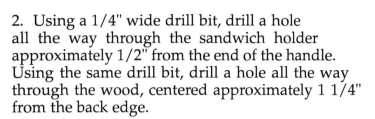

2. Using a 1/4" wide drill bit, drill a hole all the way through the sandwich holder approximately 1/2" from the end of the handle. Using the same drill bit, drill a hole all the way through the wood, centered approximately 1 1/4" from the back edge.

3. From the underside of the base, enlarge the drilled hole using a counterbore bit. The counterbore bit needs to be slightly larger than the diameter of the wing nut, and the hole should be drilled deep enough to completely recess the wing nut.

4. Attach the parts together, referring to drawing for wing nut placement:

a. Screw a wing nut (wings first) onto the threaded metal rod until it is about one inch from the end.

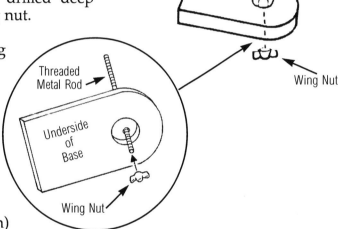

b. Push the 1" end of the rod down through the wooden base and put on a second wing nut (wings down) from underneath the base to secure the rod tightly.

c. Screw a wing nut (wings down) onto the top of the threaded dowel, until it reaches the desired height for the sandwich holder. Push the sandwich holder onto the rod and then screw on the fourth wing nut (wings up), tightly securing the sandwich holder to the rod.

Idea conceived by Sheryl Zelten, OTR/L,
and built by Val Greene, B.S.Ed., Industrial Arts Teacher at Cotting School.

SANDWICH HOLDER SPLINT

DESCRIPTION: An adapted radial bar wrist cock-up splint with a 3" flat hair clip attached to it to hold a sandwich. The clip can be attached to the splint by a flexible wire that allows the clip to be spatially adjusted, or with rolled thermoplastic material. The sandwich holder splint is most effective when a quarter of a sandwich is placed in the clip at a time, although it can hold a half of a grilled cheese or similar well-held-together sandwich.

PURPOSE:
To enable a student who has poor wrist stability and/or poor grasp to hold a sandwich. This device is used when commercially available sandwich holders have failed. The sandwich holder splint stabilizes the wrist in a more optimal position to promote a better hand-to-mouth pattern and eliminates the need to grasp.

Caution: This device should be fabricated by a qualified occupational therapist or orthotist, after it has been determined that this device, including the particular splint design, would be the optimal solution for the student. If an alternative splint design better meets the needs of a particular student, perhaps the design could be adapted with a sandwich clip in a similar fashion.

MATERIALS:
1. Low temperature thermoplastic material, enough to make a wrist cock-up splint.
2. 6" of pressure-sensitive Velcro hook tape
3. 12" of 1" or 2" wide splint strapping material
4. 6" of 1/8" thick galvanized wire (wire must be galvanized to prevent rusting). Thermotube (available from North Coast Medical, Inc.) can be used instead of a wire to attach clip to splint, if desired. Follow the manufacturer's directions to attach this to the thermoplastic material.
5. 3" wide plastic hair clip (Note: Choose a flat clip with approximately 1/4" long prongs, not a cylindrical type clip. Goody brand hair clips have been used successfully.)
6. Optional: dowel to mold handle around (not in finished product)

☞ Some types of low temperature thermoplastic materials require special solvent or light abrasion before bonding can occur. Please follow manufacturer's directions.

TOOLS:
Splinting pan or electric frying pan and water, sharp scissors, wire cutter

ASSEMBLY FOR DESIGN 1 (which incorporates a dowel handle):

1. Make your pattern:
    a. Position the student's hand on a long piece of paper towel and draw a custom pattern (from a splinting book) for a radial bar wrist cock-up splint. [1]
    b. Using diagram as a reference, draw a line 1/2" below and parallel to the line that connects the MP joints. Extend this line approximately 1 1/2" from the radial side of the hand, and approximately 3/4" from the ulnar side of the hand. This is line W.
    c. Beginning at each end of line W, draw a line perpendicular to line W, ending just shy of the tips of the fingers. These are lines X and Y.
    d. Draw a line (Z) to connect the ends of lines X and Y. The lines W, X, Y, and Z now form a closed rectangle.
    e. Cut out the adjusted splint pattern and trace it onto the thermoplastic material.

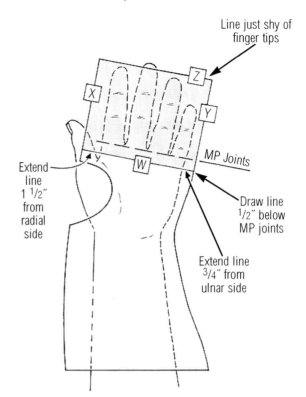

2. Heat material and shape the splint:
    a. Following the manufacturer's directions, heat the splinting material in the splinting pan and water until pliable and mold the splint to the forearm as for a typical wrist cock-up splint.
    b. Next, form the splint against the radial base of the palm, making sure the wrist is positioned correctly. (Usually, the correct position is with the wrist slightly extended and in neutral deviation; however, this will need to be determined by the therapist, based on the needs of the student). Abduct and oppose the student's thumb to get a fold in the material that will mark the medial border of the thenar eminence. Roll this edge over.
    c. Form the WXYZ rectangular portion of the material over a dowel that is slightly smaller than the desired diameter of the dowel handle for the sandwich splint. Carefully remove the dowel (while maintaining the shape in the material) as

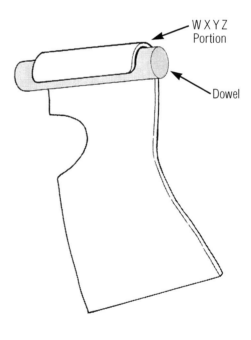

soon as the material is formed over it, so the dowel does not stay imbedded in the material. Trim excess material and then bond the material to the underside of the splint.
    d. Smooth all edges of the splint.

3. Reposition the student's hand in the splint to evaluate the splint for correct fit, absence of pressure points, smooth edges, etc., following standard evaluation procedures, and make adjustments as necessary.

4. Attach the wire to the splint:

   a. Make a small L-shaped bend at the end of the wire.

   b. Resoften the bottom, radial side of the dowel-shaped handle and insert 2" of the galvanized wire (including the bent portion) into and against the softened bottom surface.

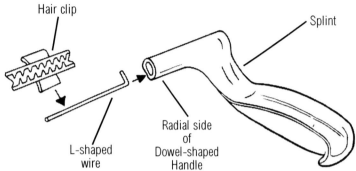

Hair clip

Splint

L-shaped wire

Radial side of Dowel-shaped Handle

   c. Press a softened strip of thermoplastic material over the wire and against the softened bottom surface of the dowel-shaped handle to secure it in place.

5. Attach the hair clip to the other end of the wire:

   a. Determine desired length of wire and trim off the excess.

   b. Position the end of the wire along the bottom portion of the clip (which is pressed to open it), and wrap a softened narrow strip of thermoplastic material around this entire bottom portion, covering the wire and squeezing hard to secure it.

6. Bend the wire to adjust the position of the clip.

ASSEMBLY FOR DESIGN 2, which is a standard radial bar wrist cock-up splint without a dowel handle:

Fabricate a radial bar wrist cock-up splint following the usual procedure, except cut out a much longer extension to fit through the web space and do not form it around to the back of the hand. Instead, form the extension straight through the web space. Either attach the clip directly to the extension using additional softened thermoplastic material or attach a wire or thermotube to the extension using heat bonding procedures. Attach the hair clip to the other end of the wire as described in step #5 above.

☞ Some students have better control using a sandwich splint when the inside or outside of their upper arm is stabilized against the armrest of their wheelchair or arm chair. This provides a stable base to allow smoother gradations of movement at the elbow.

Both versions of this device were designed and fabricated by
Sheryl Zelten, OTR/L, Occupational Therapist, while working at Cotting School.

MOTHER CARE (OR MAROON) SPOON WITH VERTICAL HANDLE

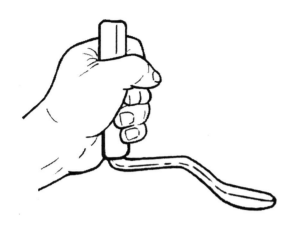

DESCRIPTION: A plastic Mother Care spoon with an extended, vertical handle made of low-temperature thermoplastic material. The vertical handle of the spoon is approximately 3" high; the spoon extends 4" horizontally.

☞ Mother Care spoons have become difficult to find; however, spoons with similar designs can frequently be found in catalogs that sell adaptive eating utensils, such as the Maroon Spoon sold by Therapro, Inc.

PURPOSE:
To enable self-feeding for a student who demonstrates a fisted grasp with forearm in neutral position.

MATERIALS:
1. Mother Care spoon or similar plastic spoon

2. Low temperature thermoplastic material, approximately 6" x 3"

☞ Some types of low temperature thermoplastic materials require special solvent or light abrasion before bonding can occur. Please follow manufacturer's directions.

TOOLS:
Splinting pan or electric frying pan and water
Heat gun
Scissors

ASSEMBLY:
1. Heat the end of the spoon handle with a heat gun and bend it upward until it is vertical.

2. Soften the thermoplastic material in a splinting pan and water (following the manufacturer's directions) and wrap it around the vertical portion of the spoon handle, bonding it to the layer of thermoplastic material beneath. When the handle reaches the desired thickness, cut off the excess material. Press to smooth the edges.

Contributed by
Suzi Collins, M.S., OTR/L, Clinical Supervisor, Franciscan Children's Hospital, Brighton, Ma.
(Designer Unknown)

ANGLED SCOOP DISH STABILIZER

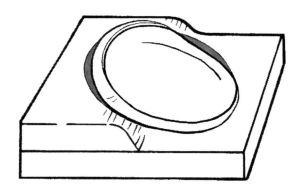

DESCRIPTION: A thick block of hard foam carved to stabilize the scoop dish in an angled position with the high lip raised. A thermoplastic covering makes cleaning easy.

PURPOSE:
To enable certain students who have neurological impairments to scoop food independently, by accommodating their particular movement patterns.

MATERIALS:
1. Two blocks of polyethylene (hard) foam, one 11" x 11", one 11" x 6"
2. Low temperature thermoplastic material, 14" by 14"
3. Contact paper to coordinate with color of thermoplastic material
4. Clear waterproof tape

☞ Some types of low temperature thermoplastic materials require special solvent or light abrasion before bonding can occur. Please follow manufacturer's directions.

TOOLS:
Steak knife
Heat gun
Splinting pan and water
Scissors
Pen
Optional: Electric knife

ASSEMBLY:

1. Cut blocks of hard foam to the dimensions described above, using an electric carving knife or steak knife.

2. Position the smaller rectangular block so one 11" long edge lines up with one side of the larger block.

3. Using a heat gun, follow procedures for heat bonding polyethylene foam pieces together, described in the chapter on Materials and Processes, to attach the smaller block to the larger block.

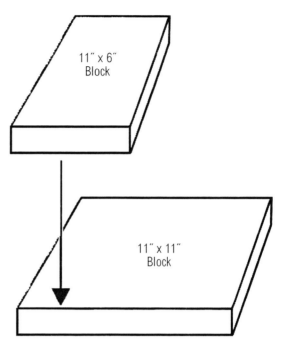

4. With the steak knife, carve a circular depression into the block combination that is just big enough to hold the scoop dish. Angle the depression so it slopes downward from the higher block to the lower block. Occasionally place the scoop dish in the depression, removing it and making adjustments until it fits snugly at the desired angle.

5. Soften the thermoplastic material in the splinting pan and water, following the manufacturer's directions, and place it over the top of the carved out block, pressing it so it conforms to the shape of the surface. Press the scoop dish against the depression before the plastic hardens to insure that the shape remains correct.

6. Once the thermoplastic material has hardened, cover the edges and bottom of the block with contact paper, overlapping the contact paper onto the thermoplastic top surface by about an inch. Then seal the edges of the contact paper with clear plastic tape.

7. Place the scoop dish in the depression so the high lip is at the high end.

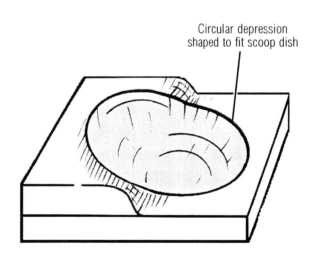

Circular depression shaped to fit scoop dish

Designed and fabricated by
Amy Houghton, OTR/L, Occupational Therapy Team Leader, Cotting School.

HARD FOAM CUP HOLDER

DESCRIPTION: A block of polyethylene (hard) foam with a cup shaped hole carved into it.

PURPOSE:
To stabilize a cup for students who have poor motor control and are apt to tip over their cups.

MATERIALS:
1. Square block of 2" thick polyethylene (hard) foam. Each side of the square should be slightly less than twice the diameter of the cup's base.

TOOLS:
Steak knife
Heat gun

ASSEMBLY:
1. Slice the block of hard foam in half crosswise to make two 1" thick blocks.

2. Trace the base of the cup onto the center of one of the blocks, and cut out the circle using a steak knife.

3. Heat bond the two block slices back together again using a heat gun, making sure the blocks are lined up in their original positions. Follow procedures for heat bonding polyethylene foam pieces together described in the chapter on Materials and Processes.

☞ It is possible to simply dig a hole in a 2" thick block of foam, but the result is rougher.

Contributed by
Sheryl Zelten, OTR/L, Occupational Therapist, while working at Cotting School.

HOLDER FOR MILK OR ORANGE JUICE CARTON

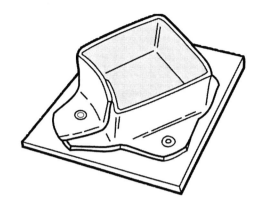

DESCRIPTION: A holder for a milk or orange juice carton made using brightly colored thermoplastic material.
The same design can be used for juice boxes by simply altering the dimensions.

PURPOSE:
To stabilize a carton of milk or juice for students who have poor motor control and are apt to tip it over.

MATERIALS:
1. Brightly colored low temperature thermoplastic material, 6" x 12"

2. Optional: Pressure-sensitive Velcro to attach holder to lap tray

☞ Some types of low temperature thermoplastic materials require special solvent or light abrasion before bonding can occur. Please follow manufacturer's directions.

TOOLS:
Splinting pan or electric frying pan and water
Heavy duty scissors, ruler
Optional: rivet gun and rivets, heat gun

ASSEMBLY:
1. Using a ruler, draw a 5" x 5" square on the thermoplastic material for the base (adjust dimensions if making a holder for a juice box). Also draw a rectangle that is 3" x [circumference of carton plus one inch], which will form the holder for the milk or juice carton. Heat thermoplastic material in the splinting pan and water, following manufacturer's directions. Cut out both pieces of material.

2. Heat the second piece of thermoplastic material again and form it around the carton, so that it overlaps the carton by about 1 1/2" with the excess extending off the bottom of carton. Snip triangles off each corner of the material that extends off the carton, forming 4 triangular tabs extending below the carton.

3. Reheat material. Fold the extensions outward. Place this piece on the square base, so that the triangular tabs are pointing to the corners of the base.

4. Attach the pieces together in one of the following ways:
   • Use a rivet gun, putting one rivet in each tab.
   • Bond the pieces with heat, using the splinting pan and water or heat gun.

5. **OPTIONAL:** Add pressure-sensitive Velcro to the bottom of the base and to the wheelchair lap tray if desired, or attach Dycem to prevent it from sliding.

Contributed by Suzi Collins, M.S., OTR/L, Clinical Supervisor,
Franciscan Children's Hospital, Brighton, Ma. (Designer unknown.)

ADAPTED PLACEMAT

DESCRIPTION: A laminated paper placemat with a picture of a place setting, and communication symbols, directions and/or reminders on it.

Some useful placemat inclusions are:
- meal-time communication boards
- step-by-step directions to assist with task set-up
- behavioral reminders

The size of the placemat can be increased to accommodate any customized combination of communication symbols and/or directions. Just remember: If the placemat doesn't fit on the table, there are too many lunchtime goals!

PURPOSE:
1. To increase a student's level of independence at lunch.

2. To allow conversation for students whose communication books cannot fit on the table while eating.

3. To improve social skills and behavior.

MATERIALS:

1. Two large sheets (at least 12" x 18") of different colored paper: one for the placemat and one for paper cut-outs of plate, cup, napkin, and utensils

2. Clear contact paper

3. Optional: Sheet of communication symbols. These should be designed with input from the student's speech and language therapist.

4. OPTIONAL: Direction sheet to assist with organizational skills or behavior during lunch. Directions can be written, pictorial, or described with other communication symbols - whichever is most appropriate for the student.

TOOLS:

Gluestick

Pencil

Scissors

ASSEMBLY:

1. Draw the appropriate shapes on one sheet of colored paper to represent the plate, napkin, utensils, and cup. Draw them actual size.

2. Cut out the shapes and glue them in the appropriate positions on the uncut sheet of paper. Add name labels if desired.

3. Glue on the communication sheet and/or the direction sheet, if desired. Position them wherever the particular student can best access them (this may vary depending upon the student).

4. Cover the placemat with contact paper to protect it from spills.

Designed by
Beth Jackson, M.S., OTR/L, Occupational Therapist,
and Deena Gulezian, M.S., CCC-SLP, Speech-Language Pathologist, at Cotting School.

TABLE-CLEARING BUCKET

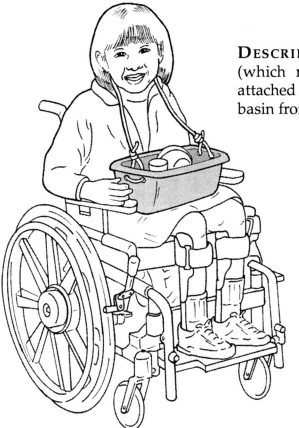

DESCRIPTION: A 12" x 12" washbasin (which rests on the student's lap) with an attached canvas neck strap, which prevents the basin from falling off the student's lap.

Caution: To prevent injury to the student, under no circumstances should the basin hang freely from the neck strap!

PURPOSE:
To enable some students who use wheelchairs to clear their dishes from the table independently.

MATERIALS:
1. 12" x 12" plastic washbasin
2. Approximately 1 1/2 yards of 1" wide canvas strap or other suitable strapping material
3. Approximately 8" of 2" wide foam padding, 1/4" thick, such as Soft Touch Velfoam Loop (available from Sammons Preston)

TOOLS:
Sharp knife
Heavy duty scissors
Sewing machine (or needle and thread)

ASSEMBLY:

1. With the bucket positioned on a table (not the student's lap!), use the sharp knife to cut two 1" long horizontal slits on each side of the bucket. Slits should be about 1 1/2" from the top edge of the bucket, and approximately 7" apart.

2. Thread the strapping material through one of the slits, threading from the inside to the outside of the bucket. Run the strap along the outside of the bucket and thread it into the other slit on the same side, this time from the outside to the inside of the bucket. Knot or sew this end to the part of the strapping material that was not threaded through the slits, a few inches above the basin, so it forms an upside down "Y" shape.

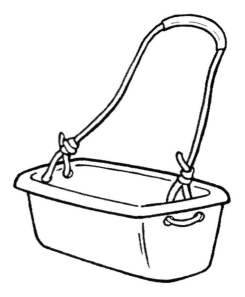

3. Position the bucket on the student's lap so the slit that was threaded first is closest to the student's body, as shown in the illustration. Position the loose end of the strapping material very loosely around the student's neck, and then thread it through the other side of the bucket, entering the slit closest to the body first, and threading from the inside to the outside of the bucket.

4. Run the strap along the outside of the bucket and thread it into the other slit on the same side, this time from the outside to the inside of the bucket, as was done on the first side. Knot or sew the end to the other strapping material, a few inches above the basin, making final adjustments to the neck strap length before attaching it to ensure that no pressure is put against the neck when the basin is positioned properly on the lap. Cut off excess strapping material.

Caution: It is a safety hazard for the strap to be either too tight OR too loose. If it has several inches of slack, it could allow the bucket to slide off the lap and thus yank the neck. If it is too tight, it will put pressure on the neck, possibly causing injury. Please adjust carefully!

5. Pad the portion of the strap behind the neck with foam padding, such as 2" wide Velfoam Loop. Fold the 2" padding lengthwise over the 1" strapping material and use a needle and thread or sewing machine to sew it onto the strap.

Designed by
Helen Denham, Program Aide, Perkins School for the Blind.

RESOURCE DIRECTORY

Following is a list of all companies referred to in this book. For a listing of additional companies that sell adaptive devices, please refer to the most recent Buyers' Guide Issue of Team Rehab Report This guide contains the most complete listing of manufacturers and suppliers that the author has seen. It also lists companies by product categories such as Seating and Positioning Systems, Computers, Switches, Mouthsticks & Headwands and Activities of Daily Living. In fact, it includes over 65 product categories, and most have dozens of subcategories. It is quite impressive. TeamRehab Report is located at 23815 Stuart Ranch Road, Malibu, CA 90265. Telephone: (310) 317-4522.

A

Abilitations by Sportime
1 Sportime Way
Atlanta, GA 30340
(800) 850-8603

AbleNet
1081 Tenth Avenue Southeast
Minneapolis, MN 55414
(800) 322-0956

ADAMLAB
33500 Van Born Road
Wayne, MI 48184
(313) 467-1415

AdaptAbility
(see S & S adaptAbility)

Adaptivation, Inc.
224 Southeast Sixteenth Street
Suite 2
Ames, IA 50010
(800) 723-2783

Adaptive Switch Labs
P.O. Box 202756
Austin, TX 78250
(800) 626-8698

Advantage Bag Company
22633 Ellinwood Drive
Torrance, CA 90505
(800) 556-6307

AliMed
297 High Street
Dedham, MA 02026
(800) 225-2610

Attainment Company, Inc.
P.O. Box 930160
Verona, WI 53593
(800) 327-4269

B

Ball Dynamics International, Inc.
1616 Glenarm Place, Suite 1900
Denver, CO 80202
(800) 752-2255

C

Canon, Inc.
One Canon Plaza
Lake Success, NY 11042
(516) 488-6700

Childcraft
20 Kilmer Road
Edison, NJ 08818
(800) 631-6100
In NJ: (201) 572-6100

Children's Resource Center
42 Trapelo Road
Belmont, MA 02178
(617) 484-9290

ComputAbility Corporation
4000 Grand River, Suite 109
Novi, MI 48375
(800) 433-8872

Concepts ADL, Inc.
P.O. Box 339
Benton, IL 62812
(800) 626-3153

Crestwood Company
6625 North Sidney Place
Milwaukee, WI 53209
(414) 352-5678

D

Don Johnston, Inc.
1000 North Rand Road, Building 115
P.O. Box 639
Wauconda IL 60084
(800) 999-4660

Dragon Systems, Inc.
320 Nevada Street
Newton, MA 02160
(617) 965-5200

E

Edmark Corporation
P.O. Box 3903
Bellevue, WA 98009
(800) 426-0856

EKEG Electronics Co. Ltd.
P.O. Box 46199
Vancouver, British Columbia V6R 4G5
Canada
(604) 273-4358

Enabling Devices
385 Warburton Avenue
Hastings-on-Hudson, NY 10706
(800) 832-8697

F

Flaghouse, Inc.
150 North MacQuesten Parkway
Mount Vernon, NY 10550
(800) 793-7900

Funtastic Therapy, Inc.
15 Renee Court
Edison, NJ 08820
(800) 722-7375

H

Holt, Co.
24 Bedford Street
Waltham, MA 02154
(617) 647-0396

I

Innocomp
26210 Emery Road, Suite 302
Warrensville Heights, OH 44128
(800) 382-8622

IntelliTools, Inc.
55 Leveroni Court, Suite 9
Novato, CA 94949
(800) 899-6687

K

Kentucky Industries for the Blind
Louisville, KY 40206
(502) 893-0211

L

Laureate Learning Systems, Inc.
110 East Spring Street
Winooski, VT 05404
(802) 655-4755

LC Technologies, Inc.
9455 Silver King Court
Fairfax, VA 22031
(703) 385-7133

Learning Things
68A Broadway
P.O. Box 436
Arlington, MA 02174
(617) 646-0093

M

Mac Connection
528 Route 13 South
Milford, NH 03055
(800) 522-6294

Maddak, Inc.
6 Industrial Road
Pequannock, NJ 07869
(800) 443-4926

Maxi-Aids
42 Executive Boulevard
P.O. Box 3209
Farmingdale, NY 11735
(800) 522-6294

Mayer-Johnson Co.
P.O. Box 1579
Solana Beach, CA. 92075
(619) 550-0084

Microsoft Corp.
One Microsoft Way
Redmond, WA 98052
(800) 426-9400

Microsystems Software, Inc.
HandiWARE/MAGic Division
600 Worcester Road
Framingham, MA 01701
(800) 828-2600

MicroTouch
55 Jonspin Road
Wilmington, MA 01887
(800) 866-6873

N

NASCO
901 Janesville Avenue
Fort Atkinson, WI 53538
(800) 558-9595

newAbilities Systems, Inc.
470 San Antonio Road, Suite G
Palo Alto, CA 94306
(800) 829-8889

North Coast Medical, Inc.
187 Stauffer Boulevard
San Jose, CA 95125
(800) 821-9319

O

Origin Instruments Corporation
854 Greenview Drive
Grand Prairie, TX 75050
(972) 606-8740

O.T. Kids
P.O. Box 1118
Homer, AK 99603
(907) 235-0688

P

Perry Packaging
Powder Mill Road
P.O. Box 160
Maynard, MA 01754
(508) 897-5002

Phonic Ear
250 Camino Alto
Mill Valley, CA 94941
(800) 227-0735

Prentke Romich Co.
1022 Heyl Road
Wooster, OH 44691
(800) 262-1984

R

RJ Cooper and Associates
24843 Del Prado #283
Dana Point, CA 92629
(800) RJCOOPER

Rifton Equipment
P.O. Box 901
Rifton, NY 12471
(800) 374-3866

S

S & S
P.O. Box 513
Colchester, CT 06415
(800) 243-9232

S & S adaptAbility
P.O. Box 515
Colchester, CT 06415
(800) 266-8856

Sammons Preston
A Bissell Healthcare Company
P.O. Box 5071
Bolingbrook, IL 60440
(800) 323-5547

Sax Arts & Crafts
P.O. Box 510710
New Berlin, WI 53151
(800) 558-6696

Sentient Systems Technology, Inc.
2100 Wharton Street,
Pittsburgh, PA 15203
(800) 344-1778

Smith & Nephew, Inc.
1 Quality Drive
P.O. Box 1005
Germantown, WI 53022
(800) 558-8633

SoftTouch/kid Tech
4182 Pinewood Lake Drive
Bakersfield, CA 93309
(805) 837-8774

Sunburst Communications
101 Castleton Street
Pleasantville, NY 10570
(800) 628-8897

T

Tash International Inc.
91 Station Street, Unit 1
Ajax, Ontario L1S 3H2
Canada
(800) 463-5685

Tech-Able, Inc.
1112A Brett Drive
Conyers, GA 30094
(770) 922-6768

Texas Instruments
13500 North Central Expressway
P.O. Box 650311
Dallas, TX 75265
(972) 995-2011

TherAdapt Products Inc.
17W 163 Oak Lane
Bensenville, IL 60106
(800) 261-4919

Therapro, Inc.
225 Arlington Street
Framingham, MA 01702
(508) 872-9494

Triarco Arts and Crafts Inc.
14650 28th Avenue North
Plymouth, MN 55447
(800) 635-9361

U

Unicorn Engineering, Inc.
5221 Central Avenue, Suite 205B
Richmond, CA 94704
(800) 899-6687

Universal Learning Technology
39 Cross Street
Peabody, MA 01960
(508) 538-0036

W

West Music
P.O. Box 5521
1212 Fifth Street
Coralville, IA 52241
(800) 397-9378

Words+, Inc.
40015 Sierra Highway
Building B-145
Palmdale, CA 93550
(800) 869-8521

Z

Zaner-Bloser
2200 West Fifth Avenue
P.O. Box 16764
Columbus, OH 43272
(800) 421-3018

Zygo Industries, Inc.
P.O. Box 1008
Portland, OR 97207
(800) 234-6006

ADDITIONAL READING

Chapter 3: Materials and Processes

Packer, B. *Appropriate Paper-Based Technology (APT): a Manual.* London: Intermediate Technology Publications Ltd., tel. 44-0-171-436-9761. 1995.

Chapter 4: Positioning

Bergen A. F., H. Presperin, and T. Tallman. *Positioning for Function: Wheelchairs and Other Assistive Technologies.* Valhalla, N.Y: Valhalla Publications. 1990.

Cook, A.M, and S. M. Hussey. *Assistive Technologies: Principles and Practice.* St. Louis, MO.: Mosby Year Book, Inc. 1995.

Zacharkow, D. *Posture: Sitting, Standing, Chair Design and Exercise.* Springfield, IL: Charles C. Thomas. 1988.

Zollars, J. A. *Special Seating: An Illustrated Guide.* Minneapolis: Otto Bock Orthopedic Industry, Inc. 1996.

Chapter 6: Communication

Rehabilitation Engineering Research Center on Augmentative and Alternative Communication. *The Guide to Augmentative & Alternative Communication Devices.* Wilmington: University of Delaware. 1996.

Goosens, C. and S. Crain. *Augmentative Communication Assessment Resource.* Birmingham: Sparks Center for Developmental and Learning Disorders,University of Alabama at Birmingham. 1986.

_____. *Augmentative Communication Intervention Resource.* Chicago: Don Johnston Developmental Equipment. 1986.

Beukelman, D. R. and P. Mirenda. *Augmentative and Alternative Communication: Management of Severe Communication Disorders in Children and Adults.* Baltimore, MD: Paul H. Brooke Publishing Co. 1992.

Lange, M. and M. Racicot. A Comparison of Wheelchair Mounting Systems. *Team Rehab Report.* June 1997.

Chapter 7: Switches

Lange, M. L. Switches. *OT Practice, Volume 1, Issue 12.* December 1996.

Chapter 8: Computers

Struck, M. Computer Access: a Link to Classroom Learning. *OT Practice,Volume 1, Issue 8.* August 1996.

Closing the Gap: Microcomputer Technology for People with Special Needs. Bimonthly newspaper. P.O. Box 68, Henderson, MN 56044. (507) 248-3294.

Lange, M. and M. Racicot. A Comparison of Wheelchair Mounting Systems. *Team Rehab Report*, June 1997.

Pogue, D. and J. Schorr. *MacWorld Mac, and PowerMac Secrets, 3rd Edition.* Foster City, CA: IDG Books Worldwide, Inc. 1996.

Chapter 10: Time Management

Haack, L. and M. Haldy. Making It Easy: Adapting Home and School Environments. *OT Practice, Volume 1, Issue 11.* November 1996.

_____. *Making It Easy: Sensorimotor Activities at Home and School.* Tucson, AZ: Therapy Skill Builders. 1995.

Chapter 12: Writing

Amundson, Susan J. *Evaluation Tool of Children's Handwriting.* O.T. Kids, P.O. Box 1118. Homer, Alaska 99603. (907) 235- 0688.

Chapter 14: Arts and Crafts

Reid, C. Craft Activity Precautions. *OT Practice, Volume 1, Issue 8.* August 1996.

Klein, M. P. *Prescissor Skills: Skill Starters for Motor Development, third edition.* Tucson, AZ: Therapy Skill Builders. 1990.

Chapter 18: Lunchroom

Morris, S. E. and M. D. Klein. *Pre-feeding Skills: a Comprehensive Resource for Feeding Development.* Tucson, AZ: Therapy Skill Builders. 1987

REFERENCES

Chapter 1- Theory

1. American Occupational Therapy Association (1972). *Project to Delineate the Roles and Functions of Occupational Therapy Personnel.* Rockville, Maryland: American Occupational Therapy Association.

2. Llorens, L. A. (1970). Facilitating Growth and Development: The Promise of Occupational Therapy. *The American Journal of Occupational Therapy, Volume 24, 93-101.*

3. _____. (1976). *Application of a Developmental Theory for Health and Rehabilitation.* Rockville, MD: American Occupational Therapy Association.

4. _____. (1982). *Occupational Therapy Sequential Client Care Manual.* Laurel, MD: RAMSCO Publishing Company.

5. Kielhofner, G. & J. P. Burke. (1980). A Model of Human Occupation, Part 1. *The American Journal of Occupational Therapy, Volume 34, 572-579.*

6. Kielhofner, G. (1980). A Model of Human Occupation, Part 2. *The American Journal of Occupational Therapy, Volume 34, 657-663.*

7. _____. (1980). A Model of Human Occupation, Part 3. *The American Journal of Occupational Therapy, Volume 34, 731-737.*

8. Kielhofner, G., J. P. Burke, and C. H. Igi. (1980). A Model of Human Occupation, Part 4. *The American Journal of Occupational Therapy, Volume 34, 777-788.*

9. Kielhofner, G. (1977). Temporal Adaptation: A Conceptual Framework for Occupational Therapy. *The American Journal of Occupational Therapy, Volume 31, 235-242.*

10. Erhardt, R. P. (1982). *Developmental Hand Dysfunction,Theory Assessment Treatment.* Laurel, MD: RAMSCO Publishing Company.

Chapter 2: Design

1. Subhashini Balagopal. (1998) Conversation with the author. Franciscan Children's Hospital, Brighton, Ma. (5 January).

2. Kerr, T. (1997) Paper-Based Technology Comes of Age in Africa. *ADVANCE for Occupational Therapists.* (31 March).

Chapter 3: Materials & Processes

1. Stiles, D. & J. Stiles. (1996). *Woodworking Simplified, Foolproof Carpentry Projects for Beginners.* Shelburne, VT: Chapters Publishing Ltd.

2. Jackson, A., D. Day, and S. Jennings. (1994). *The Complete Manual of Woodworking, a Detailed Guide to Design, Techniques and Tools for the Beginner and Expert.* New York: Alfred A. Knopf, Inc.

3. Department of the Army. (1971). *Craft Techniques in Occupational Therapy.* Washington D.C.: Department of the Army, Superintendent of Documents at (202) 512-1800, Order # 008-020-01018-9.

4. Groneman, C. H. (1982). *General Woodworking: 6th edition*. New York: McGraw-Hill

5. North Coast Medical. (1977) Poster insert from *1997 Hand Therapy Catalog*. San Jose, CA: North Coast Medical, Inc..

6. Trombly, C. A. (1983). The Materials and Methods of Construction of Temporary Orthoses. *Occupational Therapy for Physical Dysfunction: 2nd edition*. Baltimore, MD: Williams & Wilkins.

Chapter 4: Positioning

1. Waugh, K. and F. Saftler. (1997). Mat Exam for Seating: Guide to Taking Basic Measurements. Handout from Therapeutic Seating Workshop, RESNA.

2. Bergen, A. F., and C. Colangelo (1985). Positioning the Client with C.N.S. Deficits: The Wheelchair and Other Adapted Equipment. Valhalla, NY: Vallhalla Rehabilitation Publications.

3. Ward, D. (1984) Positioning the Handicapped Child for Function. Chicago, IL: Phoenix Press.

4. Benbow, M. (1991). Kinesthetics, a New Approach to Hand Skills. Workshop lecture notes. (15-16 November).

5. _____. (1990). *Loops and Other Groups: a Kinesthetic Writing System*. Tucson, AZ: Therapy Skill Builders.

6. Levine, K. J. (1991). *Fine Motor Dysfunction: Therapeutic Strategies in the Classroom*. Tucson, AZ: Therapy Skill Builders.

7. Boehme, R. (1987). *Improving Upper Body Control*. Tucson, AZ: Therapy Skill Builders.

8. J. Case-Smith and C. Pehoski (Eds.) (1992). Myers, C. A.: Therapeutic Fine-Motor Activities for Preschoolers. *Development of Hand Skills in the Child.*. Rockville, MD: American Occupational Therapy Association.

Chapter 6: Communication

1. Angelo, J. (1997). *Assistive Technology for Rehabilitation Therapists*. Philadelphia, PA: F. A. Davis Company.

2. G. Church and S. Glennen. (1992). Augmentative and Alternative Communication. *The Handbook of Assistive Technology*. San Diego, CA: Singular Publishing Group, Inc.

3. Mann, W. C. & J. P. Lane. (1991). *Assistive Technology for Persons with Disabilities: the Role of Occupational Therapy*. Rockville, MD: The American Occupational Therapy Association.

4. C.A.M.A. (1995) Lecture notes and manufacturer brochures from workshop: Innovations in Augmentative and Alternative Communication Aids. C.A.M.A. Educational Workshop, Andover, MA. (21 September).

Chapter 7: Switches

1. Massachusetts Hospital School (1985). Options in Electric Mobility. Workshop lecture notes, Randolph, Ma. (18 May).

2. Mann, W. C. & J. P. Lane. (1991). *Assistive Technology for Persons with Disabilities: the Role of Occupational Therapy.* Rockville, MD: The American Occupational Therapy Association.

Chapter 8: Computers

1. Erhardt, R. P. (1985). A Neuro-Developmental Approach to the Treatment of Hand Dysfunction. Continuing Education Opportunities Workshop, Cambridge MA. (28-30 September)

2. Berberian, B. (1997). Adaptive Computer Access, the Role of the Occupational Therapist. Full-day workshop. Department of Occupational Therapy, Sargent College, Boston, MA. (1 March)

3. Angelo, J. (1997). *Assistive Technology for Rehabilitation Therapists.* Philadelphia, PA: F. A. Davis Company.

4. Church, G. and S. Glennen. (1992). *The Handbook of Assistive Technology.* San Diego, CA: Singular Publishing Group, Inc.

5. Mann, W. C. & J. P. Lane. (1991). *Assistive Technology for Persons with Disabilities: the Role of Occupational Therapy.* Rockville, MD: The American Occupational Therapy Association.

6. AliMed (1996). *Ergonomics and Occupational Health, Issue 2.* Dedham, MA: AliMed.

7. Words+ (1995). The Key: The Augmentative and Alternative Communication Newsletter. Volume 7, Number 2. Palmdale, CA: Words+. (April through December).

C.A.M.A. (1995) Lecture notes and manufacturer brochures from workshop: Innovations in Augmentative and Alternative Communication Aids. C.A.M.A. Educational Workshop, Andover, MA. (21 September). These materials were used throughout the chapter when describing many of the commercial devices.

Chapter 9: Pointers & Mouthsticks

1. Erhardt, R. P. (1982). Developmental Hand Dysfunction, Theory Assessment Treatment. Laurel, MD: RAMSCO Publishing Company.

2. _____. (1985). A Neuro-Developmental Approach to the Treatment of Hand Dysfunction. Continuing Education Opportunities Workshop, Cambridge MA. (28-30 September)

3. Angelo, J. (1997). *Assistive Technology for Rehabilitation Therapists.* Philadelphia, PA: F.A. Davis Company.

Chapter 11: Reading

1. Greene, V. E. and M. L.Enfield. (1987). *Project Read: Report Form Comprehension Guide.* Bloomington, MN: Language Circle.

Chapter 12: Writing

1. Rosa A. Hagin (1983). Write Right or Left: A Practical Approach to Handwriting. *Journal of Learning Disabilities.*

2. Amundson, S. (1996). Handwriting: Evaluation and Intervention in the Educational Setting. Pacific Northwest Education Workshop, Marlboro, MA. (25-26 October).

3. Williams, M. S. and S. Shellenberger (1994). *"How Does Your Engine Run?" A Leader's Guide to the ALERT Program for Self-Regulation.* Albuquerque, NM: TherapyWorks, Inc.

4. Oetter, P., E. W. Richter, and S. M. Frick. (1988). *M.O.R.E.: Integrating the Mouth with Sensory and Postural Functions, second edition.* Hugo, MN: PDP Press, Inc.

5. Mary Benbow. (1991). Kinesthetics: A New Approach to Hand Skills. Workshop (15-16 November).

6. Case-Smith, J. and C. Pehoski, (eds.). (1992). Amundson, S.J.C.: Evaluation and Intervention in School Settings. *Development of Hand Skills in the Child.* Rockville, MD: American Occupational Therapy Association.

7. Levine, K. J. (1991). *Fine Motor Dysfunction: Therapeutic Strategies in the Classroom.* Tucson, AZ: Therapy Skill Builders.

8. Thurber, D. (1985). *D'Nealian Manuscript.* Novato, CA.: Academic Therapy Publications.

9. Joe, B. E. (1994) Try It! You Might Like It. *OT Week*, (10 November)

10. Benbow, M. (1990). *Loops and Other Groups: a Kinesthetic Writing System.* Tucson, AZ: Therapy Skill Builders.

11. This contributor offered this solution at the Amundson workshop (reference #2).

12. Boardman, C. H. (1994). Reasonable Answers to Commonly Asked Handwriting Questions: the First in a Series of Five. *Occupational Therapy Forum*, (16 September).

13. _____. (1994). Teach Printing with the Box and Dot Method. *Occupational Therapy Forum*, (19 August).

Chapter 13: Math

1. Erhardt, R. P. (1982). *Developmental Hand Dysfunction: Theory Assessment Treatment.* Laurel, MD: RAMSCO Publishing Company.

2. _____. (1985). A Neuro-Developmental Approach to the Treatment of Hand Dysfunction. Continuing Education Opportunities Workshop, Cambridge MA. (28-30 September)

Chapter 14: Arts and Crafts

1. Case-Smith, J and C. Pehoski (eds.) (1992). Schneck, C. and C. Battaglia: Developing Scissors Skills in Young Children. *Development of Hand Skills in the Child*. Rockville, MD: American Occupational Therapy Association.

Chapter 15: Music

1. Hickman, L. (1995). Two Clinical Stories of Sensory Integration. *Sensory Integration Special Interest Section Newsletter, Volume 18, Number 1*. (March).

Chapter 16: Industrial Arts

1. American College of Sports Medicine. (1997). *Exercise Management for Persons with Chronic Diseases and Disabilities*. Champaign, Il: Human Kinetics.

2. Department of the Army. (1980). *Craft Techniques in Occupational Therapy*. Washington D.C.: Department of the Army, Superintendent of Documents at (202) 512-1800, Order # 008-020-01018-9.

3. Erhardt, R. P. (1982). *Developmental Hand Dysfunction: Theory Assessment Treatment*. Laurel, MD: RAMSO Publishing Company

Chapter 17: Home Economics

1. Jackson, B. (1998.) *The Stepwise Breakfast Cookbook*. Framingham, MA: Therapro, Inc.

2. Jackson, B. (1998.) *The Stepwise Lunch Cookbook*. Framingham, MA: Therapro, Inc.

3. Marcus, E. F. & R. F. Granovetter(1986) *Making It Easy: Crafts and Cooking Activities*. Palo Alto, CA: Vort, Inc..

4. Steed, F. R. (1974) *A Special Picture Cookbook*. Austin, TX: ProEd.

5. Sudol, E. (1990.) *Home Cooking Cookbook*. Verona, WI: Attainment Company, Inc.

6. Sudol, E. (1990.) *Home Cooking Cookbook Plus*. Verona, WI. Attainment Company, Inc.

7. Sudol, E. (1990.) *Color-Your-Own Cookbook*. Verona, WI. Attainment Company, Inc.

8. Sudol, E. (1985.) *Look 'n Cook*. Verona, WI, Attainment Company, Inc.

Chapter 18: Lunchroom

1. Pedretti, L. W. (1981) *Occupational Therapy: Practice Skills for Physical Dysfunction*. St. Louis, MO: The C. V. Mosby Company.

ABOUT THE AUTHOR

Lynn Ciampa Stoller graduated with a Bachelor of Arts degree in Education from the University of Massachusetts, Amherst, in 1978. She earned a Master of Science degree in Occupational Therapy from San Jose State University in California in 1984. She is board certified in pediatrics, and is also certified by Sensory Integration International to administer the Sensory Integration and Praxis Tests.

Her passion for working with individuals who have physical and/or developmental challenges was lit while working as a Sensorimotor Intern at Belchertown State School in Massachusetts in 1977, She progressed through the ranks to the position of Assistant Director of Sensorimotor and Adapted Physical Education Services at this residential institution. In 1980 she caught California Fever and moved to the Long Beach area, where she accepted an administrative position as Program Director of a ninety-nine bed residential children's facility. However, she sorely missed providing direct services and subsequently returned to graduate school to become an occupational therapist.

Upon graduation in 1984, Lynn accepted a position as Pediatric Occupational Therapist/Therapy Department Coordinator at Cotting School, providing direct services to students and managing a small department of four staff members. She gave up her coordinator role and significantly reduced her hours following the birth of her first child, and continues to work part-time at Cotting School to this day. This work is supplemented by providing occupational therapy services in other settings, which have included early intervention programs, a residential children's school, group homes, a school collaborative program and a public school program.